THIRD EDITION

TEACHING CHILDREN DANCE

Theresa Purcell Cone, PhD

Stephen L. Cone, PhD

Rowan University

Human Kinetics

Library of Congress Cataloging-in-Publication Data

Cone, Theresa Purcell, 1950-
  Teaching children dance / Theresa Purcell Cone, Stephen L. Cone. --
3rd ed.
      p. cm.
  Includes bibliographical references.
  ISBN-13: 978-1-4504-0253-8 (soft cover)
  ISBN-10: 1-4504-0253-4 (soft cover)
  1. Dance for children--Study and teaching. I. Cone, Stephen Leonard.
II. Title.
  GV1799.P87 2012
  792.8083'4--dc23
                                    2011030815

ISBN-10: 1-4504-0253-4 (print)
ISBN-13: 978-1-4504-0253-8 (print)

The web addresses cited in this text were current as of July 15, 2011, unless otherwise noted.

Acquisitions Editor: Gayle Kassing, PhD; **Managing Editor:** Amy Stahl; **Assistant Editor:** Rachel Brito; **Copyeditor:** Jan Feeney; **Permissions Manager:** Dalene Reeder; **Graphic Designer:** Joe Buck; **Graphic Artist:** Kathleen Boudreau-Fuoss; **Cover Designer:** Keith Blomberg; **CD Face Designer:** Susan Rothermel Allen; **Photographer (cover):** © Human Kinetics; **Photographer (interior):** Photos courtesy of Theresa Purcell Cone and Stephen L. Cone, unless otherwise noted. Photos on pages 3, 21, 35, 53, 65, 79, 111, and 155 © Human Kinetics; **Photo Asset Manager:** Laura Fitch; **Photo Production Manager:** Jason Allen; **Art Manager:** Kelly Hendren; **Associate Art Manager:** Alan L. Wilborn; **Illustrations:** © Human Kinetics; **Printer:** McNaughton & Gunn, Inc.

Printed in the United States of America   10 9 8 7 6 5 4 3 2 1

The paper in this book is certified under a sustainable forestry program.

Human Kinetics
Website: www.HumanKinetics.com

United States: Human Kinetics
P.O. Box 5076
Champaign, IL 61825-5076
800-747-4457
e-mail: humank@hkusa.com

Canada: Human Kinetics
475 Devonshire Road Unit 100
Windsor, ON N8Y 2L5
800-465-7301 (in Canada only)
e-mail: info@hkcanada.com

Europe: Human Kinetics
107 Bradford Road
Stanningley
Leeds LS28 6AT, United Kingdom
+44 (0) 113 255 5665
e-mail: hk@hkeurope.com

Australia: Human Kinetics
57A Price Avenue
Lower Mitcham, South Australia 5062
08 8372 0999
e-mail: info@hkaustralia.com

New Zealand: Human Kinetics
P.O. Box 80
Torrens Park, South Australia 5062
0800 222 062
e-mail: info@hknewzealand.com

E5320

Contents

Part II   Learning Experiences for Children's Dance..... 109

Preface

Writing this third edition has been an opportunity to reflect on how we can improve our goal of making dance teaching accessible to educators and future educators. Whether you are a physical education teacher, dance teacher, grade-level classroom teacher, or student, we hope that your interest in dance is expressed in the enthusiasm you bring to your students when you offer dance in your program. Dance has become popular as the result of a recent flood of television shows and commercials that share the process of learning and performing and the strong message of dance as a means of expression and communication. An increasing number of students are talking about dance, dancing during recess, and using dance as a way to stay fit. Dance is now the cool activity to do. Students enjoy re-creating new moves they see on television and in videos. They view dance as a way to have fun and celebrate with friends and family. This opens the door for dance to be a welcomed activity in the school curriculum.

This edition of *Teaching Children Dance* brings a new perspective focused on dance as an inherent component of a child's education. Since our 2005 edition, educational issues have refocused on students' gaining knowledge and skills that can be applied to all aspects of their lives. Dance is one mode for learning that involves using the body and the senses to gather information, communicate, and demonstrate conceptual understandings. Teachers are interested in gaining new strategies for assessing what students learn in dance. They want inclusive approaches to designing lessons for students with disabilities, and they want to develop learning experiences that encourage creativity, positive social interactions, and development of motor skills.

The revisions in this edition include a section on dance and the whole-child education initiative; a discussion on how the 21st-century skills that promote creative thinking, collaboration, communication, global awareness, and self-direction are inherent in dance education; and a description of the link between dance and the 2008 Physical Activity Guidelines. We have developed 13 new learning experiences and expanded chapter 6 on assessment to include a menu of assessment instruments and additional examples. A new chapter, Including All Children in Dance, contains strategies for teaching students with disabilities and eight dances that promote inclusion for elementary-aged children. This edition also includes a bound-in CD-ROM with all the learning experiences, assessments, figures, and tables that can be used, adapted, and reproduced for classroom application. The materials appearing on the CD-ROM are highlighted in the book with a CD-ROM icon in the margin. On pages ix-x is a list of the materials that appear on the CD-ROM.

As in the second edition, this edition is divided into two parts. Part I contains the foundational content and strategies for developing dance learning experiences. We have updated our elements of dance and added new photos, figures, and tables. You will find ideas for planning a yearlong program, a dance unit, or a single lesson. We also include suggestions for class management, advocacy, assessment, and interdisciplinary teaching. At the end of each chapter, you will find revised questions for reflection that are applicable to both teachers and university students enrolled in dance courses.

Part II presents 23 detailed descriptions of creative dance learning experiences organized into two grade-level categories: kindergarten to second grade and third to fifth grade. The instructions for each dance learning experience are similar to the dialogue you would use with your students. As you read the instructions, you can imagine yourself in your teaching space with your students. Each learning experience includes the psychomotor, cognitive, and affective outcomes; equipment needed; ideas for the introduction, development, and culminating dance; and assessment suggestions that are directly linked to each outcome. There are suggestions for interdisciplinary teaching and ideas for varying the learning experience to meet your students' abilities and interests.

One of our challenges in writing this edition was to provide a clear description of the essential dance content and instructional strategies that are feasible and can lead to your success in teaching dance. Our hope is that, as a result of this book, more children will gain the opportunity to learn, create, perform, and respond to dance and that more educators will include dance as a cultural, social, and creative form in their programs. If you have used the previous edition of *Teaching Children Dance*, we know you will find this edition more comprehensive. If this is your first copy, we know this book will help you find the joy of teaching dance and help your students find the joy of learning dance.

How to Use the CD-ROM

The CD-ROM bound into the back of this book includes all 31 learning experiences with the suggested assessments. Also included are tables and figures and questions for reflection that can be reproduced or adapted for classroom application. The contents are listed as follows by chapter, and a CD-ROM icon 💿 appears next to them in the book to remind you of what appears on the CD-ROM.

A Framework for Teaching Children's Dance

Part I provides answers to the following questions: What is children's dance? Why should it be taught? How does one design and assess a dance program? Educators ask these foundational questions frequently when developing dance programs. We hope that in the following seven chapters you find the information that will help you understand children's dance and develop the skills to enhance or initiate dance as part of a physical education or arts education curriculum. An overview of the content in each chapter is as follows:

Chapter 1, Understanding the Importance of Teaching Children's Dance, addresses the essential content for teaching dance. It provides a description of what is considered children's dance and explains the significance and benefits of a children's dance program. Included in this edition

is information on how dance addresses the 2008 Physical Activity Guidelines, 21st-century skills, and whole-child education initiatives.

Chapter 2: Presenting Essential Content for Children's Dance. In this chapter, the elements of dance are described: the body, space, time, effort, and relationships. Also explored are the forms of children's dance and how they contribute to a comprehensive dance program.

Chapter 3: Designing a Dance Program. In this chapter are the nuts and bolts of program construction and delivery. We include examples for planning a yearlong program and a dance unit and lesson outline. The section on making interdisciplinary connections between dance and other subject areas continues to be an important component, and specific subjects are identified at the end of each learning experience in part II.

Chapter 4: Creating a Dance Education Setting. This chapter includes a discussion on tailoring a dance program to fit various teaching settings. Teachers are frequently faced with justifying to their students, parents, administrators, and other colleagues why dance should be included in the curriculum. To make such justification easier, we include advocacy strategies for maintaining and developing a program.

Chapter 5: Making Teaching Effective. The way you teach is as important as what you teach. In this chapter, we discuss how teaching and learning styles affect the success of a dance experience. Also included are strategies for establishing protocols and rules that lead to a safe and productive learning environment and strategies for student feedback, demonstrations, and observations.

Chapter 6: Assessing Children's Learning in Dance. Assessment is essential to all learning experiences. In this edition, we include more examples of assessment in dance and a menu of assessment instruments for teacher, peer, and student self-assessment.

Chapter 7: Including All Children in Dance. This is a new chapter on teaching children with disabilities. The chapter focuses on the importance of creating an inclusive teaching environment that recognizes the abilities of all children. Teaching strategies for success are included along with descriptions of dances that can be used in an inclusive dance class as well as a self-contained dance class.

Understanding the Importance of Teaching Children's Dance

Imagine a class of young children running as fast as they can, waving red streamers over their heads, and then spinning around and slowly descending to the floor with the streamers floating down beside them. Through these dance movements, children might be expressing their interpretations of a fast-burning flame slowly flickering out, or they may be pretending to sprinkle red paint all over a room. Now, imagine yourself as the teacher who designed and presented this dance idea to the class. The children responded with great enthusiasm, and you feel successful in sharing this experience with them. It would be wonderful if every dance experience resulted in this feeling of success for both the student and the teacher. The goal of this book is to provide you with the content to design and present a dance experience to students that

will be successful. All the learning experiences in chapters 8 and 9 have been taught by the authors, and many have been adapted by those studying dance pedagogy and experienced educators in dance or physical education. The success of a dance learning experience is in making relevant and developmentally appropriate content choices combined with a passion for teaching. The first step is to decide what you want students to learn and what benefits they will gain from the opportunity to participate in a dance learning experience. Clarifying the final outcome will guide you in selecting, planning, and implementing a meaningful learning experience for you and the students.

Teaching children dance may be a new area of study or an area in which you would like to improve your current knowledge and skills. It does not require being an accomplished dancer or knowing everything about every dance form; however, some experience with dance is helpful. Everyone has had the opportunity to experience dance either as a participant or a spectator. Think about the times you heard a piece of music and you could not resist the urge to move. Perhaps you have been at a social gathering where everyone is having fun dancing, and you are drawn into the energy of the group and find yourself moving your feet, laughing, and enjoying a moment of friendship and fun.

Teaching dance does require an educator who is dedicated to delivering a high-quality dance program and who believes that dance is essential to students' overall education. Even if you agree that dance is important, you may not be sure where to start. We ask you to consider the experiences, knowledge, and skills you already have and use them as a foundation for teaching dance, whether you are taking your first steps or reaching for the next level.

As a dance educator or physical educator, you enjoy physical activity in many forms. You like creating new possibilities for movement, such as developing a new game strategy, exploring how to express a poem through movement, or developing a new line dance. You value creativity and view it as a skill that students need in order to learn problem-solving and critical-thinking skills. Your enthusiasm for physical activity and positive attitude about exploring various ways to move provide you with a strong foundation for planning and teaching dance.

You can also rely on your teaching and dance experiences as a background for selecting the types of dance activities that are appropriate for the students. Find out about students' dance experiences. Begin by asking them where they have participated in or watched dance. This information can help you anticipate their acceptance of the dance experiences you have planned. Your experiences interacting with children have taught you that children enjoy creating new ways to move and that they are eager to share their accomplishments. You acknowledge that each student needs to learn in a caring and nonthreatening atmosphere. You may have already planned and implemented successful movement experiences and you know that if one idea does not work, you may need to try another and maybe even another.

These experiences with children, in a variety of settings, apply easily to teaching dance; all you may need are some ideas for lessons and a planning process.

Be confident in the knowledge and skills you bring to the dance learning experience, and be open to students' suggestions for dance content. Students' involvement in the content selection will increase their motivation to participate. Learning to teach dance begins with a willingness to try something new, to take a risk, and to persist so you can improve. Teaching will offer challenges—you may encounter reluctant students, require new teaching materials, or need additional professional development. But, why not make your teaching career full and exciting? Be open and willing to accept the challenges of learning something new, just as you ask your students to do every day.

WHAT IS CHILDREN'S DANCE?

Dance is a unique form of moving that holds various meanings for each of us, depending on how and why dance is a part of our lives. It is purposeful, intentionally rhythmic, and culturally patterned. It goes beyond ordinary motor activity because it also reflects one's aesthetic values (Hanna 1987). In the elementary school setting, dance has many purposes and can exist in a variety of forms. Children enjoy learning cultural dances, social dances, aerobic dance, square dances, and line dances as well as composing their own dances through creative dance. No single specific dance form should be taught exclusive of others. We recommend that children have an opportunity to experience many dance forms throughout their education.

Children's dance is a way of knowing that fully integrates all aspects of being human. Kinesthetically, intellectually, socially, and emotionally, children learn about themselves and others through the medium of dance. Ruth Murray (1963), a pioneer educator of elementary school dance education, noted the following:

Perhaps the best interpretation [of dance] is one that emphasizes not only body mastery and discipline in movements but even more the use of such movement for expressive and imaginative purposes. Dancing may borrow from and lend to many other kinds of movement activities. It is when the ultimate concern is with the meaning of movement that the term dancing is accurately applied. (pp. 7-8)

In the elementary curriculum, dance can be taught as a discrete subject, as a component of the physical education or arts program, or as a component that is integrated with another subject area (e.g., science or language arts). In all of these contexts, regardless of the type of dance that is taught, dance exists simultaneously as an art form and a movement form (see figure 1.1). Dance becomes the means through which children develop, express, and communicate their life experiences. As a result, they gain an aesthetic awareness about how the body and its movements are connected to meaning and intention.

When dance is part of the physical education curriculum, it provides children with an expressive way to use movement in addition to fulfilling the functional purposes of games, sport, fitness, and gymnastics. Dance is the only form of moving that meets children's innate need to communicate thoughts, feelings, understandings, and ideas through movement. All other types of movement in the physical education curriculum are functional—students acquire skills, such as throwing or kicking a ball, to improve their motor skills and ultimately use the skill in a game to perhaps score points (see figure 1.2a). In

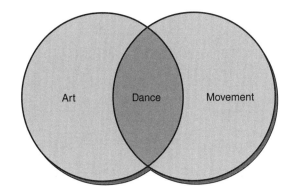

Figure 1.1 Dance, as a discrete subject, is simultaneously a movement and an art form.

gymnastics, children may learn the principles of balance to perform a handstand (see figure 1.2b). Although similar movements may appear in a dance, they are detached from their functional purpose (e.g., raising the arms high to catch a ball or to get a stretch through the body) and instead become movements that illustrate or express an idea, thought, understanding, or feeling, such as the feeling of reaching toward the sky (see figure 1.3). Both functional and expressive movements are necessary so children can use them for expression and communication of ideas and feelings in addition to developing a healthy, active lifestyle.

Children's dance involves more than exploring various ways to make a shape or learning a series of steps to use; it is a way of expressing understandings and feelings. This ability

Figure 1.2 Functional movement: *(a)* shooting a basket; *(b)* supporting body weight in a handstand.

Figure 1.3 Expressive movement: Children stretch their arms up to express the feeling of reaching toward the sky.

to use movement to express and communicate differentiates creative movement from creative dance. The purpose of creative movement is to explore movement possibilities and discover new ways to change movement. Creative dance uses the exploratory process in coming up with new movements; however, it takes the process further. After exploration, children make aesthetic choices about movements and the qualities of those movements that will best express their ideas, feelings, or understanding of a concept. These movements are then organized into a movement sequence or a dance. Children practice, refine, rearrange, and finally perform their dance individually as part of the whole class dancing or share dancing with a partner or small group. The child, as a dancer, can be compared to an artist's paintbrush as it moves on the canvas making an idea or feeling into a tangible form. Dance movements and the applied elements of dance are like the colors, lines, shapes, and textures a painter uses to express ideas. The dancing space becomes the canvas. Just as every painter might interpret a sunset, a flower, or the feeling of anger differently, children, too, will demonstrate their own unique interpretation of an idea, dance movement, or feeling using the body and its movements as their expressive tools.

Dance at the elementary level allows for personal decision making; exploration of new ways to move; and development of new ways of knowing, creating, and learning. Dance learning experiences are based on teacher- or student-selected outcomes that promote achievement in the psy-

chomotor, cognitive, and affective domains. These outcomes can guide curriculum development and help identify the benefits that students will gain as a result of participating in a dance program, unit, or lesson. Through physically learning and performing dances and creating, observing, and responding to dance, students develop their ability to physically move in different ways and understand how to create and adapt movement, and they discover how movement can be a means of learning about others and collaborating with others to accomplish a goal.

Through participating in various learning experiences that include dance as a social, cultural, and creative movement form, students can accomplish the following:

◆ Develop the knowledge and skills to use dance for self-expression and communication of ideas, concepts, understandings, and feelings.

◆ Increase their ability to observe and reproduce movement accurately.

◆ Develop their ability to use movement exploration to create new movements or find different ways to perform a specific movement.

◆ Increase their understanding of how dance represents social and cultural traditions, values, heritage, and ways of living.

◆ Acquire collaboration skills and demonstrate respect for others.

◆ Develop an understanding and appreciation for dance as a movement form and as an art form.

◆ Understand how the elements of dance, the body, space, time, force, flow, and relationships (see chapter 2) are used in learning, performing, creating, observing, and responding to dance.

◆ Recognize how dance can be a learning strategy for acquiring knowledge and skills in other arts and other subject areas.

◆ Develop locomotor and nonlocomotor skills.

◆ Increase their coordination, balance, strength, flexibility, and cardiorespiratory endurance as well as develop their knowledge of fitness.

For many children, the elementary school dance program may be their first encounter with dance. Children may bring perceptions and opinions about dance that influence their level of participation. By offering a variety of dance forms throughout the school year, children will be able to become more comfortable with different ways that movement is used as a basic means of expression and communication.

Awakening of New Perceptions

Each time children experience dance, whether as dancers, observers, or creators, they gain new perceptions about themselves and their world. Through dance, children learn more about who they are, how they move, what they think, how they feel, and how they relate to others. They also learn that there are multiple ways to express the same idea. For example, as a result of participating in a cloud dance where the children created their own body shapes and movements to express clouds they observed in the sky, the children expanded their insights into how clouds move and observed their classmates' unique interpretations of cloud shapes and movements.

Awakening of new perceptions and understandings is an aesthetic experience. Through manipulating the elements of dance, students make aesthetic choices about what movements to use and the quality of those movements. In the cloud dance, you might suggest the following explorations to help shape students' aesthetic choices: "Find a way to use your arms to create a long cloud shape. What pathway will you use to travel across the room in your cloud shape? Change your speed to show how slow and how fast the clouds move. How can you and another person connect your cloud shapes and move together?" (See figure 1.4.)

All dance movement is the result of a series of qualitative decisions about how the elements of dance will be used to express an idea. The way the dance movement appears, using space, time, force, and the relationship of the dancers to each other, is the result of purposeful decision making. This decision making is applicable to all types of dance. Traditional cultural dances were designed in a specific way to reflect a particular aspect of a culture. The formations, dance steps, clothing, and music all reflect what a group of people hold as significant representations of their history, tra-

Figure 1.4 Young children holding hands in a circle to demonstrate the shape of a cloud.

ditions, values, and beliefs. Social dances evolve from the needs of people to move together as a community, to share in celebrations, to meet others, and to maintain a connection. Creative dances are also based on individual or group decisions about how to manipulate movement to express an idea or feeling.

Dance in the elementary school curriculum provides children with a variety of dance experiences. These experiences allow them to create their own dance movements and to learn dances created by others. Creating and learning dances help children make meaning of what happens in their lives as well as in the lives of others.

Creative Dance

In creative dance, children generate, vary, and manipulate movement using the elements of dance (body, space, time, force, flow, and relationships; see chapter 2) through the process of improvisation. Creative movement is the product of improvisation and becomes the first step used in developing movements for a creative dance. Children may select improvised movements and arrange them into a sequence or choreographic structure to form a dance. The teacher or the children generate the initial idea for the dance. The following are examples of creative dance:

❖ A kindergarten class creates a dance about the animals and people they recently saw at the circus. They dance about lions jumping through hoops, elephants balancing, tightrope walkers moving forward and backward, acrobats swinging on the trapeze, and clowns juggling colorful balls.

◆ A first-grade class is studying a science unit on bubbles. They form a list of vocabulary words that describe how bubbles move and create dance movements to illustrate the vocabulary words. Next, the children develop a three-word sequence such as *pop, float,* and *burst* to create a dance that reflects the word sequence.

◆ A second-grade class has collaborated to write several poems. They select a poem they would like to express through dance. The class breaks into three groups, and each group creates a dance to represent the selected poem.

◆ The opening of baseball season is the main story on the front page of the newspaper. A third-grade class creates a dance that reflects the movements that occur in a baseball game. They include movements that represent various ways to run, catch, bat, and pitch.

◆ A fourth-grade class creates a large-group dance sculpture representing straight, twisted, and curved shapes. They focus on how to collaborate while they change from one shape to another using various tempos.

◆ A fifth-grade class, organized into groups of three, creates dances that use movements from everyday life such as brushing teeth, riding a bicycle, petting a dog, eating a sandwich, or reading a book. The dances focus on exploring range, levels, and rhythms. They perform the dances to various types of music and discuss how the movements changed to fit the music.

Traditional and Choreographed Dances

Traditional, cultural, square, and social dances are dance forms created by people in a specific culture or from a specific time period, as are dances choreographed by a professional choreographer, the teacher, or another student. These types of dances can be handed down from one generation to the next; they can be recorded on film, on videotape, on DVD, or in a written

Children performing a traditional cultural dance, the Virginia reel.

form; or they can simply exist within the mind and body of the person who composed it. The following are some examples of cultural, social, and choreographed dances:

- ❖ A dance choreographed by one student or a group of students with designated movements and a repeatable sequence that is taught to other students
- ❖ A dance choreographed and taught by the teacher (see figure 1.5)
- ❖ A traditional cultural dance such as la raspa, troika, or Virginia reel
- ❖ A popular dance from a particular time period such as the twist, electric slide, or lindy
- ❖ A children's social dance such as the hokey pokey, alley cat, or bunny hop
- ❖ A square dance such as the Texas star or Oh, Johnny
- ❖ A contemporary popular line dance such as the cha-cha slide or cupid shuffle
- ❖ A choreographed dance by a professional choreographer in dance forms such as modern dance, jazz, ballroom, hip-hop, ballet, or tap

WHY TEACH CHILDREN'S DANCE?

Dance is an essential component of a high-quality, comprehensive physical education or arts education program. Children need to have the opportunity to develop their abilities to use movement for both functional and expressive purposes. They should participate in a full range of experiences to learn the many possibilities for movement. In the National Standards for Dance Education, dance is defined as an art form that communicates meaning and understanding through movement (Meyer 2010).

Dance addresses the needs of children to express and communicate their ideas, to understand and know themselves and their world, and to expand their own movement abilities. Using movement to express ideas is already familiar to children. Along with their language development, they use locomotor and nonlocomotor movements to support and emphasize what they want to say. This natural use of movement for expression and communication becomes a foundation for learning dance. Also, children's life experiences, culture, physical and intellectual abilities, and understanding of themselves influence how they perceive and integrate dance into their lives.

Expressing and Communicating Ideas, Feelings, and Understandings

Dance addresses children's need for expression and communication in the following ways:

- ❖ Allows children to use their natural creative instincts to make a statement about their world
- ❖ Encourages children to reach beyond the conventional response to a movement task and discover new ways to move, feel,

Figure 1.5   Learning dances created by others expands a child's movement vocabulary.

perceive, and understand themselves and others in their environment

❖ Teaches children an avenue of expression and communication in addition to writing, speaking, the visual arts, music, and theater (literacy in all these areas is important for increasing the quality of interaction with others)

❖ Develops imagination, creativity, critical thinking, and the ability to make decisions through creating new dance movements

❖ Provides opportunities for children to share with others in the experience of creating and learning together

❖ Increases opportunities for children to create, perform, observe, and respond to movement they have learned or viewed

Starting at birth, children use movement as a way to express and communicate their needs. As they grow and develop, they naturally combine movement and language to share with others what they want or have experienced. Dance fosters children's innate need for movement and offers the opportunity to expand their knowledge and skills in using movement as a way of learning about themselves, others, and their world. In many school environments, writing, reading, and math are emphasized as ways to learn. Movement, specifically dance, is a natural and essential means for learning and sharing information and experiences.

Knowing and Understanding Yourself and Your World

Dance enables children to understand themselves and the world around them in the following ways:

❖ Reinforces learning about the elements of the body, space, time, force, flow, and relationships, which are common to all movement activities in the physical education and dance education curriculum

❖ Recognizes the contributions of all cultures to the fabric of Western society through learning traditional cultural dances and creating new dances

❖ Increases understanding of how dance represents the history, traditions, beliefs, and values of a culture

❖ Enhances the skills of perception, evaluation, problem solving, observation, and concentration

❖ Defines and clarifies one's ideas, thoughts, understandings, or feelings

❖ Plays a significant role in a total education by integrating cognitive, psychomotor, affective, and aesthetic development in each learning experience

❖ Increases knowledge about the various ways to move

❖ Develops self-concept, self-esteem, and self- and group identity

❖ Helps children recognize similarities and differences among people

❖ Changes the way children perceive their world

A major outcome of education is to ensure that each student gains the knowledge and skills to live a successful and meaningful life. Understanding how to create, how to learn, how to collaborate, and how to apply new ideas and understandings is essential to being productive and enjoying all aspects of life. Through dance, students learn to explore new experiences and discover what they can do and what they want to do. They learn the process of creating, making something new, solving a problem, evaluating a product, and sharing their perspective; all these attributes are required for success in any area a student wants to pursue. Success leads to positive self-esteem and a feeling of empowerment, which contribute to further opportunities to learn about themselves, others, and their world.

Developing Movement Abilities

Dance contributes to children's development of their movement abilities in the following ways:

❖ Increasing their ability to perform locomotor and nonlocomotor movements and patterns or sequences of movements while applying the dance elements of space, time, force, flow, and relationship in a variety of ways

❖ Developing their strength, flexibility, cardiorespiratory endurance, coordination, speed, and balance

◆ Adding to the number of experiences that promote learning about the infinite ways the body is capable of moving

◆ Enhancing motor learning through repetition and practice of dance movements

◆ Learning to safely move as they express and communicate ideas, feelings, and understandings

Dance is experienced primarily through the body and its movements. Children learn to dance by observing a movement and then reproducing the movement based on their ability to perceive the details of how the movement occurs and their actual physical ability to perform the movement. They also demonstrate their ability to create through movement. The more experiences children gain in the various ways to dance, the more background they will have to draw on when they learn new movements and patterns or make movement choices. Motor skills, fitness level, and a variety of movement experiences all contribute to a child's ability to use dance to express and communicate ideas and feelings.

Children who participate in a variety of dance experiences use their ability as kinesthetic learners to discover many ways to move. As they develop physically, cognitively, emotionally, and socially throughout their elementary education, they continue to increase their motor skills and expand their understanding of how to use their bodies as instruments of expression and communication. They find joy in moving to a repetitive rhythm, running across a space and leaping into the air, and spinning around as their physical, cognitive, and creative abilities are integrated in a moment of dancing alone or with others.

WHAT ARE THE BENEFITS OF CHILDREN'S DANCE?

The chapter's opening dance scenario illustrates the joy children experience as they interpret the movement of a red streamer. Although enjoyment and celebration are apparent when children dance, they are also learning. The primary goal of dance education is for children to learn how to use movement as a means of exploring, expressing, and communicating an idea, understanding, concept, or feeling, whether a movement is initiated by them or by others. For the teacher, what

children are learning can be clearly evident and easily assessed, yet for the child, there are intangible benefits that are unique and personal and cannot be measured or observed. Children who view the world primarily through movement rely on kinesthetic thinking, in which the images and feelings that emerge are best understood when a symbolic language, such as dance, is used for translating what they have experienced (Root-Bernstein and Root-Bernstein 2000). Through multiple dance experiences, children who love to move and learn best through movement welcome dance experiences because they feel dance is a natural and fun way to learn. These children seek out movement experiences and, as a result, gain the psychomotor, cognitive, affective, and social benefits. Yet all children gain many benefits from dance. Children learn motor skills through the psychomotor domain and knowledge through the cognitive domain, and they gain an understanding of their feelings and preferences and learn how to interact positively with others in the affective domain.

Psychomotor Benefits

The dance component in a physical education or arts education curriculum provides children with the opportunity to develop and improve their fitness and motor skills, which form the kinesthetic foundation children rely on to express and communicate through dance. Jane Clark, motor development and motor learning scholar (2007), states, "Motor skills do not just come as birthday presents. They must be nurtured, promoted, and practiced" (p. 43). Motor literacy is essential to success in learning and creating dances. It also contributes to all physical activities that children pursue. Dance learning experiences are characterized by learning multiple ways to move the body through space, in time, with force, flow, and relationships. Children run, jump, twist, leap, wiggle, crawl, and roll in many directions and pathways, using different tempos with varied amounts of force. They learn to move the whole body or its parts in isolation in a safe and effective manner. Moving from one shape into another or performing a combination of locomotor movements that require body control is developed through exploration and repetition. Children gain strength, improve balance, and increase flexibility and coordination through creating movements or learning new movements. They learn to reproduce and refine movement patterns, increase their spatial and body awareness, and develop the ability to coordinate their movements with the movements of others. Dance learning experiences, taught throughout the school year, provide children with opportunities to continue their development of motor skills and to expand the use of these skills in their lives. Children become better at controlling the transfer of weight when performing locomotor movements and combinations of locomotor and nonlocomotor movements and transitioning from moving to stillness. They are able to demonstrate body control at changing levels, directions, amounts of energy, and speed. This sense of learning to master the infinite movement possibilities that dance provides enhances children's self-perception that they are capable movers. They feel comfortable trying new physical activities and understand the value of practice and persistence in learning something new.

Cognitive Benefits

The cognitive benefits of dance include learning about one's body and how it moves and relates to others and the environment. Children gain knowledge about themselves and their world through active interaction; that is, they learn best through doing. Ultimately, the way children think is influenced by the types of experiences they have in their lives (Eisner 1998). Through dance, children better comprehend the concepts of direction, range, pathways, levels, tempo, shape, force, and flow by experiencing these concepts through being physically active in the learning process.

Dance nurtures cognitive development with each task in a learning experience. Children demonstrate their conceptual understanding when they move. We refer to this as a kinesthetic answer to the task presented by the teacher. For example, when the teacher instructs the child, "Using your hand and arm, draw a curved line in the air in front of your body," the child needs knowledge of body parts, of the concept "curved," and of the frontal plane of the body; he also needs the ability to synthesize these concepts into one movement. If the child does not demonstrate the anticipated response, knowledge of one of the components of the task may be missing. The teacher will need to analyze the task, investigate what knowledge is missing, and then adjust the task to help the child

learn the concepts. Offering a variety of dance experiences will increase a child's knowledge of his body and its infinite movement possibilities. Learning to dance requires children to recall terms and movement sequences, identify movement similarities and differences, demonstrate application of concepts, analyze how the elements of dance are used in a dance, and evaluate their own and others' performances.

Critical thinking and creative thinking are other cognitive abilities used in learning, performing, creating, observing, and responding to dance. As children create, perform, or observe dances, they make an objective or subjective analysis and evaluation about the movement. An objective evaluation is clearly observed and reported in a factual manner. For example, you may ask students to observe their partners holding their bodies in a balanced shape and count how many body parts are touching the floor. Asking questions that require personal reflections, opinions, or analysis as part of the response will elicit subjective evaluations. You may ask students, "What idea do you think the dancer was expressing in the dance?" or "What was the most exciting part of the dance for you?"

Through dance, children gain an understanding of their own aesthetic preferences as well as the preferences of others. Aesthetic understanding involves how the elements of dance are manipulated into meaningful patterns of body movements that express an idea or feeling. When children laugh while viewing a dance, they may be amused by the movements, the rhythm, or the use of space in the dance. As children reflect and describe what happened in the dance that made them laugh, they gain an understanding of their own aesthetic preferences.

The process of making a dance also involves cognitive development through using the imagination to create or rearrange movements in new ways to express ideas and feelings. Children instinctively use imaginative thinking in their everyday play environment. They create new characters, act out inventive scenarios, and use everyday objects in new ways to support their play concept. We encourage you not only to attend to correct replication of movement patterns but also to cultivate the powers of innovation through encouraging the use of children's imagination and creativity (Eisner 1998).

Finally, assessment of a student's cognitive abilities—recall, comprehension, application, and evaluation—can take the form of a spoken, written, or movement response. For example, after a creating a dance about rejection and acceptance of friends, students can be asked to verbally describe a sequence of movements they created to draw the shapes used in the dance or to demonstrate a movement from the dance that used strong or light energy. The assessment of a learning experience can be most challenging, yet physical educators and dance educators are familiar with using observation and analysis to see how the students respond to a task. They know from watching children dance that the movement needs to be clarified, repeated in a different way, or changed to enhance effectiveness or safety. Children show what they know as they listen to, process, and respond to what the teacher presents. Dance is one of the only content areas in the curriculum where children can demonstrate their understanding through movement. For those children who are kinesthetic learners, dance classes are the ideal learning environment.

Affective and Social Benefits

Children need to feel successful about the experiences they pursue and accomplish. They also have a need to express their joy, fear, anger, frustration, and excitement and to communicate their understanding about their world. Dance recognizes and fulfills these needs. Through dance, children discover who they are, how they move, where they can move, how it feels to move in different ways, what movements they like to do, and how those movements are different from and similar to others. They learn to make decisions, develop their imaginations, express ideas and feelings, and share with others. The dance learning experiences, whether they are positive or negative, contribute to a child's self-concept and self-esteem.

Dancing can make children feel proud of the way they move; however, it can also make them feel vulnerable. Children who are unsure of themselves will say, "I can't do it" or "I don't know how." Children are immediately aware of what they can and cannot do as they begin to move, and they know that others are also aware of how they are moving. As a teacher, you will need to recognize children's discomfort and to encourage them gently and with sensitivity to their feelings.

The body and its movements are the medium that reveals how a child feels inside. The ways in which children move through space, use time and force, and relate to others and their environment reveal these feelings. Modern dance pioneer Martha Graham said, "Movement is the one speech that cannot lie" (de Mille 1991, p. 22). How we feel at any moment is revealed in our actions, body shape, and facial expression. Dance provides children with the means of expressing and communicating what they really feel and know about themselves and their world. For example, children can express feelings of anger by stamping their feet and pounding their hands. These movements can then be explored further and inspire a dance that demonstrates angry feelings.

Socially, children enjoy interacting with others through movement. They laugh and talk with each other while sharing an experience that is fun and personally rewarding. Dance in the school environment usually occurs as part of a whole-class experience, with the teacher facilitating the session. Children participate in dances as individuals, as partners, as members of a small group, or as part of the whole class dancing in unison. While dancing in a small group, children assume various leadership roles, learn to share ideas, practice moving together, and develop a group identity. They experience the perspectives of others and see that an idea can be expressed in a multitude of ways. The dance lesson provides children with the opportunity to participate as learners, creators, and observers. In these roles they are taught to respect different movement preferences and learn to accept or positively negotiate ideas with other students. They learn how to cooperate with a partner or small group, solve conflicts peacefully, motivate others to stay focused, and provide support for others in the process of creating or performing a dance.

The teacher plays an important role in ensuring that the dance experience is positive and successful for all children. Each learning experience must be designed to match the developmental level of the children. Dance learning experiences for 5-year-old children, for example, are very different in content and presentation than experiences designed for 9-year-old children. All children need frequent positive reinforcement from the teacher and from peers. Most children want the teacher to watch them and respond with a positive comment. Young children frequently make comments such as "Watch me," "Watch how I can do it," and "Look at me." They depend on the teacher for approval, and the positive feedback helps motivate them to stay focused on the learning experience. Positive comments followed by a specific description of what the teacher observed reinforces that the child's effort is acceptable and has value. For example, a teacher commenting on a turn may say, "That was wonderful." The teacher might then continue, "That turn was very high off the floor, your head stayed up, and you landed with control." The teacher can continue to question the child, "What did you do that helped your landing to be so smooth?" In another example, two children have designed a repetitive movement to reflect the movement of a machine part. The teacher may use the following positive comment to clarify for students what they are doing well and support their collaborative effort: "Your movements are very clear, and both of you can keep the rhythm going at the same time. That's great the way you both work together."

Teachers make a difference in the attitudes that children develop about dance. Commitment to prepare and present a dance experience that is exciting, relevant, and developmentally appropriate is essential for effective and meaningful teaching. Teaching with enthusiasm and a sincere desire to make the dance experience a positive learning moment is essential. The lesson needs to ensure that children feel comfortable taking risks, trying out new ideas, and sharing their ideas with others. Extending what you already know about teaching dance will not only be challenging but will also bring personal and professional rewards, and a positive attitude will affect your students' feelings of success.

Learning Outcomes

The content of a dance experience for children reflects the characteristics unique to each age level. Every child comes to school with a unique set of life experiences and needs. A dance curriculum that encourages and celebrates what each individual brings to the learning experience recognizes these differences. Children may meet the same outcomes; however, there may be different ways for children to demonstrate what they know and are able to do. This differentiated approach

to learning recognizes the strength of each child and the areas for continued development. The dance learning outcomes describe what a student should know and be able to do as a result of participating in a kindergarten through fifth-grade (K-5) dance program. We offer a set of outcomes as an example of guiding statements for a dance program (Cone and Cone 2003). The outcomes are divided into two levels: kindergarten through second grade and third through fifth grade.

Children in kindergarten through second grade should have the following cognitive skills as a result of the dance education program:

- ◆ Describe their movements using elements of dance terminology. For example, children may describe a shape by saying, "I am making a big shape," or describe a level when they are moving on the floor by saying, "I am moving at a low level."

- ◆ Describe the movements of others using terminology related to the elements of dance. For example, a child may say, "Briana is skipping in a circle," or "Josh is wiggling very fast."

- ◆ Recognize that dance is a way to express an idea or a feeling using movement.

- ◆ Identify various locomotor and nonlocomotor movements, body parts, and shapes used in creating and performing dances.

- ◆ Understand that an idea or feeling can be expressed through dance in many ways. For example, when the sun is the topic for a dance, one child may walk slowly in a curvy pathway and slowly fall to the floor to express how the hot sun feels and how it drains his energy, while another child jumps quickly with strong energy from spot to spot to demonstrate how she feels when moving on a hot floor warmed by the sun.

- ◆ Understand that different cultures develop and perform dances for different reasons. In the traditional Japanese dance tanko bushi, the dancer's movements represent the work actions of the coal miners. Dancers perform this when celebrating the importance of coal mining in Japanese life. Another example is the German kinderpolka, which demonstrates young children's hand games and makes fun of adults scolding children with pointed fingers. Other dances celebrate a plentiful harvest, the crowning of a king, the work actions of a shoemaker, or animals that are important resources to people.

◈ Acknowledge that dance can be used in learning or reflecting learning in the other arts and school subjects.

◈ Comprehend that dance is a physical activity that builds strength and flexibility and improves balance and coordination.

◈ Recognize that dance is a way to enjoy creating and performing with others.

◈ Understand how technology is used in viewing and recording dances.

◈ Understand how to move safely in a variety of dance spaces.

These basic understandings are essential content that is unique to dance. The knowledge is gained primarily through learning, performing, creating, observing, and responding to dances whether they are a traditional cultural dance, a fun social dance, or a creative dance about animals.

Children in kindergarten through second grade should be able to do the following as a result of the dance education program:

◈ Demonstrate various movements that exemplify one or more elements of dance. For example, when children are asked to make a round shape or jump in a forward direction, they respond to the task with the corresponding movement.

◈ Perform the basic locomotor and nonlocomotor movements.

◈ Reproduce their own and others' movement, movement patterns, and shapes.

◈ Cooperate with a partner or small group to create and perform a dance.

◈ Improvise and generate movements to express an idea or a feeling.

◈ Observe the dances of others and respond to the observation by drawing, writing, or talking about the dances.

◈ Perform age-appropriate dances from a variety of cultures and time periods.

◈ Create a dance that expresses or interprets a concept from another subject area (e.g., dance about how the planets revolve around the sun).

◈ Create a dance using a self-selected idea.

◈ Demonstrate respect for the dances created and performed by others.

◈ Demonstrate the ability to move safely to avoid bodily injury.

◈ Use technology in viewing and recording dances.

Dance is learned by physically engaging in the movements and shapes that are part of a cultural, social, or creative dance. Children learn to collaborate with others by sharing ideas for movements, learning movements from others, and practicing together to perform a dance. Learning in dance is best accomplished by actual dancing because young children are eager to use movement to express and communicate their ideas.

Children in third through fifth grade should have the following cognitive skills as a result of the dance education program:

◈ Describe their movements by applying several terms of the elements of dance. For example, children may describe a shape by saying, "I am making a stretched shape that is low to the floor," or "I am running forward using a zigzag pathway."

◈ Describe the movements or combinations of movements of others by applying several terms of the elements of dance. For example, a child may say, "Julio is rising up slowly and softly," or "Julia turned on one foot, then skipped backward, and froze in a curved shape."

◈ Observe dances created and performed by others and describe their perceptions of the dance using dance terminology such as naming the formation, dance steps, gestures, costumes, and props or describing how the elements of dance are applied.

◈ Recognize dance as an art form that uses the elements of movement as the tools to express and communicate an idea or feeling.

◈ Learn the terminology and movements specific to a form or style of dance.

◈ Acknowledge that dance is representative of a variety of cultures and historical and social contexts.

◈ Understand that dance can be integrated with other art forms and other subject areas as a way of learning.

◈ Comprehend that dance is a physical activity that can improve strength, balance, coordination, cardiorespiratory endurance, and flexibility.

◈ Understand that cooperation is needed for performing or creating dances with others.

◈ Understand how to use the elements of dance to generate movement variations.

◈ Learn about choreographic structures such as AB, ABA, chance, or narrative.

◈ Understand how to access technology as a tool for learning creative, cultural, and social dances.

◈ Understand how dance as a physical activity can contribute to a healthy and active lifestyle.

Children in third through fifth grade are capable of understanding and applying dance terminology to describe a dance sequence or a complete dance. They are able to understand the process of composing a dance related to an idea and have a greater understanding of their physical abilities in performing alone or with others. These children are very familiar with technology as a learning tool and can offer ideas for viewing, recording, and choreographing using technology.

Children in third through fifth grade should be able to do the following as a result of the dance education program:

◈ Perform combinations of the basic locomotor and nonlocomotor movements using changes in space, time, and force.

◈ Demonstrate safe technique in movement to avoid bodily injury.

◈ Demonstrate respect for dances created and performed by others.

◈ Create and perform a dance with a clear beginning, middle, and end using a self-selected idea.

◈ Create and perform a dance that represents a concept from another art form or another subject area.

◈ Reproduce the movements, sequences, rhythmic patterns, energy, and use of space with age-appropriate dances.

◈ Create a dance using one or more choreographic structures such as AB, ABA, chance, or narrative.

◈ Perform age-appropriate dances from another culture or time period.

◈ Apply the elements of dance to create multiple movement variations and revisions to created dances.

◈ Apply technology skills to learning and performing creative, cultural, and social dance.

Children at these grade levels can learn and perform more complex dances and explain the meaning of the movements. They can collaborate in small groups to compose and perform dances based on self-selected ideas and integrate technology into their choreography and performance.

Implementing the National Dance Education Standards (Meyer 2010) describes how the dance education standards can be practically applied and assessed in the school setting. These standards describe the basic knowledge and skills necessary for developing an effective dance program. They focus on the content applicable to any dance program and do not dictate methodology or a specific curriculum design. Many states have referred to the national standards as a guide in developing state-level dance standards. We suggest that you obtain a copy of the national dance standards or your state dance or arts education standards to use as a reference in planning the content of your dance program. When dance is included as part of the physical education curriculum, you can also refer to *Moving Into the Future: National Standards for Physical Education* (National Association for Sport and Physical Education 2004) as a guide in developing a comprehensive dance program. These standards describe the essential concepts and skills for participating in a variety of movement forms, interacting with others, and using movement for self-expression, enjoyment, and maintaining a healthy and active lifestyle. Also, check with your school district for the physical education or arts education standards that may need to be addressed.

APPLYING 21ST-CENTURY SKILLS TO TEACHING DANCE

The best news about the educational buzz surrounding the 21st-century skills is that creativity, collaboration, critical thinking, self-direction, problem solving, and global awareness are taking center stage in education. These skills are inherent to dance education. They form the foundation for content and pedagogy. Future employment and products will rely on the creative capacity of people to think in new ways and create new solutions that improve our lives. Through dance, children have the opportunity to explore diverse ways of moving, find multiple ways to express an idea and feeling, and use their imagination and creative-thinking skills to create a dance. Our current students will create the future in which we will live. Developing their abilities to use critical reflection about what they have learned and created will guide them to see multiple perspectives and be able to discover alternative outcomes. Children who are growing up in the 21st century need to manage the complexity and diversity of everyday living and their careers. They will need to be more fluid, more flexible, more globally aware, and more innovative (Cookson 2009). Each time a teacher asks students to find various ways to make a round shape with their bodies or move across the space using various directions and levels, the students engage in creative thinking to discover solutions to the task. As the students make the shape and move across the space, they evaluate the success of their solutions and increase their knowledge of the ways the body can move to express and communicate a concept. This self-directed moment builds on previous creative experiences and develops the children's understanding that many solutions exist through using the exploration process.

When children dance together, they collectively share in the cognitive process of remembering a movement sequence and collaborating to create or perform a dance. Students learn that each group member can offer new ideas that benefit everyone. This generation of students has opportunities to observe, create, and perform dance through new technology that did not exist a few years ago. They can see dance at any time through Internet sources from around the globe. New ideas, dances, moves, and forms of dance are created and available for viewing and invite interaction. Static, traditional definitions of dance are challenged as the body and technology blend to birth a new generation of dances and dancers. Dance educators who encourage children to voice their own ideas, embrace cultural diversity, and view dance as a conduit to teaching innovation provide learning experiences that prepare their students to be productive members of society. The body and its movements are what we all share as humans. Knowing how to collaborate with others, seek fresh insights, and value ingenuity is an achievable outcome in a dance curriculum that offers authentic learning experiences and challenges students to think beyond the conventional response.

MEETING THE WHOLE CHILD THROUGH DANCE

Every child deserves an education that addresses all the ways in which learning can occur. The arts, and specifically dance, offer children an opportunity to be active participants in their learning. Through dance, children acquire the psychomotor and cognitive skills required for expressing their understandings, ideas, and feelings. While dancing with others, they learn how they are similar to and different from others and how multiple perspectives can contribute to how a child experiences her world. The whole-child initiative is focused on five components that lead to success in school: Children need to be healthy, safe, engaged, supported, and challenged (ASCD 2011). A whole-child-oriented curriculum reflects an interdisciplinary approach with multiple ways to demonstrate acquired knowledge and skills. Pedagogy and content address children's varied interests, the ways they learn and respond to instruction, and learning experiences in all the multiple intelligences.

Dance education is whole-child education. Through dance, children are physically active as they learn and perform dances and create new movements. As a result, they can demonstrate development of body coordination, balance, strength, endurance, muscle memory, agility, and flexibility. Children learn that dancing is an activity that can contribute to a healthy and active lifestyle—and a healthy child is a better learner. A dance educator who presents developmentally appropriate content and encourages students to believe in their ability to learn provides a safe learning environment where all students are respected. In this educator's learning space, students are supported for their imagination, creative thinking, and collaboration with their peers. Children who learn to create, perform, and observe dance learn to recognize the many ways an idea or feeling can be expressed through movement. These children are engaged in making decisions about their aesthetic preferences, learning to remember movement sequences, and developing critical- and evaluative-thinking processes that are applicable to learning in all subjects. Emotionally, they are supported by an atmosphere of respect for taking risks and are encouraged to experience how a range of feelings can be explored through dance. When children are empowered to explore their ideas and know that their ideas and talents matter, they feel they are recognized for their ability equally to that of their peers (Nelson 2009). Addressing the whole child requires you as the dance educator to be knowledgeable in dance content, education theory, child development, and current education issues and to be able to integrate dance with other curricular areas and be able to collaborate with other faculty members.

LINKING THE PHYSICAL ACTIVITY GUIDELINES TO DANCE

In 2008, the United States Department of Health and Human Services issued the *Physical Activity Guidelines for Americans*. These scientifically based guidelines help Americans ages 6 and older improve their health through appropriate physical activity. The guidelines describe the types and amounts of physical activity that offer substantial health benefits and include a toolkit of resources on the health-related components of fitness and suggestions for activities. The guidelines state that when children and adults participate in regular physical activity, they can reduce their risk of many adverse health outcomes. The guidelines recommend that children and adolescents participate in 60 minutes a day of physical activity, which includes moderate or vigorous

aerobic physical activity, muscle-strengthening activity, and bone-strengthening activity. Dance is mentioned as an activity that children and adolescents can enjoy doing alone or with friends and family members. Three types of activity, as noted earlier, that contribute to a healthy and active lifestyle for children and adolescents are defined in the guidelines.

Aerobic activities involve moving the large muscles using locomotor and nonlocomotor movements in space with varying amounts of force. In dance, children can learn and repeat dances that include running, skipping, sliding, galloping, leaping, jumping, and hopping. When children and adolescents repeat the dances several times during a class session, they can increase cardiorespiratory fitness. Cultural dances such as the mayim and troika use running, grapevine, and hopping steps in quick-tempo repeated patterns. As dancers repeat these dances, they use a lot of energy, resulting in increased blood flow and oxygen consumption. A dance learning experience can include a moderate aerobic warm-up followed by exploration or learning experiences that require traveling through the space at different tempos and conclude with a complete dance that includes extended movement sequences that can involve cardiorespiratory fitness.

Muscle-strengthening activities use the muscles to engage in large movements that are rhythmic and repetitive. Learning, creating, or performing a dance uses the whole body and requires that students use strength and balance as they travel in the space and hold still shapes. Through dancing, students gain awareness of how the muscles are used and can be developed through participating in the many types of dance. For example, when students learn a hip-hop movement, they may be supporting their weight on their hands and feet while changing levels. Repeating this movement several times can strengthen the muscles in all body parts. Stopping and starting a dance movement or demonstrating a smooth transition between movements also requires strength to control coordination and balance.

Bone-strengthening activities occur when the body movements produce a force on the bones. All locomotor movements require the body use force in the takeoff and landing, which increase bone development. When children use locomotor movements in a social, cultural, or creative dance, they are participating in weight-bearing activities. For example, in a creative dance that expresses the actions of a frog, the children will explore various amounts of energy, range, and levels as they demonstrate a jumping frog exploring life in a pond. In another example, children crawl and roll on the floor to express a dance about the ocean waves as they move toward and away from the beach. As these examples illustrate, bone-strengthening activities can also be aerobic and muscle strengthening.

Dance is an activity that promotes fitness, social interaction, and cultural understanding and provides children with the skills and knowledge to pursue dance as a lifetime activity. One of the many benefits of learning and creating in dance is the opportunity to increase fitness levels.

SUMMARY

All children need to express their thoughts, understandings, ideas, and feelings. Dance fulfills this need when presented in developmentally appropriate learning experiences. These experiences should include movement that is natural for children yet teaches new movements that expand their movement vocabulary and develop skills. Dance complements the acquisition of motor skills in performing a function by teaching movement for expression and communication. Participation in dance promotes motor skill development and self-discovery, builds self-esteem, engages children in a positive opportunity to interact socially, and increases cultural understanding.

As an integral component of the physical education or arts education curriculum, dance experiences should offer opportunities for students to create dances, learn dances created by others, observe dance, and respond to dance. Planned outcomes for a dance program guide you as the teacher in developing learning experiences that address what children should know and be able to do as a result of participating in a dance program. In this way, children's learning is meaningful and relevant. For success in teaching any type of dance, you and the students must enter the learning experience together with enthusiasm, a positive attitude, and the willingness to allow the joy of dancing to envelop you.

 ## Questions for Reflection

What role does dance play in your life? Artistically? Socially? Culturally?

What is your definition of dance? How do others define dance?

What perceptions do you think your students will have about dance? What do you think influences their perceptions?

How do you think that creative dance is different from creative movement? How are they similar?

What skills and knowledge about movement and teaching do you have that can be applied to teaching dance?

Throughout children's education, they participate in many experiences that contribute to their physical, intellectual, emotional, and social development. What unique contributions does dance make to a child's development?

Presenting Essential Content for Children's Dance

This chapter presents a description of the content for dance within the physical education or arts education curriculum. In both program areas, teaching children to move and to use movement as a way to learn is the primary goal. Including dance as a significant component of the curriculum ensures that children have the opportunity to integrate their capacity to think with their bodies and to analyze its movements as a means of expressing and communicating what they know and experience. Through dance, children expand their movement abilities and use critical-thinking skills to learn, perform, create, and respond to dance.

The elements of dance—the body and its movements, space, time, force, flow, and relationships—are the foundation for the dance curriculum. All the elements are part of every movement we perform; however, dance manipulates and emphasizes specific elements in expressing an idea or feeling. Compare, for example, a box of crayons to the elements of dance. Using different crayon colors and blending them in various combinations can produce an infinite number of drawings and pictures; using different elements of dance in various combinations will produce many different dances. The specific way the elements of dance are combined depends on the intended meaning of the dance. For example, a dancer can illustrate the wind by running with fast, light, and small steps or with slow, strong, and large steps, producing a unique feeling. In a creative dance about the solar system, students may choose dance elements that emphasize slowly turning round shapes or movements that rotate quickly with strong energy. Many social and cultural dances have predetermined ways of using the elements of movement. The twist, a popular dance from the 1960s, moves the upper body and lower body in a strong, fast, side-to-side twisting movement. As soon as the music for the twist is played, everyone performs a similar twisting movement. However, a dancer can personalize the basic twisting movement by adding other dance elements to vary the level or speed. Many cultural dances delineate how the elements of dance are applied to reflect particular cultural values, traditions, or beliefs. Variations to a cultural folk dance may represent a regional style or group preference yet still contain basic characteristics of the traditional form.

In this chapter, we offer our version of the elements of dance based on the work of Rudolf Laban (1976) and other dance educators (Gilbert 1992; Wall and Murray 1989; Zakkai 1997). We have organized the elements of dance into six categories—the body, space, time, force, flow, and relationships (see table 2.1). Each element is individually defined; however, all the elements typically work in combination in every movement we make.

THE BODY

In dance, children construct infinite variations of movements to express and communicate ideas, feelings, concepts, perceptions, and meaning. The body and mind act jointly to create, perceive, and perform each movement that emerges in a dance experience. Fraleigh (1987) refers to this mind and body connection as a "minded body," in which dancing requires the whole person to be involved in the dance experience. Through dance, students explore, discover, and gain knowledge of all the infinite possibilities for movement. They increase control over their movements while developing body awareness. Children learn the names of body parts, identify where they are located, and learn the ways the body parts can move in isolation or as a coordinated whole.

Locomotor and Nonlocomotor Movements

Body movements are categorized into two basic types: locomotor movements and nonlocomotor movements. Locomotor movements are movements in which the body travels from one place to another in the space. Usually, we think about traveling on the feet as in running, jumping, walking, skipping, sliding, hopping, galloping, or leaping; yet other body parts can also be used for traveling (see table 2.1).

Nonlocomotor movements describe the actions of the whole body or its parts (see table 2.1). They are performed while the body is stationary or combined with a locomotor movement. For example, the whole body or only one arm can shake while stationary or both arms can shake while combined with skipping. Other nonlocomotor movements include twisting, bending, stretching, curling, turning, swinging, rocking, pushing, pulling, kicking, punching, pressing, rising, and sinking. Two or more nonlocomotor movements can be combined to create a new movement such as swinging the arms side to side as the torso twists. Also, locomotor and nonlocomotor movements frequently are combined to form more complex movements that allow for a greater interpretation of an idea, thought, or feeling. Picture a student running and leaping to express the idea of a leaf blowing in the air. Yet, when the student adds a swinging arm movement to the leap, she or he increases the movement complexity and further defines the shape of the leaf or the path of the wind as the leaf floats in the air. Combining locomotor and nonlocomotor movements increases a student's movement vocabulary beyond what he already knows while challenging him to create, learn, and practice new ways of moving.

Actions of Body Parts

Body parts are involved in movement in three ways: in isolation, leading a movement, and supporting the weight of the body. Isolated movements occur when one body part is moving and the rest of the body is still. This type of movement, which appears quite simple, is actually difficult for young children. Balance, strength, and concentration are required to keep the body still while a single body part moves. When a body part leads a movement, it will initiate the movement and the rest of the body follows with the same movement. A body part can also lead the rest of the body through space, as in running forward with the arms reaching forward. The third way is when a

Table 2.1 Elements of Dance

Body parts isolated, combined, leading, supporting	Body actions and movements		Body shapes: still (static), moving (dynamic)
Head, face, neck, shoulders, elbows, hands, fingers, forearms, chest, arms, upper arms, wrists, back, hips, waist, abdomen, legs, thighs, knees, shins, calves, ankles, feet, toes, heels	**Locomotor** Walk, run, jump, hop, skip, leap, slide, gallop, crawl, roll, move on different parts	**Nonlocomotor** Twist, shake, bend, stretch, turn, wiggle, swing, collapse, sway, rock, push, pull, vibrate, pivot, bounce, curl, press, float, punch, dab, flick, slash, glide, wring, gesture with hands or feet	Balanced, off balance, straight, curved, twisted, wide, narrow, angular, symmetrical, asymmetrical, round, elongated
Space	**Time**	**Force or energy**	**Flow**
Personal and general space **Levels** High, medium, low **Size or range** Big, medium, small, far, near **Directions** Forward, backward, sideward, up, down, diagonal, clockwise, counterclockwise **Pathways (in air and on floor)** Straight, curved, zigzag, circular, angular, spiral, arch	**Tempo or speed** Fast, sudden, slow, sustained, accelerated, decelerated **Rhythm** Even beat, uneven beat, percussive, patterns	**Strong** Heavy, firm, hard, powerful, explosive **Light** Soft, fine, gentle, delicate, smooth	**Free** Ongoing, unrestrained, uncontrolled, continuous, relaxed **Bound** Stoppable, restrained, controlled, tense

Relationship to others, objects, and the environment				
Who	**How**	**Where**	**Formations**	**What**
Individuals, partners, groups (small and large)	Contrast, copy, echo, follow, connect, mirror, lead, shadow, unison, alternate, call and response	Above, below, apart, together, behind, in front, side by side, meeting, parting, over, under, between	Scattered, lines (short, long), circles, curves, square, semicircle, triangle, rows, rectangle, X-shape	Objects, furniture, props, equipment, walls, ceiling, ground, floor

body part supports body weight. In many cultural and social dances, the feet primarily support the body weight. Yet, in some dance forms such as break dancing and creative dance, other body parts such as the hands, head, back, knees, and shoulders can be used to support body weight.

BODY SHAPES

The body is capable of forming an infinite variety of shapes. The body always takes a shape, whether moving or in a still position. Most body shapes, used in everyday life, are for functional purposes, such as sitting at a computer or standing in the shower. Certain body shapes send powerful messages, however, such as pointing a finger at someone, slumping in a moment of sorrow, or hugging a loved one.

Shapes that are created or reproduced in a dance experience are classified into three general categories: straight, curved, and twisted (see figure 2.1). Straight shapes can be formed with the whole body or its parts. By bending the elbows, knees, wrists, fingers, and spine, the body can make an angular shape composed of many smaller straight shapes. The second shape category is curved. In this shape, the body can be rounded through curving the spine forward, backward, or sideward. Also, arms and legs can be individually curved or curved as part of the whole body shape. Other words frequently used to describe a curved shape are *rounded, squiggly, curled, wavy, arched,* or *spiraled.* The third category describes twisted shapes in which the body rotates in two opposing directions at the same time. Most twisted shapes begin at the waist with the legs and hips twisted in one direction and the upper body in the opposite direction. A single body part can form a twisted shape by rotating in an opposing direction to the rest of the body, such as twisting an arm away from the torso or both legs twisted around each other.

Two additional shape categories are symmetrical and asymmetrical. Symmetrical shapes in dance are positions in which the left and right sides of the body are in exactly the same shape. Asymmetrical shapes are positions in which the two sides of the body are different.

Shapes can be expressed through stillness, like a stone sculpture or a frozen statue. Shapes are also inherent in all locomotor movements. Some shapes appear naturally as the body travels, and other shapes are intentional. For example, a straight, symmetrical arm shape may be combined with a jump, or a curving shape of the back may be combined with a skip.

SPACE

We are always moving in space, mainly for functional purposes (e.g., walking forward to turn on a light switch). In dance, a person moves in space as the result of a series of choices that express an idea or a feeling. Changing levels from high to low can represent the action of a wave moving toward the beach. Skipping forward on a curved path may express the wind blowing from side to side, or it can express happiness. Space for a dancer can be compared to the canvas of an artist. As the dancer moves in various directions, levels, pathways, and ranges, she or he creates a spatial design. In many cultural or social dances, the space is designed in circles or lines to represent a community of people sharing an experience together. When children engage in a creative dance experience, they develop new spatial designs that reflect their meaning of the movement. The element of space is further delineated through its six interrelated components: personal space, general space, levels, directions, pathways, and range.

Personal Space

The term *personal space* describes the space immediately surrounding the body—that is, the space that is always around us everywhere we move and when we are stationary. Although the size of one's personal space changes with each dance activity, it is generally thought of as an adequate amount of space around the front, back, top, and sides of the body so the student can move without touching another person or object. The image of a

Figure 2.1 In creative dance, children explore various ways to make straight, twisted, and curved shapes.

giant bubble around the body is an effective way to describe personal space to children. They can find the limits of their personal space by reaching out with their hands and feet in the immediate space around the body and sensing that they have adequate space for their movement.

General Space

General space refers to all the space outside of personal space that is available for movement; everyone shares this space. In a dance where students are running and leaping, each student leaps in the shared general space, but an individual's leap occurs within the limits of his or her personal space. Dancers carry their personal space with them as they move in the general space. Whether students are creating their own dances or learning a dance from another person, the general space has a defined boundary. As a teacher, you may designate the boundary by the lines on the floor or cones marking an outside space. In a cultural or social dance, the general space is usually determined by the formation required for the dance, such as a circle, square, or single line.

Levels

The term *level* in dance implies three different heights—low, medium, and high—in which the body moves and makes shapes. A low level is considered close to or on the ground—that is, the space below the knees. Movements such as crawling, rolling, or stretching on the floor occur at a low level. The medium level is the space midway between high and low or generally between a person's knees and shoulders. Movements such as walking or running can occur at a medium level. The space above the shoulders is considered a high level. When students are asked to reach for the sky, raising their arms above the shoulders, or to jump and leap, they are using space at a high level.

Directions

When students dance, their bodies move in six general directions in space:

- ◈ Forward, defined as the front of the body leading the movement
- ◈ Backward, where the back of the body leads the movement

- ◈ Sideways to the right or left, in which the right or left side leads the movement
- ◈ Up and down, defined as moving up toward the sky or down toward the ground

The first four basic directions (forward, backward, right, and left) can be combined with the up and down directions in many ways, some of which form a diagonal direction (e.g., forward and to the right). A student can move forward and up as in a leap or forward and down by lowering the body to the ground. The same movement performed in each of the directions will have a different feeling and communicate a different idea. For example, reaching forward and up with the hands and arms can illustrate reaching toward the sun to express how wonderful the warm sun feels after a cold winter season, whereas the same reach in a sideward and down direction can demonstrate reaching to help someone who has fallen.

Fourth graders make a sculpture using the three levels—low, medium, and high.

Pathways

Pathways describe the way space is shaped as the body moves in space. Two types of pathways occur in dance. The first type, floor pathways, is created by traveling movements (such as running in a circle or skipping on a straight line), and the second type, air pathways, is created by a body part or parts moving in the space around the body (as in drawing a zigzag line in the air with an elbow). If a student stepped in a puddle of water and then ran in a circle, the result would be a pathway of footsteps that describe the shape of where the body traveled. All pathways are composed of straight and curved lines or a combination of both. In dance, the student makes a decision about the pathway for movement or learns a specific pathway that has already been designed for a dance. Examples of air and floor pathways are illustrated in figure 2.2.

Range

Range defines the size of a movement. Another word used interchangeably with range is *extensions*. Descriptions about how large or small, long or short, or wide or narrow the movements are all relate to size. The steps to a cultural dance may require the students to take large running steps in a circle, whereas in another dance the students might perform small, swinging arm movements.

TIME

The time element in dance refers to the tempo and the rhythm of the movement. Time also refers to the duration of the pauses between movements. Dance is composed not only of movement but also of the stillness between movements. For example, in a dance that explores different ways to jump, the student may hold a still shape for a long time between a repeated series of three quick jumps. The next sections describe tempo and rhythm.

Tempo

Tempo is the pace of a movement (that is, how fast or slow the movement occurs). In the action of clapping hands using a steady beat, the tempo may be fast or slow. Walking can also demonstrate a steady beat—the beat of the steps can be fast or slow, and the number of steps can be short in duration (with only a few steps) or longer in duration (walking for 30 seconds). Tempo can

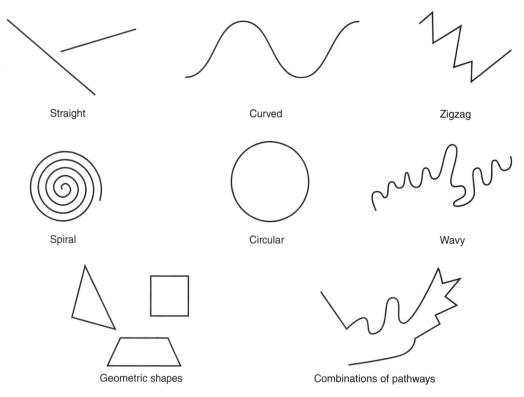

Straight   Curved   Zigzag

Spiral   Circular   Wavy

Geometric shapes   Combinations of pathways

Figure 2.2   Students can choose from several air and floor pathways when creating a dance.

change abruptly from fast to slow or vice versa, and tempo can change gradually through acceleration and deceleration. The increase or decrease in speed can occur over a long duration or very quickly. In the familiar social dance the alley cat, the foot pattern accelerates toward the end of the dance to challenge the dancers to repeat the pattern faster and faster. The dance ends with a deceleration of the pattern to the original speed. In a creative dance that interprets a rainstorm, the movement may begin at a slow speed to demonstrate the beginning of a rainfall. The speed of the movement may then accelerate to illustrate a strong rainstorm and end with a deceleration of speed to represent the final raindrop.

Rhythm

Dance movements are organized through rhythm in much the same way that sound in music are organized. Rhythm is the underlying pattern that gives order to music and dance (Fowler 1994). The most basic rhythm is a beat (pulse), which occurs at regular intervals. This beat is what we feel in the body when we hear a piece of music. Movement, whether it is the bouncing of the head or tapping of the feet, translates the sound we hear into a kinesthetic and visual response. The pulse becomes the foundation for a dance, supporting other even or uneven rhythms. Rhythm is also the combination of long and short sounds or slow and quick movements such as a dance using the rhythm, slow-slow-quick-quick-quick. Cultural dances have rhythms inherent to the culture from which the dance originated. These rhythms represent ways in which people move in that culture or how they work, play, worship, celebrate, and express their ideas. As students learn various cultural dances, they discover that some of the rhythms in the dance movements feel comfortable, whereas other rhythms may be difficult to perform. We all grow up in a culture that has its own rhythm. Learning the rhythms of another culture can be challenging, but it can lead to an understanding of the similarities and differences between and among cultures.

One aspect of rhythm is *accent*. Accent is an emphasis placed on a beat. As the emphasis is repeated in a series of beats, a rhythmic pattern of stronger and weaker beats is established. A regular accent (called the *downbeat*) falls at the beginning of a pattern, whereas a syncopated accent (or *upbeat*) is placed on the weaker beats in the pattern. In dance, an accent becomes evident by a change in the movement or quality of the movement. The accent can be represented through a movement that is stronger, bigger, higher, or faster. An accented dance step may move in a different direction, or the accent may appear as a movement of an isolated body part. For example, a folk dance may call for a strong stamp on the first beat of a pattern of steps, or a short dance composed of 12 beats may require reaching into the air on the first and fourth beats. Students will notice the accented movement in a dance; it will feel different and perhaps be exciting to express or challenging to coordinate.

In music, repeating patterns of beats are referred to as a *meter* or a rhythmic measure of a certain number of beats (Fowler 1994). Dance also uses these terms to describe a phrase of movements that contains a certain number of beats. In many cultural and social dances, the pattern of dance movements corresponds to the rhythmic measures in the music. Creative dance uses regular repeating rhythmic patterns as well as rhythmic patterns that are not regularly structured. For example, an 8-beat repeating rhythmic pattern of movement can be R-step, hop, L-step, hop, R-run, L-run, R-step, and L-leap. In another case, a dance may begin with a measure of 4 beats, then follow with a measure of 7 beats, and continue with a measure of 2 beats.

FORCE

Force is the amount of energy expended in a movement. It can be strong, as exhibited in a punch, or light, as expressed in a floating movement. When we move about in our daily routines, we use force to be efficient and effective. Washing out a crystal glass requires a different force than scrubbing a burned pan. We have learned to use the appropriate amount of muscular energy to complete a task. In dance, too, we learn to use different amounts of force depending on the intention of the movement. Using strong force with tense, firm muscles results in a powerful movement that may express the movement of a stalking lion. Using light force with loose, relaxed muscles results in soft, gentle movements that can capture the feeling of stepping on a cloud.

In a cultural dance, the dancers may perform a pattern that uses several strong foot stamps and then several quick, light kicks. A social dance like the hokey pokey may use a strong movement to emphasize placing a body part in or out of the circle followed by a soft turning movement with arms and fingers moving lightly from side to side. Children in a creative dance unit can use strong force to illustrate the powerful sound of a thunderstorm or use light force to express a story about a butterfly visiting a garden of flowers.

FLOW

Flow refers to how force is controlled in a movement. The two words commonly used to describe flow are *free* and *bound*. In free flow, the mover is not completely in control of the energy of the movements and may feel out of control, unrestrained, or unable to stop. This use of force implies taking some risks with balance and experiencing some uncertainty in how space is used. Students may create a dance that has a section where the movement feels out of control and then returns to a sequence of defined dance steps. Bound flow denotes controlling the energy of the movement. The student can stop the movement at any time. For example, in a dance using eight slides to the right and eight slides to the left, the students will need to use bound flow to change from the eighth slide to the right to the first slide to the left. Many dances use bound flow when changing the direction of a movement, pausing in a shape, ending the dance, or dancing with another person.

RELATIONSHIPS

Dance includes various types of relationships. Relationship terms include *near, close, far, away, over, under, through, in front, in back, alongside, around, between, inside, outside, above, below, together,* and *apart*. The definition of this element includes three parts: the relationship of a person's body parts to his or her other body parts; the spatial and temporal relationship of individuals organized into partners and groups; and the relationship of one's body to props, equipment, and the dance environment.

Body Parts

As children move their body parts into various relationships, they make various body shapes.

A hand may be held over the head or behind the back in a cultural dance, or the head is placed close to the knees depicting the curled shape of a caterpillar. Each body part is capable of many movements that occur in the personal space around the body and in relation to other body parts. When students perform a dance in which they gallop and swing their hands in front and in back of their bodies, they are using body-part relationships. In a creative dance where the students begin as small flower seeds under the earth, their body parts would be close to each other in a small round shape. As the seed begins to sprout, their hands and feet will begin to reach away from the torso to demonstrate the plant growing toward the sun.

Partners and Groups

When students dance with a partner or as a member of a group, they relate to each other in space and time. Partners or groups can move in a spatial relationship to each other such as side by side, facing each other, back to back, one behind the other, or side to back (see figure 2.3). They can also move in a temporal relationship to each other: in unison (moving exactly at the same time) or with a time delay between one person's movement and the other person's movement. The following movement relationship descriptions characterize a variety of uses of space and time.

◈ Shadow (also known as follow or copy): One student is behind another and follows the student, performing the same movement at the same time. The right and left sides of the body move in the same way as

Partners mirroring a still shape.

the leader (see figure 2.3, one in front and one behind).

◆ Mirror: In this relationship, students face each other and perform the same movement as if they are looking in a mirror. When the leader moves the left arm, the follower moves the right arm using the same movement. The movements of the follower occur at the same time as the leader's movements. A slow tempo is recommended to allow the follower to stay in unison with the leader (see figure 2.3, facing each other).

◆ Echo: The leader performs a movement and the follower observes the leader and then repeats the same movement after a very short delay between the movements. When a group does a sequence of echo movements, the effect is like falling dominoes or the wave. Dancers can use any spatial relationship.

◆ Unison: Two individuals or a group all perform the same movement at the same time. Dancers can use any spatial relationship.

◆ Call and response: This relationship is similar to having a conversation with words, where one person speaks and the other person responds. One person or a group makes the first movement, considered the call, and then the other person or group makes a movement, the response. The movements of the caller and the responder are usually completely different or a variation of each other movements. Dancers can use any spatial relationship.

◆ Contrast: Students perform a movement or make a still shape that is opposite to the movement of a partner or another group. A stretched-out movement can be contrasted with a closed and rounded movement, a forward movement can be contrasted with moving backward, or strong movements can be contrasted with light movements. The contrast can also appear in the use of time; for example, one person can be moving

Figure 2.3 Partner spatial relationships can include side by side, facing each other, back to back, one behind the other, or side to back.

rapidly while the other moves slowly. Dancers can use any spatial relationship.

◆ Connected: Two or more students move or make a still shape connected by one or more body parts. Dancers can use any spatial relationship.

◆ Supported: One or more students hold some or all of the body weight of another student, as in leaning on another person or lifting someone into the air. Dancers can use any spatial relationship.

◆ Meeting and parting: This relationship describes how students move toward and

away from each other in space. Dancers can use any spatial relationship.

Spatial Formations

The formation of the dancers in the space reflects the intent of the dance. In traditional cultural and social dances, students frequently dance in circles, squares, and line formations. These formations may express the feeling of unity as the dancers move using the same steps to the same rhythm. This type of dance fosters a feeling of acceptance and identity with a group. Other dances use formations that are like the spokes of

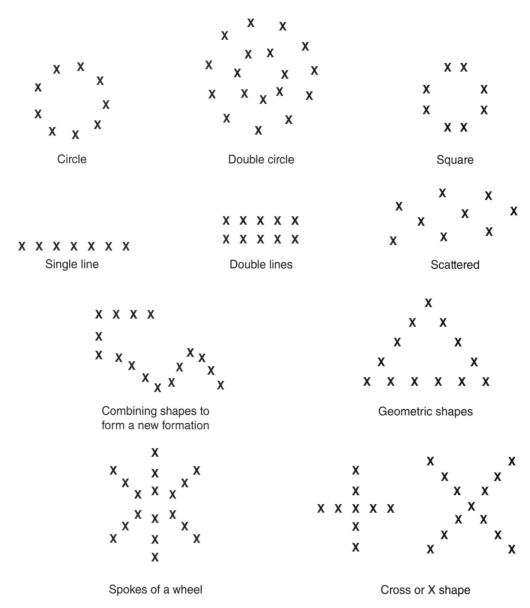

Figure 2.4 A variety of dance formations that are commonly used in traditional cultural and social dance.

a wheel, an *X*, or a cross shape. Creative dance also uses these formations in addition to scattered and geometric formations (see figure 2.4). One formation can be used for the entire dance, or the formation can change with different rhythmic patterns or to express different ideas in a dance.

Props, Equipment, and the Dance Environment

The relationship element is used here to describe the spatial relationship of an individual or group to a prop, piece of equipment, or the dance environment. Children relate to a prop by moving it in the personal space surrounding the body, to equipment by moving in the space surrounding the equipment, and to their environment by moving toward or away from the perimeter or center of the room or dance space. Children dancing with scarves in a creative dance experience, for example, can explore the space in front or in back of the body, over the head, between the legs, or around the waist. In another lesson using a piece of equipment such as a chair or a cardboard box, the children may explore ways they can move around, over, or under the equipment. A cultural dance may use long colorful ribbons held between the hands of dancers in a circle while other dancers move under and over the ribbons. The dance environment can be used imaginatively and become the sky as students run around the perimeter, or a circle taped in the center of the space can be used as a place to dance inside, outside, around, or to move toward and away.

DANCE FORMS

This section of the chapter describes the dance forms that are included in a dance curriculum: dances created by the students, defined in this book as creative dance, and dances created by others, such as social and cultural dances. A complete and inclusive dance program will provide students with experiences in creative dance, cultural dances, and social dances. Students will also have an opportunity to learn and create dances as individuals, in partnerships, and as a member of a group.

Creative Dance

In creative dance, children generate their own dances to reflect or interpret an idea, thought, or feeling. Through the process of improvisation, students can manipulate movements using the elements of dance and then select and arrange the movements into a sequence to form a dance (see figure 2.5). Creating new dance movements is often a challenge to both the student and the teacher. Students must rely on their personal backgrounds to create something new. This process is not always easy for them. Young children may not have an extensive vocabulary of ideas and movements to use. They may look to you as the teacher to provide examples of movements until they develop a stronger vocabulary. Alternatively, some children have a wealth of movement experiences and are always eager to offer new ideas. You need to establish a supportive atmosphere that encourages children to be creative and willing to share their ideas. Older children with a richer resource of life experiences may also encounter difficulty creating new movements. They may feel self-conscious and concerned about what their peers will think. The challenge for you as the teacher is to design a learning experience that encourages creativity and risk taking. Students need clear tasks that define what is expected yet are open ended to allow for a creative response.

For students with limited dance experience, a specific task approach is recommended. This approach gives students a clear understanding of what the task requires and still leaves room for personal decision making. For example, in the task "Find a way to do three consecutive jumps, each one moving in a different direction," a student can choose the shape of the jumps, the direction of each jump, the height of the jumps,

1. Explore movements using the elements of dance.
2. Select movements from those explored.
3. Choose a movement sequence.
4. Decide where the movements will happen in the space.
5. Practice the sequence and make changes.
6. Practice the new sequence.
7. Perform the completed dance.

Figure 2.5 Creative process used in creating a dance.

and the force of each jump. The task can be more specific if you require that all the jumps be high with strong energy and use a designated rhythm.

The term *personal dancing* refers to the experience of students creating their own dance movements based on a teacher-presented task. The task may be broad, such as "Make up your own way of moving to this slow music," or specific, such as "Find a way to rise slowly from the floor using a turn." Students make personal decisions about what movements they will use and how they will perform the movement within the guidelines of the task. They use their creativity, point of view, and resources to move in new ways to express a feeling or idea (see figure 2.6).

Personal dancing offers students the opportunity to discover what movements they like doing, what movements they may feel comfortable doing, how well they can do a movement, and what movements they would like to perform better. An example of personal dancing in a large-group experience is the floating clouds and rain showers dance experience (see page 117 in chapter 8). The dance experience begins with a discussion about the various cloud shapes and how clouds move in the sky. The students might describe cloud shapes as long, wide, puffy, big, or round and cloud movements as slow, floating, fast, or light. Next, each child creates a personal dance in response to the following task: "Think about the words you used to describe the clouds, and make shapes with your body that demonstrate cloud shapes. How many cloud shapes can you make with your body? Begin moving your body in its cloud shapes around the space. Move your shape forward and backward and turn it as you travel. Keep changing to different shapes as you float in the sky." In this dance experience, each child develops a personal dance

Figure 2.6 A creative dance that reflects the shape of a leaf.

even though the whole class responds simultaneously to the same task.

It is not only important to provide the opportunity to create individually but it is also critical to learn to create with others. Children spend most of their time in school interacting with others. They cooperate on science projects, eat lunch together, tutor each other, participate in the school band, and play together at recess. Working together to create a dance, whether with a partner or a group, requires cooperation and active involvement. Not all children are ready for this type of interaction. As a teacher, you need to keep in mind the motor-skill level of each age, the cognitive level of the students, and their ability to cooperate with others socially. Clearly defined tasks that include assigned roles will help the students to be successful. Young children need to gain some control and understanding of their own bodies before they can interact with other students of their age. They work more easily with a partner than in a group. Older children who are more coordinated and have a broad range of movement experiences are capable of creating partner and small-group dances when they are given a clearly defined task that encourages creating in a cooperative atmosphere. You need to make sure, however, that students have the social and collaborative skills (see figure 2.7). They will need to create and perform dances. This means that teaching children how to work together is as important as teaching the dance content.

Traditional and Choreographed Dances

In this type of dance, the student is the performer or learner, not the creator. Students can learn and perform the following types of dances:

◆ Personal or group dances created by a student or the teacher and taught to others in the class

◆ Dances created by a professional choreographer

◆ Social dances such as the twist or chicken dance that may reflect a particular time period

◆ Cultural dances that represent a particular country or ethnic population (sometimes referred to as folk dances)

Give everyone a turn to share their ideas.

Listen to one another's ideas.

Agree on a group idea through consensus or vote.

Compromise and blend ideas.

Encourage group members through the use of positive comments.

Remain focused on the task and practice together.

Figure 2.7 Collaborative skills for creating a group dance.

A description of each type of dance follows.

Dances Created by the Students or the Teacher

Student- and teacher-created dances can be created by an individual or a group and then taught to other individuals or groups. They are new dances created as a result of an idea presented and developed during a learning experience. The student or teacher organizes the movements into a sequence with a definite beginning, middle, and end. The dance is taught in a way that is developmentally appropriate and ensures a positive learning environment. The dances can be recorded in a variety of forms: on videotape or DVD, as a written record, or in a series of pictures.

Dances Created by a Professional Choreographer

Students may have the unique opportunity to study dance in their school with a professional choreographer or dancer, a guest artist, or an artist in residence. Complete dances or excerpts of dances from the dancer's or choreographer's repertoire can be taught to the students and adapted to meet the students' developmental level.

Social Dances

This form of dance emphasizes using dance as a means of experiencing the joy of moving with others. Social dances exist within a cultural and historical context and represent one of the ways in which people share, celebrate, and experience life as a community. They are dances that have become popular and are performed at many social occasions in groups. Examples include the cupid shuffle, lindy, twist, hip-hop dances, salsa, and electric slide. Students are always ready to teach a new dance that is popular, and they enjoy learning dances from other eras.

Cultural Dances

This dance form focuses on how dance represents events, traditions, and cultural heritage. Through these dances, students learn about what is important to another culture—its traditions, values, beliefs, history, and lifestyles. The dances are like stories passed down from one generation to another. They hold history and heritage in every movement and formation. Students need to learn more than the sequence of steps; they should be informed about the cultural background of the dance. It is important to teach about the environment and the people from which these dances emerge to promote appreciation and respect for the culture. In this book, American square dance is considered a cultural dance because it reflects how the diversity of cultures in various geographical areas of the United States contributed to the evolution of square dance.

Choosing dances created by others requires thoughtful selection of developmentally appropriate dances. Many cultural dances require dancers to perform movements in unison, in structured formations, or in time to a specific piece of music or rhythm. Young children may not be able to accurately reproduce the movements in the correct rhythm as a large group. As the teacher, you will need to find dances that are suitable for the ability of your students or adapt a dance while maintaining the integrity of the movements and formations. When possible, teach traditional cultural dances as they were originally intended. If you make numerous changes to the steps, gestures, and formations, the characteristics that make it representative of a culture can be compromised, and the authenticity of the dance is lost. As you teach dances from a variety of cultures, be aware that your personal culture will influence your presentation. The best situation is to have someone from the cultural group teach the dance; however, this is not always possible. You can research information on the Internet, in a library, or through pictures, videos, DVDs, and artifacts that will make the teaching and learning experience accurate and meaningful.

SUMMARY

Children's dance, as a medium of expression, is manifested through the body and its infinite variations of movement. The elements of dance—the body, space, time, force, flow, and relationships—have an impact on how the movement is designed and performed. Movement in dance has meaning—it expresses an idea or the intention of the performer or creator. When children participate in creative dance, they explore, improvise, and discover new ways to move. They also learn dances created by others—another student, the teacher, a professional choreographer—or dances from a specific historical period or ethnic population. The three forms of children's dance—creative, social, and cultural—make up a comprehensive dance program that provides students with opportunities for learning to create, perform, and respond to dance.

Questions for Reflection

How many ways to walk can you create using the elements of dance? For example, walk forward quickly using a curvy pathway or walk slowly taking big steps. What additional ideas can you think of?

If you were creating a dance about the water cycle, how would you use space, time, and force to create movements that represent evaporation, condensation, and precipitation?

Teaching dance within a cultural and historical context provides students with an understanding of how the dance movements and formations reflect traditions, values, beliefs, and ways of living. What are some strategies you would use to teach a cultural dance? How can technology be integrated into your teaching?

Think of several instances in which you participated in a cultural dance or a social dance. What did you enjoy about the experience? Who was dancing? What types of movements did you perform or observe?

three

Designing a Dance Program

Teaching dance is both challenging and rewarding. Deciding on the best way to organize and present a learning experience or a unit of study is a constant learning process. In every lesson you teach, you learn something new about the content, the task sequence, and the response from your students. You are constantly evaluating your teaching and making changes for the next session. In this chapter, we offer ideas for developing a yearlong program, specific units of study, and the individual lesson. Your school may already have a dance curriculum to guide your teaching, or you may be starting a curriculum. In either situation, planning is essential. Begin by getting to know your students, understanding the school's goals, and determining what is critical to the dance program. Review national, state, or local education standards that are required for your program. These standards provide a guide to the content that students should be able to do and know as a result of learning in a dance education program. You will not be able to teach everything in depth, and some content may not

be addressed each year. You will need to make decisions about what students need to know and experience.

What is important, however, is that children have the opportunity to learn, perform, create, and observe dances as well as respond to their own performances or creation of dances and the dances of others. The components of the artistic process form the foundation of a comprehensive dance program that addresses the psychomotor, cognitive, and affective domains inherent in all dance learning experiences. Teachers choose the appropriate content that meets their learning outcomes and incorporate two or more artistic processes into the unit or lesson development and implementation. For example, in a unit on cultural dances of the South Pacific region, the first lesson would be on learning about the history, customs, traditions, and characteristics of the people. Students observe a video, a teaching artist, or the dance teacher who presents the movements of a traditional dance. Next, students learn to reproduce the dance movements, rhythms, and formations through repetition and practice. The lesson concludes with the students' performing the dance to traditional music. Additionally, students can observe each other performing the dance and then respond through a discussion about what parts of the dance were most successful.

Following are the five components of the artistic process:

◆ **Learning** requires observation, reproduction, and repetition of movements through practice.

◆ **Creating** refers to generating new movements or movement variations through improvisation and exploration and also composing dances.

◆ **Performing** involves physically demonstrating dance movements or complete dances.

◆ **Observing** includes watching dances performed live and on DVD, video, or online sources.

◆ **Responding** engages students' critical-thinking skills to reflect on their performance, a dance they created, or an observation of a dance performed by others. Students can respond through discussion, writing, demonstration, or drawing.

PLANNING A YEARLONG DANCE PROGRAM

The dance content taught in the span of a school year for each grade level may be determined by the school district's curriculum for dance education. When a predetermined curriculum is not available, the dance educator or physical educator may be responsible for designing and implementing the dance program. Planning a dance program can be an overwhelming task. Knowing what type of dance to teach and how to organize the learning experiences requires combining knowledge of how children learn with knowledge of the dance content. Each dance learning experience focuses on several outcomes that emphasize some or all of the artistic components of dance—that is, learning, performing, creating, observing, and responding. These outcomes are met through a sequence of lessons that develop and refine the knowledge and skill that children

need in order to express and communicate ideas, thoughts, and feelings through dance. The specific theme for the learning experience, such as traditional West African dance or creating dances about the planets, must be relevant to the students in order to make their participation personal and meaningful.

As a full-time dance educator you might teach the same classes for the entire school year, or you might be scheduled to teach different classes that rotate every few weeks. The amount of time available determines the amount and depth of the content. In an elementary school where the children attend a dance class once a week for 45 minutes, you might plan 5 to 10 units delivered in 4 to 8 lessons per unit. The units can be different lengths depending on the content and age of the children. We recommend that children have the opportunity to learn about dance from creative, social, and cultural perspectives within the yearlong program.

When dance is part of the physical education program, it may be delivered in one or more units during the school year. This requires you as the teacher to make some tough decisions about what to teach within the time allotted for dance. Even with a limited time, children need to experience dance as a creative, social, and cultural form of expression. We recommend that dance be taught several times throughout the school year.

One approach to developing a yearlong program is to design one or more units for each grade level in each of the dance forms: creative, social, and cultural. In this approach, grade levels could be clustered for units such as kindergarten to first grade, second to third grades, and fourth to fifth grades. An example of a second- and third-grade dance program in the physical education curriculum might be as follows:

❖ Creative dance could involve a four-lesson unit focused on exploring and creating a dance about various water forms. In the first lesson, students identify five water forms such as a river, the ocean, a waterfall, a rainstorm, and a stream; they then explore movements that represent the characteristics of each water form. In the second lesson, students organized in pairs select two water forms and create a dance that demonstrates a change in levels, pathways, and tempos using the movements they learned in the first session.

The third lesson is focused on small groups of students collaborating to select one water form; they create a dance that includes a beginning group formation, uses locomotor movements in different directions, and ends in a group formation. In the final session, each group begins the class by practicing and refining their dance and then shares their dance with other groups while you conduct the assessment.

❖ Social dance could involve a three-lesson unit focused on learning social dances from the 1950s and 1960s. In the first lesson, students learn three dances from the 1950s. The second lesson presents three dances from the 1960s. In the third lesson, students, in small groups, choose three of the six dances they learned, practice together, and then videotape themselves for a self-assessment or show their dances to another group.

❖ Cultural dance could be a unit focused on learning three dances from Uganda connected to a social studies unit taught by the third-grade teacher. The unit contains four lessons in which a dance artist, hired by the school, teaches the first two sessions. During these sessions, the students learn three traditional dances from various parts of Uganda. In the third session, you set up three dance stations, one for each dance learned in the first two sessions. The students, organized into three groups, visit each station and practice the dance identified with that station. In the fourth session, the students perform the dances for another third-grade class and write about how the movements reflect the Ugandan culture.

A second approach to a yearlong program, applicable for the dance and physical education program, is to present units that include all three dance forms. These units are centered on a theme or one or more elements of dance. In this way, students gain a comprehensive understanding of how the theme or elements can be addressed from creative, social, and cultural perspectives (see figure 3.1). For example, a unit based on the outcomes that children demonstrate respect toward others and increase body coordination can include two lessons on learning popular social dances, two lessons on learning dances from a culture not represented in the school, and two lessons on creating dances about friendship. Respect is taught through learning to cooperate and dancing with others, and coordination is increased when children learn and repeat patterns of movement present in all the dance forms taught in the unit.

A third approach is to choose a dance form as the primary focus and include another form as an extension. The extension provides a more in-depth study and demonstrates how the dance forms are interrelated. For example, in a five-lesson unit focused on social dance, the children learn four line dances in the first three lessons. In the fourth and fifth sessions, creative dance is used as an extension in which the children create their own line dances (Johnson 2002). Another example in a three-lesson unit focused on the dances of the Southwest Native Americans is to teach two social circle dances performed by the people during celebrations in the first lesson. During the second lesson, you can add a creative element by performing the dances using a different formation, and in the third lesson you can use creative dance in extending the social dances by having the children create two new dance steps to add to the dances they have learned.

A fourth approach is to plan teaching one dance form for the entire year to all grade levels. Each grade level or grade cluster would learn different dances that represent the selected dance

THEME: BIRTHDAYS

Creative	Social	Cultural
Students create partner dances about making a birthday cake.	Students learn a line dance to the song "Happy Birthday."	Students learn a cultural dance performed at a birthday celebration.

Figure 3.1 An example of a theme-based dance unit that incorporates creative, social, and cultural perspectives.

form. For example, if social dance is selected for the yearlong plan, the unit could consist of three lessons for the kindergarten and first grade, four lessons for second and third grades, and five lessons for fourth and fifth grades. Content for the social dance units for each grade cluster could include the following:

Kindergarten and First Grade

Lesson 1: hokey pokey, chicken dance, and seven jumps with a partner

Lesson 2: meet and greet dance (see page 102 in chapter 7), the bunny hop, and the animal dance

Lesson 3: one new dance, the barnyard get-together based on Boynton's (1993) *Barnyard Dance*

Students select their four favorite dances and perform each dance.

Second and Third Grades

Lesson 1: meet and greet dance using locomotor movement variations, friendship mixer dance (Cone and Cone 2011), and bandanna dance (see page 105 in chapter 7)

Lesson 2: partner dances combining social and creative dance using mirroring, shadowing, echoing, and call and response

Lesson 3: three teacher-selected simple line dances

Lesson 4: students organized in small groups agree on one favorite dance and practice and share it with their peers

In this lesson, the students can perform the dance for peers or lead their peers in performing the dance together.

Fourth and Fifth Grades

Lesson 1: cha-cha slide, cupid shuffle, and a line dance selected by you

Lesson 2: double circle mixer (see page 102 in chapter 7), a review of one dance from lesson 1, and a line dance selected by you

Lesson 3: dances from the 1950s, '60s, and '70s

Lesson 4: review of selected dances taught in the first three lessons

Lesson 5: students teach new popular social dances and select dances taught in the first

three lessons and create a variation to the formation or add new dance steps

In this approach, the following school year could focus on cultural dances appropriate for each grade level. Finally, in the third year, creative dance would be the focus of the yearlong plan. In this way, over three years, the children have had the opportunity to learn dance in all three forms.

Finally, as part of the planning process, consider the following criteria as a checklist to ensure that you have designed a comprehensive, developmentally appropriate, and meaningful dance learning experience:

❑ The annual plan, units, and lessons are aligned with national, state, or local standards.

❑ Each unit and each lesson contain clear outcomes and assessments.

❑ The selected content is relevant to the age and interests of the students.

❑ The collection and organization of teaching materials are feasible.

❑ Cultural dance units and lessons are integrated with accurate and relevant information about the culture.

❑ Lesson tasks follow a sequential progression that builds skills and knowledge.

❑ The dance space is appropriate for students' learning and safety.

PLANNING A DANCE UNIT

A unit of study in dance is a series of lessons that focus on a set of instructional outcomes (see chapter 1). The unit outcomes describe what children will know and be able to do as a result of participating in the lessons. Each lesson also contains more specific outcomes that can be achieved in a single session, but single-lesson outcomes still relate to the broader unit outcomes. There are many ways to plan and implement a unit; however, what is common to all units is a thoughtful and meaningful design that provides for skill development, social interaction, attainment of knowledge, and understanding of culture. For example, if pathways have been selected as the topic for a creative dance unit, the unit outcomes will state that students learn to identify various types of pathways and create ways to move using pathways. The unit is planned to occur in four dance lessons and specific lesson outcomes are as follows:

- ❖ Session 1: Children will explore locomotor and nonlocomotor movements using straight, curved, and zigzag pathways on the floor and in the air.
- ❖ Session 2: Children will explore locomotor and nonlocomotor movements using straight, curved, and zigzag pathways on the floor and in the air that represent numbers and letters of the alphabet.
- ❖ Session 3: Children and the teacher will collaborate to create a whole-class alphabet dance that uses pathways on the floor and in the air.
- ❖ Session 4: Children will collaborate with a partner to create a dance about letters or

numbers that uses two types of pathways that demonstrates a change in direction, tempo, or level.

Using the elements of dance as a topical theme for a creative dance unit is one strategy for selecting a unit topic. Numerous other interesting topics can be selected (see table 3.1) depending on the age and interests of the students.

When planning a unit, decide what dance form will be taught, the broader outcomes of the unit and specific lesson, and how to assess learning. Then plan the progression of tasks for each lesson (see figure 3.2). This process is called a backward-design planning process (Wiggins and McTighe 2005). Wiggins and McTighe, educational researchers and consultants who developed the popular Understanding by Design

Table 3.1 Topics for Learning Experiences in Creative Dance

Theme	Topics
Literature	Poems, novels, picture storybooks, folk tales, stories, and poems written by students
Holidays	National holidays, cultural holidays, religious holidays
Special events	Birthdays, graduation
Machines	Car wash, homework machine, computer
Day-to-day activities	Getting ready for school, family dinners, playing games
Media	Films, television programs, online videos
School activities	Eating in the lunchroom, recess, walking in the halls
Feelings	Sadness, fear, joy, anger, excitement
Seasons	Fall leaves, snow and ice, spring flowers, summer fun at the beach
Friendship	Name dances, partner dances, dances about acceptance and helping one another
Circus	Horses, tightrope walkers, acrobats, clowns, lions
Animals	Bears, dogs, birds, fish, monkeys
Weather	Tornadoes, clouds, wind, rain, lightning, a sunny day
Action words	Wiggle, burst, float, punch, press, melt
Sports	Basketball, soccer, tennis, swimming, football, baseball, hockey
Environments	Mountains, water forms, desert, rainforest, icebergs
Social issues	Rejection, acceptance, fighting, discrimination, bullying
Historical events	Baseball World Series, inauguration of a governor, war
Life experiences	Losing a tooth, welcoming a new student into the class
Current events	Front pages of the newspaper, sports news, popular culture
Dance maps	Designing pathways and movements
Other academic subjects	Science, social studies, math, language arts, music, visual art, theater

curricular development process, suggest that teachers identify the desired results, determine what evidence demonstrates learning, and then design the activities. For example, planning a dance unit for first-grade students focused on pathways would begin with identifying the outcome: Students will learn to identify various types of pathways and be able to create movements that travel on pathways. Next, the type of assessment is determined. A teacher observation checklist can be used in noting whether students can move on various pathways when asked by the teacher, or students may draw pathways to demonstrate their understanding. Additionally, students can write the names of the movements or draw pictures of themselves moving on the pathway. Another assessment strategy requires children to verbally describe a pathway danced by a peer or demonstrate and identify a pathway they created.

The next step in unit design is to delineate how the content will be presented. How many teaching sessions are needed or how many sessions are available? Next, an outline or a detailed description for each lesson is developed. Remember, as you plan, include sufficient time for children to fully engage in the processes of learning, performing, creating, observing, or responding to the dance content. Students' performances and assessment of their work can occur at any point in the unit; however, these activities are some-

- Identify grade level.
- Review national, state, or local dance standards.
- Determine the dance form.
- Select a dance topic or theme.
- Develop a unit outcome.
- Identify the number of lessons in the unit.
- Develop outcomes for each lesson.
- Decide on the assessment type and instrument.
- Plan the content and progression.
- Collect instructional materials, music, or props.

Figure 3.2   Unit planning outline.

times used as a closure activity. Before the unit starts, collect or order music, props, equipment, costumes, or other required materials. At the beginning of the unit, communicate your expectations to the students, and be clear about what they will be learning. Your planning should reflect a thoughtful sequence of learning tasks that facilitates meaningful and successful learning.

Finally, after you have presented a dance unit, take time to reflect on the teaching experience. Reflective teaching (Brookfield 1995) is a critical analysis of students' responses, the framework of the unit, and what the teaching experience was like for the teacher. What parts were most frustrating, satisfying, unexpected, or challenging? The insights gained from reflection will help to refine your teaching practice and offer you an opportunity to reflect on your own attitudes, beliefs, assumptions, behaviors, and perceptions. Ongoing self-observation and self-evaluation help you to make changes and deepen the rationale for content selection, design, and teaching techniques.

PLANNING THE DANCE LESSONS

Once you have identified the dance form, content, instructional outcomes, and assessment of the dance unit, you can design the lessons and tasks that will occur in each dance lesson. A similar planning process is appropriate for teaching creative dance, social dance, or cultural dances. Each dance lesson includes four main sections: introduction, development, culminating dance, and closure activity. These sections are discussed next. The dance lesson also emphasizes one or more specific outcomes that relate to the broader outcome of the unit. Generally, lessons may be completed comfortably in one session; however, you can decide based on how your students respond to the content if more time is needed. If appropriate, use a second session, or even a third, to complete the lesson, giving students a chance to fully explore the concept. This may result in adjusting the amount of content you can teach in the unit.

Introduction

The introduction serves as a transition for children between the activities they have just experienced (perhaps a math lesson or lunch) and the dance learning experience. You can offer several approaches to these first moments of class. One option is to provide an instant activity where students, as they enter the space, are immediately engaged in practicing skills, viewing posted instructions, or obtaining materials to be used in the lesson (Graham 2008). This teaching technique allows time for a transition as well as time for children to talk informally with you. During this time, you can play the music that will be used in the lesson to familiarize children with the music's tempo, mood, and style. Another way to begin a lesson is to gather the children in a designated listening spot and start the lesson with a brief verbal introduction.

Here, you tell the students what they are going to learn, why you chose the topic or theme, and how it relates to them. One way to begin is by asking the students what they know about the topic or theme. As a result, you gain insights into the students' understanding and experience regarding the topic or theme. Another part of the introduction can include a review of skills and concepts taught in a previous lesson or a question about what students remember. In this way, students develop an understanding about how lessons are related to one another as part of a planned sequence. It is also appropriate to accompany the verbal introduction by showing a movement that will be taught, an object, video, book, map, or pictures related to the topic.

The introduction for teaching a cultural dance should include background information on the origin of the dance and its relationship to the culture or ethnic group. The information presented can be supported with a video, pictures, maps, clothing, artifacts, books, newspapers, music, artwork, crafts, food, the language, religion, or other materials that provide a context for the dance. Communicate how the values, traditions, lifestyle, environment, and history of the culture influence the movements, music, and formations of the dance. Avoid stereotyping a culture or making biased comments, and present accurate information based on reliable resources.

The beginning of a social dance lesson can emphasize concepts of respect, responsibility, cooperation, leadership, kindness, or being helpful to others. Children can talk about their understanding of what these words mean to them and how they can demonstrate these concepts

through dance. This type of introduction sets the expectation for the learning outcome and places the enjoyment of socializing through dance in a broader context. When possible, include historical information about the social dances and discuss the types of social gatherings where they occur.

You can introduce a creative dance lesson in many ways. You can begin with a story, a photo, a prop, a book, or perhaps a news event. Children are always curious when they come to class and usually ask, "What are we going to do today?" The first response sets the tone for the day. Be enthusiastic. For example, to introduce the spaghetti dance (pages 131-134 in chapter 8), you might say, "Today we are going to dance about straight and curved shapes. I chose these two shapes because they are everywhere in our world. Let's begin to find these shapes by looking at our clothes." As the students are looking at their clothes and pointing to shapes, you can quickly assess whether they can identify shapes. You can use a prop, such as a rope, to illustrate the straight and curved shapes, or you can draw the shapes on a poster or whiteboard.

After the verbal introduction, a body warm-up follows. The warm-up is directly related to the type of movements students will be doing in the dance lesson and prepares the body for safe and active participation. The warm-up can be a series of movements that warm up the muscles and increase the body's blood flow. The students can begin with locomotor movements such as walking, galloping, or skipping in the space and then continue with nonlocomotor movements such as stretching, bending, twisting, or swinging the whole body or its parts. If the students will be running, leaping, twisting, and bending during the dance learning experience, the warm-up should include movements that prepare the body for those actions. Movements in the warm-up should be whole-body actions that include both locomotor and nonlocomotor movements.

A warm-up for a cultural dance may include moving to the music used in the dance or performing specific movements from the dance. Students can move body parts in isolation, such as moving the head from side to side, the shoulders up and down, and the hips in a circle; bouncing through the knees lightly; reaching the arms up and out to the side; stepping in place with the feet;

and twisting the torso from side to side. Warm-ups for social dance can follow a format similar to that of the cultural dance. To emphasize the social aspect, students can do the warm-ups with partners or in small groups and then change to another warm-up group. A warm-up for a creative dance can include a short aerobic section; isolated body part movements; and bending, stretching, and twisting movements. If the lesson is on pathways, you can incorporate the words and types of pathways into the warm-up. In the spaghetti dance (see chapter 8), for example, the warm-up may include instructions related to shape making: "Walk around the room and look for straight and curved shapes. Where can you find them? Look high and low. When you find a shape, imitate the shape with your body. Find another shape and another." Here, the students are using walking as the whole-body movement and making shapes with their bodies. To summarize, through the introduction, the dance topic is presented, students' prior understanding of the selected topic is revealed, topic relevancy is established, and the students are prepared physically to participate.

Development

During the development section, students experience new ways to move, whether through patterned movements from a cultural or social dance or a series of movements they have created. You can create a sequence of tasks, which is a coherent progression, that leads the students to learn and create movements relevant to the lesson outcomes. Students learn, explore, improvise, and create movements that express and communicate concepts, ideas, thoughts, and feelings. During a lesson on learning a cultural or social dance, students would be learning the sequence of movements and the formations inherent in the dance. Usually this is presented using the part–whole or whole–part teaching strategy (see chapter 5). If the lesson focus is on creative dance, the task sequence needs to be relevant to the topic. Just asking students to make up a dance or dance to the music is too general and does not provide for focused learning. However, this general task does have value if you want to see what the students could create, and you can use it as a preassessment or as a culminating dance after a lesson (Cone 2002). When the focus is on

an element of dance such as contrasting fast and slow tempos, students will explore a variety of movements using the different tempos. The tasks can be specific ("Find a way to walk eight steps forward using a fast tempo, then walk eight steps backward as slowly as you can.") or more open-ended ("How can you change levels, alternating between a fast and a slow tempo?"). This task may evolve into a dance or a selected sequence of movements that represent an idea, or the lesson can focus on a topic, such as a circus, a sport, a poem, or celebrating a birthday. The students explore movements that interpret the actions, events, or feelings relevant to the topic or theme. Here, the elements of dance are applied to the topic as tools in developing the type and quality of movements. Instead of saying, "Act like a lion, or be a seed," extend the imagery to included a description of the movement shape or quality with the emphasis on the movement (Kaufmann 2006). Change it—act like a lion to move low and slow like a lion stalking its prey. In this way, the movement quality is the focus and children can increase their variety of movement responses to the task. For example, in a dance about zoo animals, you would ask each child to choose an animal. You then present the following as exploratory tasks related to the elements of dance (EOD; see table 2.1 on page 23). The tasks guide students as they create their movements:

- ❖ Demonstrate three ways your animal moves. Does the animal walk, run, jump, gallop, swing, twist, stretch, slither, wiggle, shake, or kick? (EOD: body actions)

- ❖ Show me how your animal moves its arms, head, shoulders, back, legs, and feet. (EOD: the body)

- ❖ Have your animal move using very small steps . . . now huge steps. (EOD: space, range)

- ❖ Find a way your animal can move in different directions. Can it move forward, backward, and sideward? (EOD: space, direction)

- ❖ Find a partner. One of you be a leader and the other a follower and slowly mirror your partner's animal movements and then switch roles. (EOD: relationships)

◆ Show me how slow your animal can move. Can your animal begin moving slowly and increase its speed? (EOD: time, tempo)

◆ Create three still shapes that show different actions your animal does. Is your shape twisted, round, or straight? (EOD: body shape)

◆ Demonstrate how your animal moves very lightly and then moves with strong energy. (EOD: force)

◆ Decide if your animal moves smoothly and slowly or sharply and quickly, and then practice the movement. (EOD: force and time)

◆ Find a way for your animal to move on a straight pathway. Now change to a curvy pathway. Change the pathway to a zigzag. (EOD: space, pathway)

By exploring the creative dance topic through the elements of dance, students broaden their movement vocabulary. They learn to find multiple ways to express movements that go beyond their initial action. The next step would involve creating a dance about animals. In this way, students are performing a sequence of movements that can be repeated and refined. The dance may follow a short story designed by you, or the students may suggest an idea for the animal dance. The students would then choose movements they have explored in the dance. For example, in this teacher-designed dance, the animals begin by sleeping in a shape low to the floor; then they slowly wake up and move in general space to meet other animals. They play follow the leader with a partner and finally return to where they started and fall asleep again. Although the students follow the sequence of your story, they are choosing the type and quality of the movements their animal makes.

The development section is an important component of the learning and creative process and relates directly to the culminating dance or final product and outcome of the unit or lesson. This section is the journey children take as they create, learn, practice, and refine new movements. Hawkins (1988) tells us that "This core of the learning period should foster new understandings and growth. The content may be new material or new developments of previous experiences. Activity should be designed with

a clear relationship to the focus of the lesson" (p. 128). Knowing the desired result—whether it is a specific line dance, a creative dance about force, or the words of a poem expressed through a dance—is a key element to planning meaningful tasks. In some creative dance experiences, the exact form and sequence of the culminating dance may be unknown until after the children explore and improvise movements; however, a general framework or outline of the final outcome should be planned. Here, Wiggins and McTighe's (2005) concept of backward design in unit planning, described earlier, can also be applied to each lesson.

The sequence of tasks in the development section is presented in what Mosston and Ashworth (2002) refer to as guided discovery. The tasks are designed and sequenced to prepare and lead the students to create and learn movements that are evident in the culminating dance. One approach to developing an appropriate sequence of tasks is to analyze how the elements of dance are used in the culminating dance. The following questions guide the analysis of the culminating dance:

◆ What movements of the whole body and its parts are used in the dance?

◆ How are levels, pathways, range, and direction used?

◆ What is the speed and rhythm? Are there accents in the movements? Will the movements accelerate or decelerate? Is there a pause in the movements? Will everyone be moving on the same beat? Is there a contrast in speed? Do the rhythms change?

◆ What type of force is used? When are the movements strong or light? Do they change force?

◆ Is the flow of the movements free or bound? Does the flow change?

◆ How will the students be organized—as individuals, partners, or small groups? Will they follow each other, connect, support, or mirror? What formations will they use? Will the relationships and formations change during the dance?

Chapter 8 includes a description of the culminating dance for the spaghetti dance lesson, which focuses on making straight and curved shapes and movements with the body. From reading the description, you can anticipate the sequence of movements, changes in quality, and formations used in the dance. During the development section, the presentation of the tasks uses the guided discovery strategy to lead students to experience and create the types of movements that are included in the culminating dance. In the culminating spaghetti dance, children begin in a straight shape and travel on a straight pathway to a pot of water. During the development section, children explore making straight shapes with their bodies and find various ways to travel on a straight pathway. Through the exploration process, you guide the children to experience movements that are used in the culminating spaghetti dance.

A similar analysis for task construction can be applied to cultural and social dance, in which you have prepared the culminating dance. The following example demonstrates the first two tasks presented while teaching the Russian troika dance during the development section of the lesson.

❖ Task 1: "Each person will take 4 running steps forward and stop. Now try it again, beginning on the right foot, and take the 4 running steps moving diagonally to the right." This task teaches the first 4 steps of the culminating dance. The elements of movement to be emphasized are running, direction, and moving in a specific rhythm and tempo.

❖ Task 2: "I will organize you into groups of 3. Join hands and practice the 4 steps diagonally right, then left, and then take 8 steps forward." In this task, the students are learning to move in unison connected by their hands. These 16 steps make up the first section of the culminating dance of the troika. The elements of dance highlighted are running, a connected relationship, tempo, rhythm, and direction.

Each task prepares the students for the way they will move in the culminating dance and emphasizes one or more elements of dance.

Culminating Dance

The culminating dance brings together the movements experienced in the development section. In this part of the lesson, structure is given to the movements that were created and learned. Students select, organize, and perform movements individually, in small groups, or as one large group. The dances may follow a choreographic structure such as round, narrative, ABA, AB, chance, and theme and variation (see figure 3.3) (Sprague, Scheff, & McGreevy-Nichols 2006). Keep in mind that it may be appropriate for young children to participate in large-group culminating dances until they are ready to work more independently to create their own dances. Large-group dances are also appropriate for older students with little dance experience, because they often feel more comfortable if everyone is doing the same dance at the same time. The large-group culminating creative dance is similar to everyone performing a cultural or social dance as a group.

AB—A two-part composition. A represents a movement and B represents another movement.

ABA—A three-part composition. The A movements are performed, then the B movements are performed, and the A movements are repeated.

accumulation—A dance that begins with one movement, then another is added, then another, each time repeating all the movements from the beginning before another movement is added.

narrative—A dance that tells a story or series of events.

theme and variations—A movement that is then changed but still is related to the original movement.

round—A dance that is like an echo. The same dance is performed but it is started by another dancer at a different time shortly after the first dancer begins.

chance—A dance that is composed spontaneously with random movements.

rearrange—A dance that has the dance movement sequence changed to a different order.

retrograde—A dance that is performed in reverse order.

Figure 3.3 Choreographic structures used in dance.

Culminating dances usually have a recognizable beginning, middle, and end. The dance may be a narrative form or express a range of feelings. It may be a sequence of movements that show how a round shape can change size, move at different tempos, or travel in the different pathways. The dance can begin and end in a formation such as a circle, a line, or scattered around the perimeter of the space. In the middle section, students may maintain a formation or change to one or more formations. In addition to formation changes, the rhythm, movements, force, flow, and relationships of the dancers can change. Another approach for creating the culminating dance may be a spontaneous performance of movements experienced during the development section. For some young children, the act of spontaneously creating dance movements is their dance. They do not make a definitive distinction between the process of creating and the final dance (Cone 2002). In a spontaneous culminating dance, there is no set choreographic structure; instead, the dance is more organic in nature, where the dance is created moment to moment while the children are dancing. The dance may end when the children decide they are tired, or they may keep dancing until you tell them the dance is over.

As the teacher, you may want to create your own new culminating dance for a creative dance instead of using a previously created dance like the spaghetti dance. In this situation, you would outline your vision of the dance through a written description or through drawings and notes. You may envision a dance about fall leaves and develop a dance that expresses the action and qualities of the leaves as they fall from the tree and blow around the field. Then, analyze the anticipated movements, changes of quality, and use of space, and plan a series of tasks for the development section that will guide students toward this culminating dance.

Consider the following questions when developing your own culminating dance:

◆ What do you want students to gain as a result of learning this dance?

◆ What is the image, theme, story, piece of literature, idea, or feeling that will be expressed in the dance?

◆ What is the sequence of movements in the culminating dance?

◆ What specific elements of dance can be emphasized to support the movements of the dance?

◆ What formations will be used? Lines? Circles? Scattered?

◆ How will the dance begin?

◆ Where and how will the students move in the middle of the dance?

◆ How will the dance end?

To create the spaghetti dance, we began with the idea that we wanted students to learn how to make straight and curved shapes with their bodies and to travel on straight and curved pathways. Making different shapes and finding different ways to travel would be suitable for exploring the concept; however, we believed children would understand the concept better if we created a story about what happened to a box of spaghetti. We knew the image of spaghetti was familiar to the students, and they would find humor and interest in dancing the imagined event of the spaghetti as it cooks. The culminating dance expresses the events of the story. In this dance, the students travel as straight pieces of spaghetti on a straight pathway from an imaginary box to a pot of water and then jump in. They change from straight to curved shapes as they cook and move around in the pot among the other pieces of spaghetti. A giant bubble appears and pushes the spaghetti out of the pot. The spaghetti runs and leaps in a curved shape as it flies around the kitchen and becomes stuck in a curved shape on the wall. Finally, the curvy cooked spaghetti slowly moves off the wall, walks in a curved pathway, steps onto the dinner plate, and ends lying down on the plate in a curved shape. The students experience a change of levels while cooking, flying around the kitchen, and falling onto the dinner plate; a change of tempo; a change of shape; and a change in relationship, moving close together and far apart. The entire class dances the sequence at the same time yet each uses his or her own unique ideas about how to express straight and curved shapes and pathways.

Closure Activity

A closure activity is appropriate at the end of each lesson as well as the end of the unit (Graham 2008). The activity may be a performance of culminating dances, a review of all the dances learned during the unit, a written response or drawing of the experience, or a discussion focused on what students learned. This activity brings a conclusion to the lesson or unit and is one way in which you can assess students' learning and check for understanding. Children should have a moment to reflect and recall what they experienced during the lesson or unit and think about what knowledge and skills they acquired. The nature of the ending can vary, but provide time for a meaningful closure. Remember that how you end is as important as how you begin.

SAMPLE UNIT AND LESSON OUTLINE

We offer an outline of an initial planning document for a creative dance unit. This unit is taught during the fall season to correspond with the falling leaves and the science teacher's unit on environmental changes.

Grade Levels: Kindergarten and First Grade

National standards (Meyer 2010) are as follows*:

- 2: Understand choreographic principles, processes, and structures.
- 3: Understand dance as a way to create meaning and communicate meaning.
- 7: Make connections between dance and other disciplines.

*The National Dance Standards are reprinted from the Consortium of National Arts Education Associations 1994.

Dance form is creative dance.

Dance topic is leaves in the fall season.

Unit outcome is that children will create and perform a dance that represents leaf shapes and movements.

Number of lessons in unit is three.

Outcomes for Each Lesson

Lesson 1: Children will create still shapes to represent the various leaf shapes and use various locomotor movements to demonstrate how the leaves fall from the trees and blow in the wind.

Lesson 2: Children will create a personal dance that uses three still leaf shapes and three locomotor movements.

Lesson 3: Children will perform a dance story created by the teacher about the fall leaves.

Unit assessment: The checklist used in lesson 2—assess the personal dances that include three still shapes and three locomotor movements.

Lesson 1 Outline

Introduction and warm-up: Teacher shows leaf shapes gathered from school property and the book *Fall Leaves Fall* (Hall and Halpern 2000).

For warm-up, students walk around the space; on a signal, students freeze in various shapes designated by the teacher.

Development: Students explore making their bodies into the shapes of the leaves using levels and range.

Students explore rocking and turning movements in various directions and range using their leaf shapes to represent the leaves swaying in the wind while attached to the tree.

Students explore locomotor movements using various pathways to express the leaves blowing in the space.

Culminating activity: Students dance a sequence of movements designed by the teacher, such as balance in leaf shape 1, leaf shape 2, and leaf shape 3, then slowly rock forward and backward to express the leaf blowing in the wind. Then they run on a curvy pathway to show the leaf flying around the yard and freeze in leaf shape 1 to end the dance.

Closure: Students discuss their favorite leaf shapes and locomotor movements.

Lesson 2 Outline

Introduction and warm-up: Students are asked to relate the movements in the previous lessons. "What do you remember we danced about in lesson 1?"

For the warm-up, students walk around the space; on the teacher's signal to freeze, students freeze on a leaf shape they created in lesson 1. This is repeated several times.

Development: Each child chooses three leaf shapes and then practices making the three shapes. The teacher adds counts to hold the shapes still. Students practice. Teacher adds a count number to change from one shape to the next. Students practice.

Teacher reviews the locomotor movements and pathways used in lesson 1 and students practice. Teacher sets a specific number of steps for each locomotor movement.

Students choose three locomotor movements and choose the order and practice.

Students create a dance that uses the three still shapes followed by the three locomotor movements.

Teacher conducts the assessment while students practice their dances.

Culminating activity: In pairs, students show their dance to their partners.

Closure: Teacher asks half of the class to demonstrate their dance while the other half observes and then groups switch roles. Teacher can complete the assessment if needed.

Lesson 3 Outline

Introduction: Teacher tells students they will collaborate to create a story about the falling leaves.

In the warm-up, students repeat the warm-up used in lesson 2. Teacher adds counts to the still shapes and includes the rocking movement.

Development: The teacher and students create a story about the falling leaves. Key words in the dance are recorded on a flip chart. The students and the teacher create movements for each key word and form a dance.

Culminating activity: The teacher tells the story while the children dance. Each time a different piece of music is used. One piece of music is slow and soft and the second is fast and energetic.

Closure: The teacher asks the students how it felt to dance to different types of music.

INTERDISCIPLINARY CONNECTIONS

Many terms are used to describe an integrated learning experience, such as *interdisciplinary, connected, correlated, cross-curricular,* or *multidisci-*

plinary. These terms imply that two or more subject areas are linked together to create a learning experience that fosters enhanced learning in each subject (Cone, Werner, and Cone 2009). Interdisciplinary learning acknowledges the integrity and uniqueness of each subject area yet recognizes the interrelationships of one subject to another. Students need to have discipline-specific learning experiences as well as learning experiences that demonstrate the relationship among the disciplines (Jacobs 1989). Jacobs, an educator and scholar on interdisciplinary teaching, says, "The curriculum becomes more relevant when there are connections between subjects rather than strict isolation" (p. 5). Learning experiences are less fragmented and foster multiple perspectives on a theme or topic. Knowledge and skills in one subject area are viewed as applicable to learning in another subject area and promote creative and divergent thinking.

Dance integrates easily with other content areas. It offers children who are kinesthetic learners (Gardner 1983) the opportunity to use movement as a means of understanding and communicating their life experiences using their own unique perspectives. For all children, the body and its movements are a means of attaining and expressing knowledge and skills. As Lazaroff (2001) notes, the body can be referred to as a "potential curricular resource that can enrich and amplify learning in a variety of subjects" (p. 27). Educators who believe that dance is an essential mode of learning not only addresses the goals of a dance education program but also provides students with the knowledge and skills applicable to all aspects of their lives.

Although dance has a discrete body of knowledge, the topics children dance about are frequently related to other subject areas. In a dance about spring flowers, for example, information about how flowers grow is essential when creating a dance that interprets the growing process. Cultural dances represent aspects of how people live, what they value, their traditions, history, and beliefs. These are also concepts taught in the social studies curriculum. Dance is embedded in many cultures for a variety of reasons, and thus integrating dance and social studies becomes a viable teaching strategy for each discipline. In many classrooms, the teacher selects a common theme such as community, change, patterns,

Children demonstrating a snowflake.

conflict and resolution, or respect. The theme is explored through various subject areas, creating learning from multiple perspectives. In this thematic approach, dance plays a role in adding a kinesthetic, creative, and aesthetic dimension to learning. Children can express their understanding of a particular theme through learning or creating dances that represent various aspects of the theme (see figure 3.4).

Many of the learning experiences in chapters 8 and 9 are applicable for integration. Suggestions for interdisciplinary connections are included at the end of each learning experience. For additional lessons that integrate dance with other subject areas, we encourage you to check the suggested readings section of this book to review the work of Benzwie (2011, 2002, 2000, 1987); Brehm and McNett (2008); Cone (2000); Cone, Werner, and Cone (2009); Donnelly (2002); Gilbert (1977); Kane (1998); Overby, Post, and Newman (2005);

Rovegno (2003); and Stinson (1988). These educators offer many wonderful ideas for integration. Here are some other suggested strategies that can lead to developing opportunities for interdisciplinary connections:

◆ Visit the classrooms of your students to see what they are learning with other teachers.

◆ Talk with the classroom teacher, school librarian, music specialist, and art specialist, and find a way to connect what you are teaching in dance with what they are teaching in their classrooms.

◆ Ask teachers to place a note in your mailbox about upcoming units of study.

◆ Invite teachers into your class to see your program in action.

◆ Attend grade-level meetings or set up a monthly meeting to share ideas.

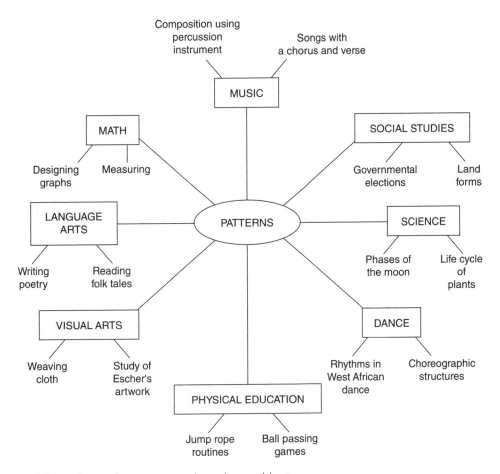

Figure 3.4 Children learn about patterns in various subject areas.

◆ Review curriculum guides for information about the content of various subject areas. This information is helpful when planning to integrate concepts and skills from another subject with dance.

The process of integrating content from other subject areas requires an examination of the discrete skills and concepts of each subject area and, specifically, the content you are interested in for an interdisciplinary learning experience. We suggest considering three models of interdisciplinary teaching that function on a continuum from simple to complex. These models are connected, shared, and partnership (Cone, Werner, and Cone 2009). The models clarify your intent and objectives and make the learning experience meaningful to the students as well as the teacher (see figure 3.5). In the connected model, the skills, topics, and concepts of the dance curriculum are the primary focus of the learning experience, and the content from another subject area is used to enhance, extend, or supplement the learning experience. For example, you are teaching European cultural dances, and you show the students a map to indicate where the countries are located and share pictures of people in traditional dress performing the dance as a means of connecting to social studies. The shared model integrates two or more subjects through presenting similar skills, topics, or concepts that are part of the content of the integrated subjects. In this model, the dance or physical education teacher would coordinate with other subject-area teachers to look for common areas that can be taught at the same time. A dance lesson might be shared with a math lesson on fractions. In dance, the students are learning about quarter, half, three-quarter, and full turns, and in the math class children are introduced to the concept of fractions. The third model, partnership, is an equal representation of two or more subject areas taught simultaneously. The line between the subject areas is completely blurred and the learning activities fuse content seamlessly. For example, the dance, visual arts, and music teachers collaborate to teach a partnership unit focused on hip-hop culture. All three teachers teach the unit as a united team. They use their expertise in their respective subject areas to create common outcomes and assessments. During the experience, students learn and create music, dance, and visual arts and discuss other cultural artifacts associated with the topic. This model requires considerable planning and a willingness to view content from a new and different perspective.

As educators, we seek to make connections between what children experience in their lives and the content of dance. Teaching from an interdisciplinary perspective offers an opportunity to deliver knowledge and skills holistically to help children transfer what they learn in one subject area to another. Interdisciplinary learning experiences recognize and promote multiple ways of knowing a concept or skill and enlarge our view about what we can experience in our world. Eisner (1998) believes that what students learn is shaped by the experiences presented to them in their education. Teachers are responsible for providing learning experiences that challenge conventional methods of learning and embarking on a journey with their students to explore the world through a myriad of paths.

SUMMARY

A successful dance learning experience is the result of planning an appropriate sequence of tasks that leads students to learn how movements can communicate an idea, a tradition, or a feeling. You will choose an idea for the learning experience that is relevant to the students, has meaning in their lives, and emphasizes the elements of dance.

Each learning experience can make a significant impact on the way children view dance. The learning experience must be well crafted so that students can develop an idea that is logical and well planned. This process begins with a verbal and physical introduction to the idea; provides time to explore, learn, or create movements related to the idea; and ends with composing or performing a completed dance. The culminating dance belongs to the students as they become

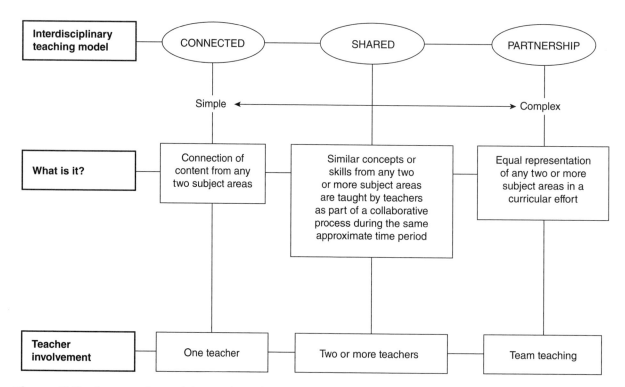

Figure 3.5 A comparison of three selected interdisciplinary teaching models.

Adapted, by permission, from T.P. Cone, P. Werner, S.L. Cone, 2009, *Interdisciplinary elementary physical education*, 2nd ed. (Champaign, IL: Human Kinetics), 11.

fully engaged and find personal meaning in the movements.

Dance should play a vital role in the school's curriculum. It can be taught as a single learning experience that occurs frequently throughout the school year or as several units that focus on a particular theme. Both creative dance and dances created by others need to be included in the dance program each year at the primary and intermediate levels. Providing students with the opportunity to create, learn, observe, perform, and respond to dances offers them a comprehensive program that includes all dimensions of dance as an art and movement form.

Questions for Reflection

Where do you obtain your ideas for a unit of study? Are they prescribed in the curriculum, or do you design your own units within a framework of school outcomes?

What parts of a unit are easy to plan? Why? What challenges do you encounter when planning a dance unit? How do you resolve the challenge?

How would you prioritize the content you will teach for a yearlong plan in dance?

The components of a lesson described in this chapter are one way to organize and develop the content. What ideas can you add to the lesson design?

What do you see as the significance of teaching an interdisciplinary unit that integrates dance with another subject area? What other curricular areas can you integrate with dance?

four

Creating a Dance Education Setting

Teaching would be much easier if we could teach in what we consider an ideal environment. Then, our planning and implementation would easily fall into place. The fact is that your teaching situation most likely does not have everything you need and you adapt your ideas to make student learning meaningful, safe, and effective. We all share some similarities . . . and some definite differences! These differences include class size; frequency of class meetings; length of class period; facilities; equipment and materials; community; and a broad range of ages, abilities, and special needs within the same class of children (Newnam 2002). In 1995, the National Dance Association, in collaboration with the Consortium of National Arts Education Associations, published the *Opportunity-to-Learn Standards for Dance Education*. These standards describe the physical and educational conditions necessary for enabling students to learn and achieve in dance. Topics addressed in the standards include curriculum, scheduling, materials, equipment, facilities, and staffing. As guidelines for developing a dance program, the standards present criteria for providing an environment that facilitates effective teaching and learning. This chapter presents strategies for planning and delivering dance content in various teaching situations to best meet the needs of the children and heighten their enjoyment of learning.

CLASS SIZE

Although the National Association for Sport and Physical Education (2009) recommends that physical education or dance classes contain the same number of children as the classrooms (e.g., 25 children per class), some schools and districts schedule two or three classes at the same time. This means a physical education or dance teacher might teach 60 or more children during one session. Although this makes teaching a challenge, you can find ways to deliver the content to provide children with positive learning experiences. For example, the use of stations or learning centers is an efficient way to organize large groups of children. Each station can contain written instructions, pictures, or diagrams about how to perform a specific movement of a line dance or traditional cultural dance. After visiting each station, the students can put all the steps together in the correct sequence. Another set of stations can focus on tasks that explore an element of dance. A station about the element of time might include the following tasks:

◆ Find a way to walk in a circle as fast as you can.

◆ Next, walk in a circle as slowly as you can or begin walking in the circle slowly and accelerate to running and then decelerate to walking.

◆ Find a partner and practice mirroring each other's movements.

Safety is an important consideration when many children are moving at one time. The children can keep themselves from bumping into other children or objects in the space by being aware of their personal space (the space immediately surrounding their bodies; see chapter 2). You must teach and reinforce this concept in each dance lesson. Another way to organize a large class is to place the children into lines. Keep the number of children in the line to a minimum to reduce waiting time and increase activity. Creating a balance between allowing for movement that is fully expressive and ensuring that children can move without injury requires careful planning and a willingness to make the appropriate modifications to the lesson.

Teaching a large group will be more effective when your voice is amplified so the students can hear the instructions. Also, it's a good idea for children to use a microphone when asking and answering questions. In this way, the entire class can hear without your needing to repeat the comments. To present instructions and information needed for the lesson, consider using posters, a whiteboard, an overhead projector, a slide projector, or a liquid crystal display (LCD) projector.

EQUIPMENT AND TEACHING MATERIALS

The addition of equipment and materials such as music, props, and costumes enriches the dance learning experience. These items can be used as the stimulus for creating dances or as the accompaniment to a dance. Music and dance are frequently partnered in a learning experience. The voice, percussion instruments, and recorded music support the rhythm of the movement and set an environment for dancing. Props help illustrate the meaning of the movement, exaggerate the movement, and create a visual component that complements the dance. Most props are light, handheld objects that students manipulate while moving through space. Sometimes students dance around, over, or under larger objects; these larger objects help establish an environment for dancing. Costumes are also a wonderful addition to a dance. Children enjoy dressing up as a character, an animal, a tree, a monster, or any other idea from their imaginations. Every dance program should have access to a variety of teaching materials. DVDs, CDs, MP3 players, books, photos, posters, and computers for accessing websites, applications, and videos can be the catalysts for new dance ideas, present information on cultural and social dances, and support the dance concepts that are emphasized in the learning experience.

Music

Most dance experiences use music to accompany the movement, whether it's the voice, percussion instruments, or live or recorded music. Music can stimulate ideas for dance, support the tempo and rhythm, provide a mood or atmosphere, or provide structure to a dance. The voice is one instrument that we always have with us. It can generate sounds and words that express the qualities of a movement. Even the way the voice is used when giving instructions can make a difference in how students respond. To illustrate this point, think of how these action words can be expressed differently to elicit a specific way to move. You

Beginning shape for a scarf dance.

can say "splat" in a loud, fast, and sharp voice; "press" in a loud and sustained voice; and "fall" in a voice that begins at a high pitch and ends at a low pitch.

Students can also use their voices to sing songs as accompaniment for dances. Consider using a familiar song, such as "Row, Row, Row Your Boat," as the accompaniment for a dance structured on a round (also known as a canon). Students can create movements for each section of the song and then, in small groups, sing and perform the movements to create a dance round. Another possibility is to make up a song that describes a movement sequence. For example, in a dance about planting a garden, you and the students sing, "Seed, seed, cover up with dirt, and jump, jump." On the words "seed, seed," the children pretend to place a seed in the ground. Next, on each syllable of the phrase "cover up with dirt," the students use their feet to stamp quickly while pretending to bury the seeds. A big jump

on each word "jump" completes the phrase. This phrase is repeated several times with the students singing and moving simultaneously. You can also vocalize rhythms by making a variety of sounds with the voice. In a dance about a machine, for example, students can create sounds with their bodies or voices to accompany the machine movements. Words, poems, and stories read out loud can all involve the voice as accompaniment.

Develop a collection of percussion instruments as a readily available resource to accompany dance. Most percussion instruments can be carried easily while teaching or dancing. When planning a dance experience, consider what movements could be supported by the strong, percussive beat of a drum; the light, sustained sound of the triangle; or the quick, vibratory sounds of the maracas (see the percussion instrument dance in chapter 8 on page 138). Also, consider making instruments to create interesting and unusual sounds (see table 4.1). You don't have

Table 4.1 Percussion Instruments

Traditional instruments	Nontraditional or found instruments
Drums of various sizes	Pot lids
Triangle	Spoons
Maracas	Glasses filled with water at different levels
Gong	Plastic garbage cans
Chimes	Plastic or metal cans
Rain stick	Round oatmeal boxes
Bells	Wooden spoons
Sticks	Metal or plastic garbage can lids
Woodblock	Rocks scraped or tapped together
Guiro	Plastic buckets
Cymbals	Containers filled with beans
Xylophone	Paper bags

to be an accomplished musician to use instruments in dance. Take time to become familiar with the instruments, and explore ways to play them by hitting, rubbing, or shaking them with your hands. Ask the school's music teacher to help you learn to play a few basic rhythms. Investigate the possibility of borrowing instruments, or look for them in music stores, toy stores, museum shops, yard sales, and school catalogs.

Finding the appropriate recorded music for a dance experience is always a challenge. There is such a variety of music that it is hard to know where to begin to look. One option is to purchase music that is prepackaged with ideas for dance lessons. These types of recordings can be a way to begin to develop a personal library of music. Another option is to set some time aside to listen to music and then record selections that could be used for dance. Label the selections with ideas for future use, and then try the music with the students. Include in your collection music that

◆ has a definite even beat;

◆ offers varying tempos for slow and sustained as well as fast and percussive movements;

◆ has various rhythms for skipping, running, or jumping;

◆ produces various moods, such as feeling peaceful, anxious, or powerful;

◆ evokes images and feelings (e.g., sounds like music for strange creatures landing on the earth);

◆ represents other cultures; and

◆ denotes a specific time period.

Be sure to include a variety of music that represents a wide range of styles and cultures. Students may prefer music that is popular and familiar to them; however, use the dance experience to present many types of music to broaden the students' exposure to and knowledge of music. Your list can include classical, jazz, pop, rap, reggae, hip-hop, new age, rock, gospel, opera, a variety of vocal music, movie soundtracks, sounds of nature, children's songs, and traditional and contemporary ethnic music. Different types of dances can be paired with different types of music. African music can be used in a dance about a rainstorm, for example, or ragtime music can be used to accompany a dance about baseball. Traditional cultural dances usually require a specific piece of music as accompaniment and can help to make the experience more authentic. The music teacher can be a valuable resource for selecting music and can offer assistance with identifying rhythms and musical structures.

Once you have chosen your music, be sure to become thoroughly familiar with the selection. Play the music in the space where the dance experience will occur so that you can ensure the volume is appropriate and the audio equipment functions properly. Always acknowledge the composer, the name of the music piece, and the performer when introducing music into the dance session.

Having the proper audio equipment can make a significant difference in the quality of music used in the learning experience. Purchasing state-of-the-art equipment is not always possible; however, a CD player or MP3 player may be available in the school. When you have the opportunity to purchase new equipment, consider the following wish list:

- ◆ A CD player with an MP3 connection, a remote control, and speakers that will project into the space. The remote control enables you to position yourself easily for effective teaching.
- ◆ A portable microphone and speaker. A wireless lavaliere microphone can allow you to teach in any of the space and move with the students. You also have the ability to speak over the music to provide instructions.
- ◆ Blank CDs for creating music selections.
- ◆ Cleaning kits for CD players to keep the equipment in good shape.
- ◆ Storage cases for compact discs. Proper storage will eliminate damage.

Props

Dance learning experiences frequently require equipment or handheld props to accompany the dance. Children may manipulate streamers, hoops, elastic strips, balloons, wands, ropes, and pieces of material or scarves as they dance. Or, they may use equipment such as chairs, mats, cones, or tables to move around, over, under, on, or between. Ideally, and when appropriate, each child should have her or his own prop. When there aren't enough of the same type of prop available for each child, children can share or trade props. For example, in a lesson on making different shapes, one group uses an elastic rope, the next group uses wands, and another group makes shapes with long pieces of yarn. When choosing equipment or props, consider each child's developmental abilities to handle the

equipment or prop safely. Can the child move the prop easily? If the prop falls out of the child's hand, is there a potential for injury? Do children have adequate space in which to move with the prop?

Props are used to initiate, extend, or accompany movement. Cultural dances may use scarves, sticks, ropes, flowers, or baskets as part of the movements or to express a character or cultural artifact. In a learning experience focused on creating straight and curved lines, children can lay ropes on the floor in straight and curved lines and then match their bodies to the rope shape. Streamers or ribbons held in the hand can be imaginary brushes with which to paint letters in the air, and scarves can be flames, leaves, or flower petals (see figure 4.1). Partners and small groups can share a prop and discover ways to move together. Students can hold hoops as imaginary doorways into outer space or to connect students as rays of the sun. Curtains or long pieces of material are easy for a small group of children to use as a floating cloud, a swirling river, or the wind of a tornado. Most schools have a parachute that can be turned into a giant monster when a group holds one side of the parachute and runs in the space with the parachute floating in the air. There is no end to the ways props can be part of a dance experience. When you ask the question "What else could it be?" about any prop, children will enthusiastically offer many new ideas.

You can also use props to illustrate a concept or element of dance. Children often need a concrete

Figure 4.1 Children dancing with streamers to express the movements of a flame.

object to help them visualize the words and concepts presented in the learning experience. For example, the concept of roundness can be illustrated by showing a ball or a globe, the concept of increasing and decreasing size is best illustrated by inflating and deflating a balloon, and the feeling of strong and light force can become vivid when you wring a towel or float a piece of tissue paper. Using props to create an environment for a dance magically transforms the space and stimulates ideas for creating movements. Imagine a room filled with red and orange streamers scattered on the floor. The children immediately pretend they are dancing on the sun as they run and leap over the streamers. You can also use hoops to move in and out of as if they were different worlds, such as the fast world, shaking world, or frozen-shape world. Ropes tied to volleyball poles can form a web for a spider dance, chairs arranged in lines could depict a dance about traveling on a train or bus, and taped lines on the floor can be used for pathways. An environment created by props encourages students to use their imagination and helps to make an abstract idea real. Here are some additional ideas for creative props:

- Pom-poms (cover a paper-towel tube with contact paper, cut 8-inch [20 cm] strips of plastic, and staple 8 to 10 strips together on one end of the tube)
- Large sheets of plastic cut into various shapes (plastic tablecloths work well)
- Sheer curtains, sheets, and other pieces of material
- Stuffed animals or dolls
- Tissues or paper napkins
- Juggling scarves
- Stretchable plastic bands or pieces of elastic
- Long pieces of ribbon
- Beanbags
- Deck rings (streamers can be attached)
- Paper bags
- Rolls of toilet paper
- Beach balls

First grade girls use foam shapes as props in their dance.

❖ Umbrellas

❖ Lummi sticks (12-inch wood sticks) and wands

Costumes

Children, especially young children, welcome the opportunity to create and wear costumes while dancing. Costumes can be as simple as a scarf tied around a wrist, a piece of material draped over a shoulder, or streamers taped to a shirt. Adding a costume to a dance can help define a character, a mood, a time period, a culture, or an animal. Aluminum foil can be wrapped around the arms or molded into a headpiece as a costume in a dance about lightning bolts. Monster costumes can be made of large plastic garbage bags with a hole cut out of the bottom for the head and the sides cut into long strips. When designing costumes, consider ease of movement and safety. Make sure the costume is fastened securely and that headpieces allow the children to see and breathe.

FACILITIES

Although some teachers have adequate indoor and outdoor space, others are less fortunate. In fact, some teachers have no indoor space whatsoever. In some schools, dance may be taught in the children's classroom, outside on the blacktop, in the lunchroom, on a stage, in the foyer of the school, or on an outside grassy area. Following are some suggestions for how the content in this book can be adapted for limited indoor or outdoor space.

You can teach dance learning experiences both outdoors and indoors. Teaching dance outdoors can be inspiring, especially when using the outdoor environment as a theme for the learning experience (see figure 4.2). The challenge is to find a way to accompany the dance with music. We suggest using a battery-operated CD or MP3 player or running a long extension cord outdoors. Percussion instruments work well outdoors because they are portable and can be handheld; however, some of the sounds may not carry well in a large open space. Before you begin to teach, test your voice and musical accompaniment in the outdoor space to determine what adjustments may be needed. To keep students focused and safe in an outdoor area, you need to set spatial boundaries for the dance. Cones or ropes laid on the ground are useful as markers to define the space. Be sure the outdoor space is free from objects that children can slip on such as loose gravel, glass, or oily spots.

Most gymnasiums are well suited for indoor dance. However, a classroom or hallway is sometimes the assigned space for the dance session. These situations are not ideal. Define the boundaries of the space clearly, and check for objects that may cause injury. Not all floor surfaces are suitable for dancing, and adaptations will be necessary. Excessive jumping on concrete, turning on carpet, or moving on a waxed tile floor can lead to injury for you and the students. You are always responsible for the safe participation of your students. Be aware of the limitations of the environment, and plan lessons that are

Figure 4.2   After observing the wind blowing the leaves, children create strong, stretched movements to express the feeling of being blown around by the wind.

meaningful, appropriate for the available space, and safe for actively moving children.

Whether teaching inside or outside, use a wall or portable easel to display dance concepts, photos, students' work, articles, or drawings. A whiteboard in the space will allow you to display the lesson plan, list vocabulary words, or draw pathways and diagrams of formations. Storage space is essential for audio and video equipment, instruments, props, and other instructional materials. Also, students learn best when the facilities have good lighting, ventilation, and access to drinking fountains and bathrooms.

CLASS FREQUENCY AND LENGTH

Schools differ in the number of days per week that the children attend physical education or dance classes and the length of those classes. As one might expect, children who have physical education or dance every day for 30 minutes will learn more content and enjoy more of the physical benefits of regular exercise than will children with less contact time. Realistically, the goals that can be achieved in the dance program are determined by the total amount of time children participate in dance during the school year. When planning, keep in mind school vacations, class trips, assembly programs, and special events that affect the regular school schedule. One approach is to obtain an annual school schedule and note how many sessions are available and the time frame for each marking period. Then plan units that fit into the available time.

Dance, as part of the physical education curriculum, can be presented in several units of concentrated experiences or in single class sessions several times throughout the school year. Sometimes, a single learning experience can be completed in a 30-minute session; at other times, it may be necessary to continue in additional sessions. Students may need more time to learn and practice a dance or to complete the process of creating a dance. When a learning experience is continued over several sessions, students will need time to review what happened in the previous session. This connection between the sessions is important for a meaningful experience to occur. Consider that a high-quality experience may be more important than staying on a set schedule.

Having children feel a sense of accomplishment in the learning experience will lead to increased understanding of the value of the dance experience. This understanding builds positive attitudes toward dance in the physical education and dance curriculums.

COMMUNITY CHARACTERISTICS

The characteristics of the community in which you teach are important elements to consider when planning and delivering a dance program. A community includes not only the city or town but also the school community. Every town, city, and regional area has its own culture, traditions, history, and ways in which the community functions. The values and beliefs of a community have a direct impact on the children who grow up in the community.

As a teacher, you should know the community in which you teach. Learn about how and what the community celebrates, where your students live, what types of recreational activities are available, what religious institutions are located in the community, and what languages are spoken. Become familiar with what it is like to live in the area. As a teacher, you must be sensitive to the communities in which you work, especially if the customs and traditions of a community are not part of your background. Sensitivity implies understanding the socioeconomic and ethnic composition of the community as well as what the community values in education. Each community has a vision for its children, and this vision is reflected in the schools' goals. You need to be aware of these goals and ensure that your dance program is in alignment.

As a means of expression and communication, dance helps students understand the unique composition of their community and how it relates to other communities around the world. A specific ethnic population in the community may request that students have the opportunity to learn dances from their ethnic heritage (see figure 4.3). Reach out to the community as a resource if you are not sure how to teach these dances. Parents are usually willing to share their ethnic customs and dances with the class. Religious values of the community are another consideration. Dancing and specific topics for dance that focus on cel-

Figure 4.3 Folk dances can offer students the opportunity to learn about their own or others' ethnic heritages.

ebration are not part of every religion. You may need to eliminate or change certain dances so children do not feel they must compromise their own beliefs in class. Look to parents and other community members as a resource for cultural and social information that will help you understand what is appropriate and make your dance experiences meaningful to the students.

SCHOOL POLICIES

Every school has policies and procedures for dealing with a variety of situations. This means the school has planned how to address unexpected situations or has carefully anticipated what emergencies could occur and planned accordingly. As a responsible teacher, you must know the school policies and protocols and be prepared to act when necessary. This information may be available in a school handbook or provided by the administration. All schools have requirements to practice fire drills, school lockdowns, and evacuations. Review the procedures and discuss and practice with your students the appropriate behaviors for complying with an emergency event. There are three parts of a school's emergency plan that you should know (Tanis and Hebel 2010). During the crisis, you should know how to make contact when help is needed, how to address a student's injury, and who should be involved in decision making. The second part occurs after the crisis and is related to completing accurate reports; gathering evidence of the event or injury; and communicating with parents, administrators, and school staff. In the third part, you evaluate the incident and assess whether procedures were followed and make recommendations for changes in policy and procedures if needed.

Have a plan for children who are injured in your class. The initial response to an injury requires a careful but speedy assessment followed by safe and appropriate action to help the child. Seeking the advice of the school nurse about procedures for dealing with injuries before someone gets hurt is essential. To ensure a safe learning environment, the nurse should also inform you about children with life-threatening allergies or other medical conditions such as diabetes, asthma, or epilepsy.

PROGRAM ADVOCACY

You may already be teaching in a school where dance is considered an integral part of the curriculum, or you may be asked to initiate a dance program. Both situations call on you to use your knowledge about dance to communicate the benefits of offering a dance component to the physical education or arts education curriculum. Your efforts to maintain or start a dance program require you to become an advocate for dance. Serving as an advocate means that you must become the voice of support for dance in the school curriculum.

Advocacy is a planned approach to making your views count in the decision-making process. It is communication with a purpose (Alperstein and Weyl 1992). You must always be ready to clearly and concisely express the importance of dance in a child's education. Dance can be a vulnerable area of the curriculum because in many schools it is not considered part of the core curriculum and is often subject to budget cuts; thus, opportunities for children to participate in dance experiences are often minimal. Here are some tips to help you in your advocacy role. To be an effective advocate you need to be

◈ well informed about the benefits of dance for children;

◈ willing to solve problems and collaborate with others;

◈ open to listening to other perspectives;

◈ prepared when speaking to an individual or a group;

◆ sincere, optimistic, and passionate about your goals; and

◆ ready to seize opportunities to discuss dance with your colleagues, school administrators, and parents.

Advocacy in dance can be proactive or reactive. In the proactive situation, advocacy efforts are ongoing throughout the school year. Following are ideas for ongoing advocacy efforts:

◆ Submit an article, written by you or your students, about the dance program to the school newspaper or the local newspaper.

◆ Contact a newspaper photographer or reporter to cover a dance class or performance featuring your students.

◆ Collaborate with another teacher in the school to integrate dance with another subject area.

◆ Publicize dance events in the weekly or monthly school calendar.

◆ Invite parents or your administrator to observe a dance class.

◆ Prepare a fact sheet about the dance program for distribution to parents on back-to-school night.

◆ Present an in-service workshop on dance education to faculty members in your school or district.

◆ Send letters of invitation, with complimentary tickets, to members of the board of education, school administrators, and community leaders for the school's dance performances.

◆ Organize a special event such as a family dance night to promote dance as a social activity.

◆ Invite community members or parents with expertise in a specific dance form to share their knowledge and skills with your students.

◆ Attend a conference, workshop, or convention on dance education to keep updated on current issues, research, and practices.

◆ Inform parents, administrators, and colleagues of your program goals, and include the skills and knowledge that students gain as a result of participating in the dance program.

◆ Emphasize to your students what they are learning. Clearly articulate your goals, clarify your assessment strategies, and keep your students actively involved in learning during the class.

◆ Create a bulletin board to highlight what students are learning in the dance class; include pictures, students' drawings, or essays.

If you find yourself in a reactive situation, one in which there is the possibility of reduction to or elimination of the dance program, you will want to develop a plan of action. Begin planning by asking yourself the following questions:

◆ What do I see as the outcome? What do I want to occur?

◆ Why should this issue be addressed?

◆ What message about dance do I want to communicate?

◆ Who is the target audience or whom do I need to influence?

◆ What strategies can I use to reach my target audience?

◆ Who can help me deliver the message?

The best way to advocate is to deliver a solid program founded on standards and goals. A good program will be relevant to the students, have clear objectives, present information in multiple ways, and contain multiple forms of assessment. Students can be very influential in what they say to their teachers, the school administrator, and their parents about their dance learning experiences. Consider their voices as a means of advocating for the dance program. When they experience a sense of accomplishment and success, they will know how meaningful dance can be to their lives and be willing to share their excitement with others.

SUMMARY

Numerous factors have an effect on the teaching and learning environment. You may find yourself teaching a small group of children on a carpeted floor in the classroom or teaching 50 children in one part of a large gymnasium while another class meets in a different section of the gym. The best strategy for making the most of a less-than-ideal situation is to focus on your goals for the learning experience and the children you are teaching. The facilities, equipment, schedule, and class size certainly influence your planning and implementation; however, teaching is a learning experience, and the challenges you face open new possibilities for a creative teaching opportunity. There are a variety of ways to teach dance regardless of the environment. Your responsibility is to be realistic in what you can achieve, considering the educational parameters of your environment, and to continually seek effective teaching methods. Students and colleagues can be valuable resources for ideas to help you deliver your program. Ask them to help you find alternative solutions. This collaborative effort can lead to increased support for dance, especially when students are asked to contribute their ideas. Finally, dance is an invaluable learning experience for children. As a teacher of dance, you are responsible for advocating for your program and ensuring that children have the opportunity to discover the relevance of dance in their lives.

Questions for Reflection

Think about a time when you needed to make a last-minute change in your teaching facility or schedule. How did you handle it? What worked best? What could you have done differently?

How would your teaching strategies change according to the size of the class?

What do you see as a benefit of using props or equipment in a dance lesson?

Think about different spaces in which you might teach dance. How would you adapt a lesson to work in several different spaces?

What do you know about the community in which you teach? How is the community where you live similar and different?

The safety of children is of utmost importance in teaching. Are you familiar with the procedures to follow in case of an emergency such as fire, bomb threat, injury, or breach of security? What are your plans?

What do you think your students would tell their parents about their dance learning experiences? What would you like your students to say?

Why is it important to advocate for dance in your school? Have you considered the various people you would need to contact? What are some steps you might take to be an effective advocate for dance in education?

Making Teaching Effective

Effective teaching begins with planning a learning experience based on knowledge of children's growth and development, the ways in which children learn, the content in the dance program, and lesson development and implementation. The goal is to provide a meaningful learning experience that integrates the needs of children with the content of the dance program. This chapter offers strategies for making the dance experience positive for both the student and you as the teacher.

HELPING ALL CHILDREN LEARN

Every child is unique. They all learn differently, which requires you to adapt content and pedagogy to help all children be successful learners. Huebner (2010) notes, "Today's classrooms are filled with diverse learners who differ not only culturally and linguistically but also in their cognitive abilities, background knowledge and

learning preferences" (p. 79). Although you may welcome this diversity in learning, it poses a challenge for you as a teacher. Dance and physical education classes include children with a range of abilities; for some children, movement is one of the best ways for them to express ideas and feelings. These children are familiar with using movement as a means of communicating and responding eagerly to the sounds and rhythms of music. Not all children, however, respond to movement as comfortably or as easily. Meeting children's educational needs begins with learning about the students' physical, cognitive, emotional, and social characteristics. This knowledge helps you differentiate instruction through providing variations in content, teaching style, and outcomes to meet the needs of each child (Tomlinson 1999). Observe students in their classes, and talk with their teachers to identify their strengths and learning styles as well as what instructional strategies seem to be the most effective. Also, talk with the students to learn about their interests and needs. How do they feel about dancing, what are their previous experiences with dance, and what kind of dance would they enjoy? Most important, be flexible and willing to adapt your learning experiences to ensure success for all students in the class (see figure 5.1). Dance educator and scholar Karen Kaufmann (2002) notes, "All students deserve new opportunities to express their thoughts and feelings kinesthetically in a safe and supportive environment" (p. 16). Teaching students with a broad range of abilities and learning styles presents challenges that can result in gaining new insights about teaching dance.

In addition to ability level, teachers need to be aware of students' cultural, ethnic, linguistic, and social backgrounds. The whole-child approach requires that you honor cultural traditions and understand that students' lives may be different from yours. The way children learn, behave, and feel about learning is culturally influenced by their families' values and experiences. One strategy is to let parents and guardians know that you want to maintain frequent communication about the children's progress. In this way, parents hear the good news about achievement as well as share concerns if they arise. Invite family members to your class to observe and share their dances, music, and cultural heritage. When children have the opportunity to share family celebrations and events, they become empowered and view their

ideas as equally valuable to others' ideas. Most important is that you have established a learning environment that is respectful and safe for everyone. Set high expectations for all children. Believe that all children can learn, be leaders, help others, take responsibility, and have a perspective that needs to be acknowledged. McCarthy-Brown (2009) relates the importance of culturally relevant dance education as follows: "Learning is stifled in a space where individuals do not feel welcome. Everyone has an entry point; and if the paradigm is circular rather than linear then all entry points are valid and valuable" (p. 122). There is no one-size-fits-all approach to teaching. If you view each lesson as a learning moment for you and your students, they will see how your acceptance of other ways of living and specifically dancing is an essential concept to learn. Notice the types of pictures, videos, DVDs, and books you use to support teaching dance. Teach dances from cultures around the world, use music from many cultures in creative dance lessons, and use music from different time periods. Are both sexes and many cultures represented? Can students relate to your teaching materials as well as learn new perspectives? Use culturally diverse and relevant teaching materials and pedagogical approaches, and use feedback that is culturally responsive to your students.

You may have students who are not able to physically participate in class because of a temporary medical condition or injury, or they might

Figure 5.1 Students bring their own background of movement experience and creative potential to the dance learning experience. As the teacher, you offer information about the elements of movement and the process of learning about dance.

not be prepared for class. These students, who frequently sit out on the side of the space and watch their peers, need to be engaged in learning the content in a way that is appropriate. If the child's physical participation is restricted, you can plan in each lesson an activity that addresses cognitive and affective learning. Children can listen to your instructions, observe their peers' dances, or contribute ideas to a group dance. You can develop observation forms that enable students to focus on the movements and formations or how the elements of dance are used. Students can be peer assessors for parts of the lesson: They can list dance terms they hear used in the class and share their lists with the students at the end of the lesson. They can draw or make pipe-cleaner shapes they see their peers using or draw shapes they would use if they were physically participating. Sometimes students who are not dancing can help with the MP3 or CD player or play a percussion instrument for accompaniment. The most important thing is that the students learn. In this way, they will feel included and ready to continue with the content when they are able to physically participate.

USING VARIOUS TEACHING STYLES AND STRATEGIES

Skillful educators know and use a variety of teaching styles that may be different from the way they learn. You must see learning from your students' perspectives and develop content that is developmentally appropriate and meaningful to the students. You should also understand that there are common strategies that can be applied that are appropriate for many students (Ball and Forzani 2011). Choosing the best teaching style to present a dance movement or complete a dance depends on what you want to accomplish in the lesson. A teaching style that is appropriate for presenting a social dance or cultural dance that has established movements and formations may be different from a creative dance lesson where exploration and spontaneous movement are involved. It may be appropriate to use several teaching styles within a single learning experience to address the task and students' individual learning styles.

One common teaching style that is effective for teaching social, cultural, or aerobic dance or doing a set warm-up is the command style. In this style, you lead all the movements and the students follow, reproducing the movement. You decide on the movements, how they are performed, the sequence, and the number of repetitions. This style is useful when teaching movements in which everyone is dancing the same step at the same time. A natural follow-up to command-style teaching is practice style (Mosston and Ashworth 2002). After you demonstrate the movements or complete dance, you ask the students to practice the movements or complete dance while you circulate among the students to offer corrective or affirmative comments.

You can use a problem-solving teaching style when asking the students to create or rearrange dance movements. Graham (2008) describes this style as divergent problem solving, in which there are many ways to solve the problem. This style is the preferred methodology in teaching creative dance (Stinson 1998). Students make decisions about how to move within the limits of the task. Exploration and improvisation are frequently associated with problem solving. Exploration is a thoughtful response to a task in which the student finds a variety of answers. In the task "Find various ways to move on your hands and feet," for example, students think about a way to accomplish the task, try out the movement, then think of another way, try that idea, and continue to think about and perform different answers to the task. Improvisation is a spontaneous response to a task, evoking an immediate physical action. In the task "Move in a way that expresses the word *splatter*," the student immediately responds by moving his or her body with the first idea that comes to mind.

When using the problem-solving teaching style, be open to students' responses. Even if you can anticipate some of the responses, you may be surprised when the children try out something new and unexpected. You can elicit a variety of responses from students by repeatedly asking them to find another way to accomplish the movement task. When you first present the task, students will move in ways that are familiar to them, but as you continue to ask for different responses, they will begin to explore and create new alternatives. This is when creative thinking occurs.

Presenting a task with a specific solution and allowing the students to discover the solution for themselves is called convergent problem solving (Graham 2008) or guided discovery (Mosston and

Ashworth 2002). This teaching style leads the students to a specific solution through a sequence of planned questions. You know the solution beforehand and choose this method to provide students with a more in-depth understanding of how to arrive at the solution. For example, the following sequence of questions leads students to discover how to achieve a balanced position with another person when exercising: "Stand facing your partner with your toes touching and grip each other's hands at the wrists. Now, slowly begin to lean away from each other until your arms are straight. Can you both stay balanced on your feet? How are you using your energy in the pull? Repeat the same balance with one partner pulling more than the other. What happened? When you felt yourself falling off balance, how did you change the energy of the pull to maintain a balanced position? You are now experiencing countertension. What do you think makes it work?"

When students understand the concept and principles of using countertension, switch to a problem-solving task that requires them to demonstrate their understanding through application. For example, direct the class as follows: "Find another way to balance with your partner using countertension. What other body parts can you pull with instead of your hands? Create a countertension balance that uses four people." Students can share their solutions to the problem with others, and use the imitation teaching style themselves to present their solutions to other groups for duplication.

The following additional teaching strategies serve as a menu from which you can choose a variety of approaches to present dance. You can apply the strategies to small- and large-group teaching, to teacher- or student-led presentations, or when integrating technology.

❖ **Modeling.** You demonstrate the dance movement. Students observe and reproduce the movement. Modeling is also used in demonstrating a process or step-by-step plan for creating a dance. The students observe and follow the process when creating their own dances. This process is frequently supported with printed instructions.

❖ **Part-to-whole add-on.** You can teach the dance movements one at a time and then combine them into the correct sequence. You demonstrate the first movement and then the students observe and practice along with you or on their own. Then, you demonstrate the second movement and the students practice it. Next, the students combine the first and second movement and practice. Then you demonstrate the third movement and the students practice it and then add it to the first two movements. This procedure continues until you have taught the movements of the entire dance.

❖ **Show all first.** You demonstrate the entire dance before teaching the individual movements. In this way, students see the end result and understand how the individual movements they will learn fit into the dance. After demonstrating the entire dance, you teach each movement using the part-to-whole add-on strategy.

❖ **Big screen.** You project a DVD or online video of a dance onto a wall or screen so that all students can see the dance. Students follow and perform the dance movements along with the performers in the DVD or online video.

❖ **Observe and join in.** You or a student demonstrates the movements or a complete dance and continue to repeat the movements or dance several times. When the observing students think they are ready to try some or all of the dance movements, they join in and practice the dance along with you or a student demonstrator. This strategy allows students to work at their own pace for learning a dance. This strategy is often used when students are at a social event and want to join in a dance they see others doing.

❖ **Peer teaching.** This strategy introduced by Mosston and Ashworth (2002) is also known as reciprocal teaching. Students are organized into partners or small groups. They collaborate to help each other review and practice the movements or dance that was presented in class.

❖ **Photograph sequence.** A photograph of each movement is placed on the wall in the correct sequence. Students view the photographs and reproduce the movements. The photos can be used as a visual reference to help students remember the dance sequence. A printed description can be added under each photograph to further clarify how the movement is performed.

❖ **Stations.** Stations are set up in the space, which include one dance movement or one complete dance. Placed at each station is a poster with printed instructions, a video, photograph, diagram, and the accompanying music when appropriate. Students organized into small groups spend a few minutes at the station learning and practicing the movement or the dance and then rotate to a new station. The rotation continues until the students learn all the dance movements or the selected dances. Then all students join together to practice the dance or dances in the correct sequence. One idea for a social dance unit is to design stations that focus on a dance from another decade. Students rotate to the stations and learn dances or steps from four or five decades.

❖ Student leaders. A small group of students learn the movements or the complete dance before it is presented to the class. During the class session, these students teach the dance to their classmates. When teaching a line dance that faces the four walls, leaders can be located around the perimeter of the room so that when the dancers turn to face a different wall, they have a leader to follow.

❖ Student video performance. A small group of students learn the movements or the complete dance before it is presented in class and videotape themselves performing the dance. You show the video during the lesson as an instructional tool using the big screen or station strategy.

❖ Symbols sequence. A symbol is created for each movement and organized in the correct sequence. The symbols can be used as a visual reference to help students remember the dance sequence. This may look like a music score or dance notation.

❖ DVD or online video as teacher. Have students watch the complete dance or a part of the dance and then stop the video. Ask the students to remember what they observed and then reproduce the movements. Next, show the video again and ask students to observe and see if they are missing movements. Students observe and practice the dance again. This strategy is appropriate for individuals or small groups. When small groups observe the dance, each group member can contribute what they remembered; as a result the groups can collectively put the dance sequence together.

❖ Background information using DVD or online video. You can use video to present his-

torical and cultural information for cultural and social dances. Students learn about the history, customs, geographic location, political scene, or local traditions and rituals. This information is critical to teaching cultural dance and social dances that represent a culture or historical period.

❖ Line switch. When students are learning a dance where they are organized in multiple lines facing in the same direction, some students will be in the back of the space and some in the front. You can switch the lines to allow all students to dance in the front line and have a better view of you.

❖ Direction readers. Provide students with the printed instructions for performing a dance. In partners or small groups, they take turns reading instructions and collaborate to interpret the instructions and practice and perform the dance.

❖ Contextual teaching. When you present a dance to the students, include historical, social, or cultural information that supports the dance steps, formation, rhythms, and meanings of the movements. The information can include books, articles, online information, pictures, videos, personal stories, press releases, artifacts, props, clothing, maps, or music.

❖ Jigsaw. This is a cooperative teaching approach that uses small groups organized in two ways to learn movements and collaborate to create a dance. First you assign each group a letter identification, such as A, B, or C. In the letter group, each person is assigned a number beginning with 1, then 2, and so on until everyone has a number. Each letter group creates or is assigned a specific movement to learn and practice. This can be a step from a cultural or social dance or a movement they generate for a creative dance. Next, all the students with the number 1 form a new number group named number group 1. This procedure continues until all the letter groups have been reformed into number groups 1, 2, 3, and so on. As a result, each person in the number group knows a different step or movement they learned or created as part of the letter group. Then students from the letter group teach the other members of their number group the step they learned when they were part of the letter group. Now, all students have learned all the new steps and movements that can be organized into a complete dance.

❖ Mental rehearsal. After students have learned or created a dance, they close their eyes and see an imaginary video of the dance being played in their minds. The students visualize the steps, the sequence, and the formation. This strategy helps students to improve their memory and prepare to perform the dance.

❖ Verbal cueing. While teaching the dance, you call out the key phrases or words to help students remember the dance sequence. You can eliminate the cues when students become familiar with the dance.

MOTIVATING LEARNERS

All teachers have students who are reluctant to try a new activity—particularly dance. The thought of presenting a dance learning experience that some students might not receive with enthusiasm can deter you from attempting to teach dance. However, there are students in each class who do enjoy participating in a dance experience and welcome the opportunity to do so. You need to take these students into consideration as well. Engage students in the learning experience through establishing a sense of connectedness with the content (Anderson 2002). Ensure that students feel that their insights and contributions are valued and the content is relevant to their lives. When planning, be sensitive to students' conceptions of the subject matter.

Although you may ignite enthusiasm in many of your students, you will also find there are reluctant learners who are hesitant to participate in dance. Bartholomew (2008) notes, "Good instruction begins when interest and excitement are sparked. Lasting learning, by contrast, comes about when instructional challenges are carefully designed to kindle success" (p. 56). One approach to addressing students' reluctance is to acknowledge the feelings of students who say, "Why do we have to dance? I don't like dancing. Dance is not for me. I can't dance." You can respond, "I hear what you're saying. I understand that dance is not your favorite activity. I know that dancing makes you feel very uncomfortable," or "I know that you feel that you're not very good at dancing, but all the movements in today's lesson are movements you already know how to do." Then ask the students to try the dance, and set time aside at the end of the session for them to talk more about their feelings. Students may find all or part of the experience enjoyable, but some will continue to feel reluctant and may not change their minds for the entire school year.

Here are some other strategies for addressing the concerns of reluctant students:

◆ Acknowledge that there are many definitions of dance and that all are valuable representations of the way people incorporate dance into their lives.

◆ Be generous with honest praise for all students during the dance experience. The praise can help alleviate some of the "I can't" feelings. Students want to trust that you will help them.

◆ Take time at the end of each session to talk about the experience. Discuss with students what parts of the lesson were uncomfortable, what worked well, what could be changed for the next time, and what could be added to make the experience more challenging. This type of questioning allows the students who enjoyed the experience, as well as the reluctant students, to voice their opinions.

◆ Listen carefully to what students tell you. Talk with students individually about their feelings outside of the session, either in a formal conference or casually as you meet them in the hallway. In this way, you can show that you are sincerely interested in their feelings and that you want to help them feel comfortable with learning dance. According to Landsman, Moor, and Simmons (2008), "Reluctant learners need to feel that they are heard, that their stories, their voices, their questions, and their contributions matter" (p. 65).

◆ Find hooks. Have the music or a video of the dance playing when students enter the room. Add a pictorial display that represents the content or topic, dress in a relevant costume such as a sport shirt when teaching sport-themed dances, or ask students to arrive dressed for a theme or bring a prop such as a stuffed animal or favorite toy.

◈ Teach by invitation (Graham 2008). This strategy allows students to make choices. You could say, "You can choose to add percussion instruments to accompany your dance or create the dance without any accompaniment."

◈ Set a positive atmosphere in the beginning of the learning experience as you would with any area of the curriculum. Children do not want to be viewed as foolish or incompetent in front of their peers. You can tell children that you are trying this lesson for the first time, and you would like their feedback at the end of the session. Then, ask them what parts of the learning experience were the most interesting. What did they learn today about dance? What changes would they suggest for the next session? We stress that students respect the individual differences among their peers. We all bring strengths to the experience and we can all learn something new about ourselves and how we move. What is challenging to one student may not be as challenging to another. Acknowledge these differences in a positive, accepting atmosphere that helps alleviate the feeling of vulnerability.

◈ Students seem more reluctant to participate in dance than in other curricular areas. However, when you exhibit sincere enthusiasm as you introduce the learning experience, choose content that is relevant to the students, and ensure a positive atmosphere, your students will begin to understand and value dance as an important part of their experiences.

Frequently, teachers who anticipate reluctance when they use the word *dance* will begin the session by saying, "We are going to create some new movements today," or "This lesson is about moving to a rhythm in the music." They purposely avoid using the word *dance* because some children will immediately turn off from the learning experience because of their preconceptions about dance. Using other phrases or words as a substitute for *dance* in the beginning of a lesson may encourage children to participate. We strongly recommend that at some point, either at the end of the lesson or at the end of the unit, you explain that what the children were doing is called dance. When their experiences are positive, they will link a new meaning to the word *dance*. Children must know that they are dancing and that the learning and feelings of success and joy they experience are a result of a dance experience.

ESTABLISHING PROTOCOLS AND RULES

Most teachers have a series of established protocols and rules they use with their classes. Protocols are usually teacher-designed ways of operating during the class that facilitate efficient class management and allow maximum time for active participation (Graham 2008). These include ways to enter and exit the class, obtain and return equipment, stop an activity, and react to fire drills and other emergency situations. Rules establish guidelines for responsible behaviors that foster learning (Brady, Forton, Porter, and Wood 2003). Often, children can suggest rules that address respect, good listening, sharing, and cooperation, as described later. Dance learning experiences follow similar protocols and rules used in other educational experiences.

One important protocol to establish is the stop signal. Clarify your meaning of *stop*. Explain to students the specific behaviors you expect—the voice is quiet, the body is still, everyone is looking at you, props are placed on the floor, a shape is held still, or hands that are connected are let go. The signal can be you saying "stop" or "freeze," or it can be another specified signal. For example, when using recorded music, you might say, "When the music stops, I want you to stop." When using percussion instruments, you could tell students, "I am going to play a skipping rhythm on the drum. When I hit the drum loudly, like this, stop." Or you might say, "This movement will not be accompanied by music. Stop when you hear me tap the triangle three times, like this: one, two, and three." You can also incorporate a way to stop in the movement task: "Run, leap, turn, and freeze in a stretched shape," or "As you are running in the space, begin to run slower and slower until you come to a complete stop."

Another protocol that supports effective teaching is to establish a way to begin and end the dance session. To begin class, you could have students sit in a circle and take attendance by asking each student to respond with a movement or a clap of their hands. One attendance strategy that allows you to get to know more about students is to choose a category, such as colors, foods, animals, or sports, and when you call a child's name, the child responds with an answer that fits the category. At the end of the class, students can convene to talk about what they learned or to hear about what will happen in the next session. In Graham's (2008) book *Teaching Children Physical Education*, he offers strategies for establishing and maintaining effective class management protocols. Teachers can design a plan, communicate it to the students, and monitor students' reactions. Children need parameters to help them focus on learning, being safe, and respecting others.

Creating rules begins with awareness for you as the teacher and each student about the goals for learning. Ask students what they hope to learn and what they want to learn. Their comments become the foundation for developing rules that help them reach their goals. The task now is to solicit from the students their ideas for rules. During class, children can offer spoken suggestions, write or draw about rules, or work in small groups on a rule list. Encourage students to frame rules in the positive instead of beginning each rule with "Don't" or "No" (Brady et al. 2003). Consolidate the lists, and make the rules global and concise (see figure 5.2). Once the rules are developed, it is time to bring them to life. Practice the rules with students by having them experience what the rules look like and sound like in action. You can ask, "What does respect look like when you are listening to someone talk?" or "What would you say if you are sharing a prop?" Role-play with students about the situations that occur in the dance session. Here, students can connect the rules to actual situations. These moments of practice model for students the acceptable way to behave and further their understanding of the rules. Consequences for choosing to not follow rules or protocols should be logical, maintain the integrity of the children, and offer an opportunity to learn from the situation. Provide children with problem-solving techniques for settling disputes and the language to express their feelings in an appropriate manner. There is no question that it takes time to establish rules, practice rules, and discuss consequences; however, establishing classroom protocols is a worthy investment that

Rules for Dance Learning

Be kind, helpful, and caring.
Respect others and school materials.
Always try your best.
Listen to each other.

Figure 5.2   Sample list of rules for a dance class.

will establish a positive environment for teaching and learning.

CREATING A SAFE LEARNING ENVIRONMENT

In dance and physical education classes, children are always moving, and the potential for injury is greater than in a classroom where children are more sedentary. Establish a safe environment by communicating the safety protocols and rules to the students and then reinforce appropriate behavior during the session. Before you teach, review the lesson and anticipate where an emphasis on safe behaviors will be needed. For example, when asking children to huddle closely together in a group, you can anticipate that some children may push or fall and injure themselves or another child. Before the huddle, explain to the children that they need to move into the huddle slowly, remain still, and then move apart slowly. When children are traveling in the room, they need adequate space to dance freely without bumping into others. Not all children have fully developed agility and perceptual skills to make quick changes of direction and weight shifts to avoid collisions. As a result, you will need to organize students for safe movement. First, reinforce understanding of the concepts of personal space (the space immediately around the body, whether while stationary or traveling) and general space (all other available space). Developing an awareness of appropriate personal space takes practice. Many children tend to be too close to others, the walls, and objects. It may be helpful to remind students, "Look in front of you, to the sides, and in back of you to see if you have enough space to move without bumping into another person." Also, identify safety lines on the floor that border the dance space and instruct students to stay within the lines to protect them from hitting a wall, furniture, or other obstacles. Check to make sure children are wearing appropriate footwear, such as sneakers and clothing that allow for easy, safe, and effective movement.

When students are making quick traveling movements such as running or leaping, have all students move in the same direction in the space. They can be organized into lines of three or four and take turns, or they can move in a large circular path around the space, not necessarily in a single circle. With very large groups, taking turns for fast movement may be the best choice for keeping the environment safe. A balance is necessary between the time students spend moving and the time they are waiting for a turn to maintain active participation in a safe space.

You also need to stress personal safety to enable children to perform dance movements without injuring themselves. Teach children appropriate techniques to help them express themselves and avoid injury (Joyce 1984). Teach children to land softly through their feet when coming down from hops, jumps, and leaps. The toes should touch the floor first, followed by the ball and then the heel of the foot, and the knees should be bent on the landing to absorb the force. When children lower themselves to the floor, they need to use their hands to help control their body weight and avoid dropping directly onto their knees. Require children to be cautious when bending or moving backward, switching weight from one body part to another, or turning and stopping quickly. As the teacher, you are responsible for the children's safety. Anticipate problems, teach safe ways to move, and attend to injuries immediately. Always begin each session with a proper warm-up and end the session with appropriate cool-down movements.

PRESENTING DEMONSTRATIONS

In many learning experiences, movement patterns or sequences require a demonstration by either the teacher or the students. When demonstrating a specific movement or dance step for a large group, you have several choices. Facing the students with the front of the body allows you to see all the students. This requires you to reverse the right and left orientation of the movement. For example, you call for the students to step to the right yet demonstrate a step to your left side while the students step their right side, similar to looking in a mirror. Having your back to the students allows the students to match the movement identically, but it is difficult for you to see if the students are following correctly. Another possibility for demonstrating is to stand beside a student. This works well when demonstrating to one student. The student can match the movement, and you can see the student at the same time. This approach is helpful when teaching specific dance steps that are difficult for students to learn.

You can also demonstrate from the center of a large group where the students face the center of the circle. In this situation, the students will follow the movement in a general way rather than match it exactly. For example, you may say, "I am going to move very slowly. I want you to follow my movements and stop when I stop."

Be sure all students can see the demonstration. The demonstrator can repeat the movement in different places in the room or change the position of the students (Graham 2008). Those in back of the space can move to the front, or those in the center can switch with students on the periphery of the group. When teaching a large class, it may be possible to teach from a raised platform or stage to allow the students to view the demonstration easily.

Besides the appropriate location, how you present the demonstration requires consideration. Sometimes, showing the whole dance or complete sequence of movements gives students the big picture, and they can see how the individual movements are part of the whole. Then you can break down the steps or short phrases of movement. You may need to first demonstrate the movement slowly so that students can follow, and then demonstrate using the appropriate tempo and quality of movement. Finally, accompany the demonstration with verbal focus or cues to help direct children's attention to the movement (Graham 2008).

PROVIDING FEEDBACK

Frequent positive and constructive comments to children will maintain motivation and reinforce learning (Graham 2008). Because dance can be an area of the curriculum where students may feel more self-conscious and vulnerable, it is important to acknowledge accomplishments, no matter how small, and also to make corrections when necessary. Both types of comments—acknowledgment and correction—should be specific and descriptive. Acknowledge students' work with comments such as these: "That's great. I see you've used your back and arms to make a round shape." "You are using great control to lower your body carefully to the floor." "Everyone learned the steps very quickly. Your concentration and coordination are improving." When using corrective comments, acknowledge the positive aspects of the movement first, and then add a comment to help the child improve performance. Say, for example, "You are moving in the right rhythm, but you need to think ahead about which side you move to first," or "I see that you are moving at a low level. Now can you use only your hands and feet for traveling?" Always look for something positive to say to children. They value your comments and use them to reassure themselves of their progress.

In order for comments to be effective, the children must be able to hear the positive feedback. Children tend to use their voices and can be noisy when moving. To ensure that children hear your comments, move close to them. Sometimes, however, it is appropriate to comment from across the room. Making sure that children hear your positive feedback is valuable and can help them feel good about their movements. It is also helpful to say a child's name first before commenting. Doing so will gain their attention so they are ready to hear the comment. Here is an example: "Tim, I see you are using a jump in three directions to show your popping movement. That's great!"

Children also want the opportunity to talk about their experiences. Allow a few seconds after a dance is performed or a series of tasks is presented for students to talk. Frequently students share their feelings or describe their experience with their peers when performing or learning. You may hear comments such as "That was so much fun," or "I could not get that step. Did you?" Students need to be quiet when you or a child is speaking to allow everyone to hear the comment the first time. When a child answers a question or makes a comment, you should refrain from

rephrasing the comment every time. Doing so can send a message to children that their comments are not valued and that you can say it more effectively. Some children do not speak loudly enough to be heard in a big space. It may take extra time to gather the class closer and make sure they can hear a child speaking, yet you must respect the integrity of the child as the speaker. In dance, value is placed not only on the students' abilities to create and learn movement but also on what they think and say about movement.

ENGAGING STUDENTS IN PERFORMANCES

In a dance class, the purpose of performance is to share dance movement that has been created or learned with other students or with you as the teacher. Not all students' work needs to be performed; however, there are times when students' performance is appropriate. Performance provides the opportunity to communicate the intent of the dance to others. When students perform a folk dance, for example, they are communicating an event or custom of a particular culture. A dance about clouds may communicate the shapes of clouds and how they move across the sky. These performance opportunities can occur at various times throughout the learning experience. Often a teacher will ask one or more students to perform a particular sequence of movements. This pinpointing method of performance (Graham 2008) is valuable when you need to illustrate accuracy and quality in movement or demonstrate a variety of solutions to a problem-solving task. At other times, the performance will occur near the end of a learning experience to demonstrate the culminating dance that was learned or created.

Generally, you will ask all the students to perform the dance movement at the same time. This is a comfortable approach for students who are hesitant about performing. Many students are afraid to make a mistake in front of others or to show their work because they believe that their work will not be accepted, yet they are willing to perform as part of the whole class. Asking students to perform solo when they are not ready or have not readily volunteered places them in an uncomfortable situation. Do not expect children to perform solo unless they request to do so.

A trio performs a dance for their peers.

Also, if a child refuses to perform, even after your encouraging words, do not demand that he or she do so. Your insistence will only intensify the child's resistance. Respect the student's decision and find a time to talk with the child outside of class to discuss the child's feelings. Together, you and the child can explore other ways the child can share what he or she has learned.

Designing a variety of performance circumstances will allow students to communicate their dances to others, provide students with an opportunity to observe others dancing, and give you an opportunity to observe how the students complete the tasks. The following are examples of performance opportunities:

◈ A student readily volunteers to perform for the whole class.

◈ A student shares a movement or sequence of movements with a group of three or four other students. Each student in the group is encouraged to take a turn.

◈ Students paired together as partners perform for another set of partners.

◈ An individual student shares a movement idea or completed dance with one other student.

◈ Two or three small groups perform at the same time for the whole class.

◈ Half the class performs at one time while the other half observes, and then they switch roles.

◈ One small group performs for another small group, and then the groups switch roles.

◈ Individual students or small groups perform for you at a time other than during class.

◈ Students perform for you or other students at a performance station.

For reasons that are understandable, children cannot and should not sit and observe or wait for extended periods for their turn to perform. Keep the performance time short.

When the students are ready to perform, make one or two specific comments that focus the students' attention on how they will perform the dance. Offer comments such as these: "Think about what you want to express in this dance, and make each movement clear." "Be sure to feel the strong energy in your movement, especially when you jump into the air." "Take your time in the turn and fall to the floor, thinking of lightly and slowly melting." or "Listen carefully to the change in the music as the cue to change the dance formation." Request that students begin and end their performance with their bodies still. This stillness defines the beginning and end of a specific movement or a whole dance, both for the dancer and the observers. Remind students who are observing to applaud or comment in a respectful manner after the performance. A great way to show support for the performer is to have the observers applaud before as well as after the performance. Starting a performance on such a positive note builds self-esteem and encourages students who are reluctant to be more enthusiastic about performing.

OBSERVING AND RESPONDING TO DANCE

Observing dance, whether it is a professional company or student class work, is a valuable component of the dance program. Frequently, dance observation is overlooked because the emphasis of the lesson is experiential; that is, the children are actively involved in physically learning or creating dances. Observing can give children an appreciation for dance as a means of nonverbal communication and expression. It is a valuable means of learning about dance if you prepare the students beforehand so their response is thoughtful and meaningful. A general statement such as "Tell me what you liked about the dance after the performance" can precede the observation. Additionally, you can state more specific expectations by telling the students what to look for in the dance: "Pay attention to how the dancers use light and strong energy in their locomotor movements." This verbal focus makes observation more meaningful and increases comprehension of the dance.

Other suggestions for directing students' observation include asking the students to look for the following:

- ◈ The ways the dancers use straight and curved pathways

- ◈ Movements in which dancers go into the air
- ◈ How the dance steps match the beat of the music
- ◈ How the dances are similar to each other
- ◈ Whether the dance tells a story
- ◈ Movements and shapes that remind you of clouds (in a dance about clouds)
- ◈ How the dance begins and ends
- ◈ Feelings expressed by the dancers
- ◈ Answers to student-created questions for the observation

After the observation, a discussion should occur in which students respond by expressing their thoughts and perceptions and hear a variety of other viewpoints. Guide the class discussion by asking questions such as these:

- ◈ What movements did you see? Describe how the dancers were moving.
- ◈ How did the spatial formations change throughout the dance?
- ◈ How did the dancers use gestures to convey a character?
- ◈ What ideas or feelings might the dancers have been trying to express?
- ◈ What does this dance mean to you personally?
- ◈ What other possible meanings might the dance have?
- ◈ What did you see in the dance?
- ◈ What part of the dance was the most exciting and why?
- ◈ Describe the ways the dancers related to each other.
- ◈ Was there a message in the dance?
- ◈ Can you suggest another way to end the dance?
- ◈ What part of the dance would you like to dance yourself?
- ◈ What do you think about the music used for the dance?
- ◈ How did the costumes, props, or setting affect the dance?
- ◈ How did the dance relate to the title of the dance?

◆ What do you feel about what you saw?

◆ What was original or imaginative about the dance?

◆ What did the dance tell you about the time period it represents?

◆ What did the dance tell you about the people and their environment, traditions, or culture?

Children can respond to their observations through drawing pictures (see figure 5.3), writing in a journal (see figure 5.4), writing a review, composing a poem, or demonstrating their responses through movement or discussion. In a large class, it is not always possible to have the time to listen to everyone's response to a question. A strategy that is helpful for sharing verbal responses requires that students be organized into pairs or small groups and take turns sharing their comments with each other. This is referred to as the pair and share response method. Encourage children to use the movement vocabulary from the elements of dance in their comments. In this way, they will be able to extend and clarify their comments beyond stating simply, "I liked the dance," or "It was interesting." Probe for in-depth comments by asking students what they liked about the dance or what, specifically, they found interesting. Asking a follow-up question to a comment engages children's critical-thinking skills and helps them understand what they observed and increase their ability to articulate their perceptions.

SUMMARY

From the moment children step into the space to their last step out the door, the dance experience should be engaging, relevant, and enjoyable. You know the needs of the children and plan a unit and lessons that invite them to experience dance in a variety of ways. Children are recognized for their individual perspectives, learning styles, and abilities to learn and create dance movements. As the teacher, you have established protocols and rules that help children learn and grow in a safe, kind, and orderly place. Here, children feel their way of learning is respected and are willing to take risks as they collaborate with others to create, perform, and observe dances.

Figure 5.3 Drawings depict children's responses to an observation.

	May 17, 2012
○	I thought the dance assembly was very entertaining and informing about dance all over the world. The three dancers showed the movements and told us where it originated from. I liked the Brazilian dancers the best. It was fast and colorful. I wonder how the dancers remembered all the movements and dance so well together. I wasn't always interested in dancing, but now I am because of the cool moves.

Figure 5.4 Journal writing about a dance observation.

Questions for Reflection

What are some characteristics of effective teaching in dance? What would it look like and sound like in your classroom?

We can all agree that children learn in a variety of ways. What are some of the strategies that you can use to help children be successful?

What supportive phrases can you share with students as feedback to their dancing? Create a list of 10 or more comments.

What strategies can you use for including students in constructing rules for effective learning?

What suggested strategies for reluctant learners do you find appropriate for your situation? What other strategies in other content areas have you used to help students feel comfortable and motivated to learn?

Students enjoy learning new activities, yet they also need the comfort of a routine. What protocols can you use with your classes that are applicable to teaching dance?

Think about your experiences in viewing a dance. What do you look for when you are observing a dance?

What precautions do you take to ensure the children's safety during the lesson?

Assessing Children's Learning in Dance

Assessment, as a significant part of a comprehensive dance curriculum, can be conducted in a variety of ways. Most important, the type of assessment selected must be directly related to the outcomes of the learning experience. Wiggins (1998) contends that the primary goal of assessment is to educate students and improve learning, not merely audit it. As an essential component of the teaching and learning process, assessment is embedded throughout the dance curriculum. Those who teach dance are continually seeking the best ways to assess students' learning. They look at how creativity, performance, group cooperation, personal growth, and change in attitude and values can be assessed feasibly in a valid and reliable manner. Many assessments used in dance are designed by a teacher and focus specifically

on learning that occurs in a particular unit or lesson. These types of teacher-constructed assessments reflect a student's level of skill, acquisition of knowledge, and perception of what he or she has learned. The assessment offers feedback to you and the students about how the outcomes are being met. Assessments can occur before, during, and at the conclusion of a unit. All collect different types of information that can inform prior knowledge and skills and progress. To complete a comprehensive assessment, you need to access the three learning domains inherent in dance. Psychomotor assessment is one of the primary areas of dance assessment and evaluates how well the student can perform the dance movements. Cone and Cone (2005) explain psychomotor assessment for elementary level students as follows:

"This assessment looks at accuracy and clarity in performing movements; rhythmic coordination; flow from one movement to the next; or ability to change tempo, direction, levels, 'size' [range], pathways, and energy" (p. 10). You can observe how a student uses strength, balance, flexibility, cardiorespiratory endurance, body and spatial awareness, and body control to perform a dance movement or a complete dance. One example of psychomotor assessment in a creative dance about performing three different cloud shapes involves observing a student performing a sequence of three cloud shapes and assessing the student's body control as she holds each shape still for 4 counts and assessing the student's ability to move from one shape to the next with smooth control (see figure 6.1). Assessment can involve evaluating whether the student can accurately perform a sequence of dance steps from a cultural dance or perform dance movements to the music rhythm. The psychomotor domain is assessed through teacher or peer observation based on clear criteria for achievement. This domain challenges the observer to focus and remember the movements, especially during live performances. However, video recordings of a performance can offer the opportunity to view the performance several times, making the assessment easier to see how the criteria are applied. In many dance classes, video is not available and the assessment relies on your knowledge of the criteria and ability to be in a good viewing position.

Cognitive assessment determines what knowledge children have about the unit or lesson content. The assessments focus on recalling terminology; identifying dance steps or facts about a dance such as origin, formation, choreographic structure, or order of movements; explaining their perceptions and opinions of their own dance or the dances of others; and analyzing dances for commonalities, differences, or application of the elements of dance. One way knowledge can be revealed for young children is to ask them to give a movement answer to a question. When young students blend movement with language, they have a greater range of responses to use to express their understanding. You can also assess cognitive understanding by administering a written quiz or test, having students write a response to a journal question, or asking students to give a verbal response or draw a picture.

The affective domain involves feelings, reactions, attitudes, preferences, social interactions, and self-concept. Assessment of the affective domain should not be limited to assessment of participation, effort, and attitudes. Worrell, Evans-Fletcher, and Kovar (2002) note, "Teachers might consider including other elements such as personal responsibility, cooperation, compassion, self-expression, positive interaction with other students, respect for differences, and being a good team member" (p. 31). Knowing how students feel about the content or about themselves as dancers can help you to design lessons that are meaningful and relevant. In many lessons, students collaborate to learn, teach each other, respond to a peer, or create and perform a dance together. This social interaction is a critical component in

Criteria

Shapes: yes = included 3 shapes; no = included 1 or 2 shapes

Control: yes = smooth transition from one shape to another; no = hesitated, lost the flow of the movement, or fell down

Students' names	3 cloud shapes	Control
Mina	Yes	Yes
Shawn	Yes	No—hesitated
Thomas	No (only 2)	Yes
Genese	Yes	Yes
Pen Pen	No (only 1)	No—fell down

Figure 6.1   Example of psychomotor assessment.

assessing students' leadership, responsibility to stay focused, willingness to listen to other ideas, demonstration of respect, and positive negotiation and compromise. Information on the affective domain can be collected by teacher observation, student surveys, verbal comments, drawings, and journal writings.

In dance, children learn, perform, create, observe, and respond to dances; thus various types of assessments are needed. Assessment of how a student performs a dance movement or a completed dance or how a student creates a dance is usually embedded in most dance lessons and units and conducted formally or informally. Be sure to plan time for assessment to occur during the lesson or unit. Assessment may also take the form of a written test using multiple-choice questions or questions requiring short phrases or paragraphs. Other written assessments can include journal writing in response to their own dancing or the dancing of others, constructed books containing descriptions and drawings of dances, and lists of vocabulary words used in the dance lesson. Students can also respond orally to questions, lead a discussion, interview a peer, deliver a presentation on dance, or complete a project. Relying on a single type of assessment will not fit all situations and limits the information that you collect about students' learning. It is not enough to simply measure a student's ability to recall memorized facts or perform an isolated movement; instead, assessment of what students know and are able to do should include a balance of lower- and higher-order thinking skills, as represented in Anderson and Krathwohl's update of Bloom's taxonomy (Anderson and Krathwohl 2001; see figure 6.2 on page 82).

Assessing dance presents a challenge because of its ephemeral nature. Dance is a live art form that occurs in a time and space that cannot be exactly replicated. As a form of human movement and art, the dance is embodied in the dancer, and as experience affects the dancer, the dance itself is also affected. This is why conducting a single view of assessment captures only one moment, whereas a variety of assessments can provide a more comprehensive picture of what a child knows, understands, and is able to do. Taking a video of children dancing may be considered one way to address this concern; however, although a video can be a useful tool for assessment, it does have its limitations. Dance on video is taken through the view of the person with the video recorder and, as a result, may provide a limited view of the dance.

Subjectivity is another issue in dance assessment. One's background, values, and aesthetic preferences play into the interpretation of what the assessor views. Teachers, alone or in collaboration with students, need to define the criteria for the rubric. The criteria become the description of what is considered an appropriate response, and the rubric delineates the range of possible responses. Rubrics can be holistic (containing several criteria; see figure 6.3 on page 82) or analytic (in which there is a rubric for each criterion; Wiggins 1998). A rubric for five elements of choreography developed by Rovegno and Bandhauer (2000) is a clear example of how an analytic rubric can be used in making assessment less subjective. For each of the five choreographic elements—originality, transitions, expressing an idea, focus and clarity, and contrasts and aesthetic highlights—Rovegno and Bandhauer include a different range of performance levels accompanied by a description of what you would observe at each level. When rubrics are used to guide self- and peer assessment, students become increasingly aware of how to assess their work and set goals for improvement. It is okay to make adjustments in the assessment during the unit because as you teach you will also learn more about how students respond to the content.

Assessment in dance should address students' knowledge and skills as learners, creators, performers, and responders to dance. In this chapter, we address dance assessment from four approaches: teacher assessment of program and effectiveness of a unit or lesson, teacher assessment of individual student learning, peer assessment, and student self-assessment.

ASSESSMENT OF TEACHING EFFECTIVENESS

Effective teaching is the result of creative thinking, planning clear outcomes, dynamic delivery, and reflection on the teaching and learning experience. What worked and why and what can be changed for the next lesson? These questions influence a recurrent cycle of planning, presenting, and reflecting. As an ongoing part of teaching, the

Remembering: Retrieving, Recalling, or Recognizing Knowledge From Memory

Name three movements in square dance.

Demonstrate how to skip forward using a fast speed.

Observe and repeat the three movements I have demonstrated.

Understanding: Constructing Meaning by Interpreting, Summarizing, Comparing, Classifying, or Explaining

Describe the benefits of participating in a social dance.

Express anger using three different shapes.

Show me the difference between a strong reaching movement and a light reaching movement.

Applying: Carrying Out or Using a Procedure Through Executing or Implementing

Practice the dance you learned at two different tempos.

Develop a new line dance using the steps you have learned.

Organize the members of your group into a circle formation.

Analyzing: Breaking Material or Concepts Into Parts, Determining How the Parts Relate or Interrelate to One Another or to an Overall Structure or Purpose

Compare and contrast Samir's dance with Kristen's dance.

Experiment using three pathways for the leaf dance and select one that best expresses the leaves blowing in the wind.

Watch a video of a cultural dance and categorize the movements as either locomotor or nonlocomotor.

Evaluating: Making Judgments Based on Criteria and Standards Through Checking and Critiquing

After viewing a dance performed by your peers, decide what you think they were expressing in the dance.

After observing a dance video, choose a different way to begin and end the dance.

After performing your sport dance, check to see if you have included a change in level and tempo.

Creating: Putting Elements Together to Form a Coherent or Functional Whole; Reorganizing Elements Into a New Pattern or Structure Through Generating, Planning, or Producing

Create a new line dance using five of the steps you have learned.

Rearrange the steps to the cupid shuffle to create a new line dance.

Plan a dance map that shows the pathways you will use to move through the space.

Figure 6.2   Sample tasks reflecting Bloom's taxonomy.

Adapted from Anderson and Krathwohl 2001.

Circle the number that describes how well your group performed the dance.

3	Awesome	Everyone did the whole dance really great.
2	Very good	Two or three people make a mistake, but the dance was still good.
1	Try again	A lot of people made mistakes and we need more practice.

Figure 6.3   Holistic rubric created by students.

dance experience shared by the teacher and the students is evaluated based on a set of outcomes that describe what students should be able to do and know as a result of participating in the dance learning experience. The answers to the following questions provide you with valuable information to use in evaluating your preparation and presentation of a specific learning experience or the total dance program.

Questions for Reflection of a Program's Effectiveness

- Did students have experiences in all the artistic processes throughout the program?

- How was dance as a cultural, social, and creative dance form included?

- What types of assessment instruments were used in gathering evidence of learning? How were the results analyzed and what changes were planned for program improvement?

- What national, state, or local standards were emphasized and what standard needs to be strengthened?

- What new learning experiences were added to the program and what learning experiences need to be deleted or changed?

Questions for Reflection at the Conclusion of a Dance Unit

During and after the unit and lessons, you reflect on the lesson design and how it was presented to the students.

- Were the unit and lesson outcomes clear and did they address a set of standards?

- What were students expected to learn in the psychomotor, cognitive, and affective domains?

- How did the sequence of the learning experiences contribute to meeting the outcomes?

- Did the units include new information or a review of previous knowledge?

- How were the assessments implemented during the unit? Were formative and summative assessments used? What type of assessment instruments were used in assessing the psychomotor, cognitive, and affective domains?

Questions for Reflection at the Conclusion of a Dance Learning Experience

Assessment of teaching is an ongoing process. You look at the way the students respond to each task and adjust the tasks during the learning experience to ensure students' achievement of the planned outcomes. Following are questions to consider:

- Did students have time to practice and create dances? Did I rush through the content without providing adequate time for skill accomplishment and knowledge acquisition?

- Was the content too hard or too easy for students? Were students challenged or bored?

- Did the introduction provide background information?

- What did I learn about students' prior experiences with the topic or dance form?

- How did the warm-up relate to the movements used in the dances?

- Was the task progression logical and built developmentally so that students were successful?

- Did I include a culminating dance?

- Did students have time to fully perform the dance with expression and understanding?

- Did I use different ways to close the lessons? Which ways were meaningful to the students? How do I know what they learned?

A more focused approach in assessing a single learning experience is to develop a list of questions that relate to each psychomotor, cognitive, or affective outcome. For example, when teaching a cultural dance, the outcomes can be for students to learn the sequence of steps (psychomotor), understand the cultural background of the dance (cognitive), and dance with enthusiasm and in cooperation with others (affective). Questions for assessment of the learning experience could include the following:

- How many of the students can accurately perform the steps in the dance? (psychomotor)

- How many of the students could remember a sequence of steps and perform them without cues? (psychomotor)

❖ Are the students able to change direction smoothly? (psychomotor)

❖ Can they maintain the spatial formation of the dance? (psychomotor)

❖ Can they describe what the steps represent about the culture in which the dance was designed? (cognitive)

❖ Are they dancing with a sense of joy in the experience? (affective)

❖ Are the students able to relate positively to their partners and the group as a whole? (affective)

You can also include the following suggested list of general questions that are appropriate to the overall experience:

❖ What parts of the learning experience were successful and why were they successful?

❖ Which outcomes were met by all the students and what outcomes continue to be addressed?

❖ What parts of the learning experience could be changed, what indicated that change is needed, and what changes would be made?

At the end of each learning experience, it is helpful to record a few notes about each class, review the written plans, and add or delete tasks for the next learning experience. In addition, review what was successful about the way you taught the lesson. Ask yourself, "Was it the way I demonstrated a movement, how I used my voice, where I placed myself in the space, my addition of a video or picture or diagram, or my energy and enthusiasm for the topic?"

Assessment of teaching effectiveness is a form of teacher self-assessment. The reflective process of thinking about how the unit and lessons were planned and taught and how the students experienced learning challenges you to reconsider prior assumptions, attitudes, beliefs, behaviors, and perceptions and to be open to change. As a result of self-assessment, you are more informed about your teaching and can develop a rationale for better practice (Brookfield 1995; McCollum 2002). You can look at your work objectively and know with some confidence why you believe what you believe and why you do what you do.

TEACHER ASSESSMENT OF STUDENTS

Assessment of students' learning can be formal (specifically designed tests) or informal (usually conducted through observation while students are participating in the lesson). In both types, you monitor a student's progress during a single learning experience or over time. Assessing students' learning in dance requires a feasible approach that provides you with the information you need when you see many children in a limited time. Instruments and formats for collecting information of students' learning can include teacher-constructed assessments, standardized norm-referenced state or national assessments, teacher observations using a rating scale or checklists (see figure 6.4), written notes, recorded comments, and videotapes. You can

Class: Mrs. G

Dance: Line dance pattern

+ = Child is able to demonstrate

x = Child is unable to demonstrate

Students' names	Correct movements	On the beat	Changes direction
Sharia	+	+	+
Donovan	+	X	+
Robert	+	+	+
Zui	x	X	+

Figure 6.4 Teacher's checklist for a single evaluation.

Figure 6.5   Student responding to the teacher's question.

also collect information through tests, quizzes, journal writing, drawings, verbal responses (see figure 6.5), and portfolios.

Teacher assessment of students' performance begins with a discussion of the criteria and the rubric. Show students examples of good and not-so-good work and identify the characteristics of each. McTighe (1997) suggests, "If we expect students to do excellent work, they need to know what excellent work looks like" (p. 9). Articulate the gradations in the rubric, such as beginning, improving, and excelling, so students can set levels of achievement for themselves. Be clear about the criteria for each rubric level. For example, in a lesson in which students are creating a dance about geometric shapes and pathways, explain what you are looking for specifically as they perform their final dance: "I want to see you begin your dance in a geometric shape, then travel on a geometric pathway, and end in a different geometric shape. Make sure your dance contains at least one change in tempo and one change in levels. A dance with all these parts and clear shapes and pathways will be graded as excellent, a dance missing one of these parts will be graded as satisfactory, and a dance with two or more missing parts will be graded as needs more time to improve." Students understand the

levels of achievement and can set goals during their learning and creating. After watching each student's performance, you record on the rubric how well the student's dance met the criteria.

Another student assessment format is to use a form that notes the rubric and criteria and write the student's name in the rubric category (see figure 6.6 on page 86). Space is also available for writing specific comments. In addition to the performance of the dance, you can assess a student's understanding of how his or her body represents a geometric shape, for example, by asking the student to draw their body or the shape used in the dance (see figure 6.7 on page 86). Older students may write about their choreographic process for the dance (see figure 6.8 on page 87). Be aware that for some children the ability to communicate their understanding through drawing and writing may be limited by their ability to use those media of expression. Again, it is important to assess students' knowledge and experience in a variety of ways.

PEER ASSESSMENT

Peer assessment provides students with an opportunity to respond to the dancing of their classmates in a one-to-one relationship or as part of a small group. In this form of assessment, students can observe their classmates performing a dance and share what they observed through discussion, reviewing a drawing or written comments, interviewing a student about his or her process to create a dance (see figure 6.9 on page 87), or responding to a peer teaching or tutoring situation (Townsend and Mohr 2002). When students develop the assessment criteria and rubric, they take ownership of their learning and set their level of achievement. Peer assessment is a highly effective teaching strategy yet should not be used as part of a student's grade. It should be focused on improvement, not on grading (Leahy, Lyon, Thompson, and Wiliam 2005). We have used this type of assessment in a square dance unit for fourth- and fifth-grade students. During the square dance unit, students learned four dances and chose one for their final assessment. Before the assessment, the class constructed the criteria and rubric. This activity helped the students set a goal for their group's practice and performance. Small groups of students assessed one another.

TYPE OF DANCE: CULTURAL DANCE

Level of performance	Evidence of student's behavior	Student	Teacher comments
Basic	Cannot accurately reproduce all movements Loses rhythm Has steps but not arm or head movement Body parts not coordinated Moves out of formation Not focused during the dance Loses control	*Sue*	*Needs to stay focused on the lesson. Demonstrated difficulty staying in rhythm.*
Proficient	Accurately reproduces all movements Loses rhythm but can regain Remembers the dance sequence Stays focused on dance Moves out of formation but can regain Loses coordination on a movement Loses control on a movement	*Steve* *Mary*	*Remembered the sequence of the dance and recalled the names of the steps.* *Stayed focused on lesson. Demonstrated initial difficulty with coordination on the slide step; successful after continued practice.*
Advanced	Performs all movements accurately in sequence and rhythm Includes movement details and arm and head movements Demonstrates good balance and strength Stays focused Stays in formation the entire dance Coordinates movements with others	*Mark*	*Was very helpful to other students and took time to show them slides to the right and left and how to count the steps in rhythm to the music.*

Figure 6.6 Recording sheet for a cultural dance performance with rubric and criteria.

Figure 6.7 Student's drawing of a geometric shape.

The students developed the criteria for the final performance. They chose a holistic rubric (see figure 6.3 on page 82). Students observed one another and then checked the level of performance they thought the group achieved. They also added a written statement of justification for their score.

Peer assessment of a creative dance can include both objective and subjective observations and responses. For example, one student chose to create a dance inspired by water evaporation and cloud formation, and another chose to dance about an erupting volcano. After spending a session creating and practicing the dances, students worked in pairs to assess each other's dance. The teacher created two questions to focus the response to the observation: (1) Name three movements you saw the students do in their dance (objective), and (2) What part of the dance was

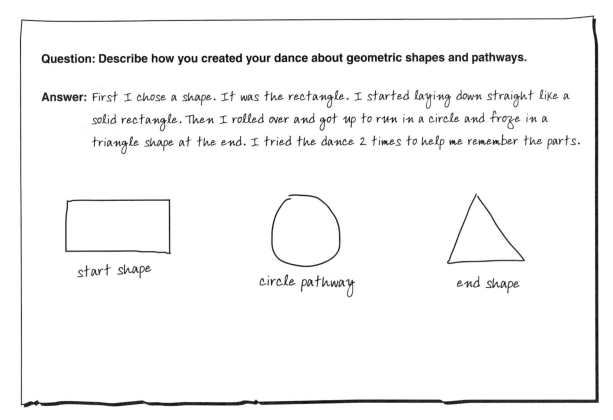

Figure 6.8 Student's writing explaining the student's choreographic process.

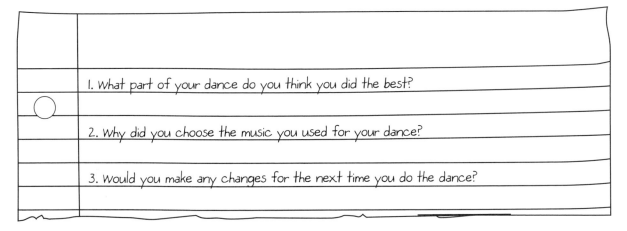

Figure 6.9 Student-constructed questions for a peer assessment.

most exciting and why (subjective)? The students wrote down their answers and discussed their comments with each other. Additional questions appear in figure 6.10 on page 88.

Young children who are not proficient in reading and writing a response can draw a pathway or shape that they observed, demonstrate a part they liked, or tell their peer what they remembered about the dance. You can provide a ques-

tion to focus the observation and facilitate the assessment.

The link between assessment and learning becomes strengthened when students have the opportunity to revise their work after peer assessment (Goodrich 1997). In this way, children can reflect on the assessment and make changes to improve the dance they created or their performance of a dance. Through peer assessment,

- What movements did the students use to show the dance idea?
- What direction, speed, or type of force did they use?
- Was there a change in level?
- Did the dancer perform the movement the way you expected?
- What changes would you recommend? Why?
- What ideas can you add to the dance?
- How is this dance the same or different from yours?
- What question would you like to ask the dancer?
- How did the dance begin and end?
- Where did the dancer move in space? Can you draw the pathway?
- What about the dance did you think was creative?
- How do you think the music went with the dance?
- What was the purpose of the props in the dance?
- What effect did the costumes have on the dance?
- Did you observe that the dancer or dancers focused on the dance?

Figure 6.10 Teacher-constructed questions for a peer assessment.

students take responsibility for their learning, become autonomous learners, and develop transferable personal skills needed for lifelong learning. This shared activity promotes the interaction of ideas and discovery of preferences about dance.

STUDENT SELF-ASSESSMENT

In self-assessment, the students evaluate themselves on what they know about dance; how well they learned, performed, or created a dance; and how they feel about dance. This type of assessment increases students' responsibility for their own learning and clarifies their understanding of expectations for achievement. Students can assess their learning through a variety of tools that include completing a questionnaire, writing a journal entry, having a personal conference with the teacher, writing a letter about their experience, drawing a picture, or recording comments. These activities all take considerable time and can occur during or outside of the session. You can also ask the classroom teacher to help with the writing and drawing portions of the assessment. We find that the students' responses to the self-assessment inform us about what the students were experiencing and learning. It also

contributed to our revision of lessons and units. Sometimes the questions are announced at the beginning or end of a unit or lesson, whereas others are asked throughout the lesson. We have developed a question bank as a resource for a variety of self-assessment situations (see figure 6.11). You can select one or two key questions from the bank that will provide you with the information you are seeking and design a tool that is easy for students to read and complete.

Portfolios are an approach that provides children and teachers with a comprehensive view of learning. This assessment tool is a chronological collection of students' work gathered throughout the year, or throughout several dance units, and used in documenting progress and achievement. McTighe (1997) describes portfolios using this analogy: "If a test or quiz represents a snapshot (a picture of learning at a specific moment) then a portfolio is more like a photo album—a collection of pictures showing growth and change over time" (p. 12). A dance portfolio might include writing samples, journal entries, drawings, notations of dances, a list of dance ideas or music, tests, audio recordings, photographs, videos, peer reviews, collections of articles and news items, and artwork. Establish and communicate

Cognitive Reflection Questions

1. What did you learn about dance today?
2. Is the dancing you did today like any other dancing you have done before? How is it the same or different?
3. What was the hardest part of this assignment? Why?
4. What was the most important thing you learned in doing this assignment?
5. What did you learn new about dance from the lesson today?
6. How would you describe your dance to someone at home?
7. What part of your dance should be changed? How would you change it?
8. Did you choose to use music? If you did, why did you choose that piece of music for your dance? If not, why did you choose not to use music?
9. Explain how you used the prop in your dance.
10. Name three different movements you performed in the dance.
11. What are some reasons that people dance?
12. Describe how the dancers used directions and levels in the dances.
13. What movements are similar in the two cultural dances we learned today?
14. Describe one movement from each dance that you think was strong and powerful.
15. What do the movements in the [name a specific dance] tell us about the culture?
16. Describe the sequence of the [name a specific dance]. How does it begin? What happens next? How does it end?

Psychomotor Reflection Questions

1. What movements did you perform best in your dance?
2. What was the most important thing you learned in doing this assignment?
3. What movements did you perform in your dance that used balance?
4. What movements could you practice so they are better the next time?
5. What movements did you perform that took a lot of strength?
6. Did you have enough energy to perform the dance without getting tired?

Affective Reflection Questions

1. What was the most important thing you learned in doing this assignment?
2. Did you offer ideas to your partner or group?
3. Did you cooperate with your partner as you moved together?
4. What was your favorite part of the learning experience? Why did you like that part?
5. Would you like to do this dance lesson again? Why or why not?
6. What parts of the learning experience did you like most? Why?
7. Would you like to perform this dance again? Why or why not?
8. What do you like most about dancing? What do you like least?
9. How do you feel when you are dancing?
10. Do you feel you can be creative in dance?
11. Do you enjoy dancing with others as part of a small group?
12. Did you feel uncomfortable in any part of the dance learning experience? If so, during what part, and why?

Figure 6.11 Sample bank of questions for student self-assessment.

What have you learned about dance this year?

What do you think was the best dance that you performed or created? Why is it your best?

What was the most difficult dance you learned this year and why?

Did you improve your ability to dance or create dances?

Comment on your abilities as a dancer or a choreographer.

What helps you do your best dancing?

What does your dancing say about you?

Did you achieve what you wanted to learn about dance this year?

Figure 6.12 Reflective questions for student portfolios.

the purpose of the portfolio to the students and take time to review and reflect on its contents frequently (see figure 6.12). In addition to providing a method of documenting students' work, portfolios provide a tangible way for students to view and celebrate what they have accomplished.

When students take their portfolios home, they can share their work with parents and other adults, which facilitates school-to-home communication about what is learned in the dance program. The management and storage of portfolios can be overwhelming and will take time for review and filing. We suggest that you provide each child with a folder and organize the folders by class in a basket or box. Then, bring the box to the dance session so that students can place their work in it and review the portfolios at the end of each unit. You will gain valuable insights into what your students think and how they can express themselves in a variety of ways.

ASSESSMENT INSTRUMENTS

Gathering assessment information before a lesson or unit is useful in ascertaining students' current skill level, knowledge, experience, or interest. This preassessment helps you prepare for adjustments you may need to make in your planned lessons or unit and can also stimulate students' interest in the dance topic. Assessment that occurs during the lesson or unit, known as ongoing or formative assessment, can occur at different times and determines skill development, understanding, and progress in meeting the outcomes. The third time that assessment can occur is at the conclusion of a lesson or unit. This summative assessment determines the extent of learning or

provides students an opportunity to reflect on their progress in skill development, knowledge gained, and feelings or attitude about the content (Cone and Cone, 2005).

Once the outcomes are established, the next step is to determine what type of assessment will yield the best evidence that the outcomes have been met. You decide when the assessment will occur, the domains assessed, who will conduct the assessment, and the best instrument for collecting evidence. Following is a list of assessment instruments that can be used for psychomotor, cognitive, and affective assessment. Remember that feasibility is important for ensuring that the assessment is easy to administer in a class of children.

❖ **Checklist.** The checklist is easy to use and contains a two-item rubric, such as yes and no, that evaluates whether the criteria are present. The format usually lists the names of the students down one side of the recording sheet and the skills across the top. Criteria for a yes and a no for the skills are clearly defined (see figure 6.13). This instrument is frequently used for assessing skills in the psychomotor domain.

❖ **Rating scale.** This assessment identifies three or more performance levels based on criteria described for each level (see figure 6.14). This instrument is an effective tool for assessing ability in performing dance skills.

❖ **Written test or quiz.** This cognitive assessment is in the form of multiple-choice, matching, fill in the blank, true or false, or short written answer (see figure 6.15). Be aware of the students' reading and writing abilities and develop a form that has adequate space for students to write.

Complete 4 side steps right, 4 side steps left, 4 kicks, and a quarter turn left to face next wall.

Repeat dance 2 times.

Yes = on the beat for both dance repetitions

No = off the beat on one or both dance repetitions

Students' names	Cupid shuffle
Rob	Yes
Sherri	No
Greg	Yes
Melissa	No

Figure 6.13   Teacher checklist for cupid shuffle dance steps.

Check how well you performed the dance you created.

Name:

Skill	I was great	I messed up once	I need a lot more practice
Remembering the moves			
Body control			

Figure 6.14   Rating scale for student self-assessment.

1. Name two dances that used the grapevine step.
2. Identify two dances that used the circle formation.
3. Choose one of the dances and explain how the dance reflects the people's culture.

Figure 6.15   Written test items for a unit on cultural dance.

❖ **Exit slips.** This assessment is applicable to the cognitive and affective domains. Students answer a question about the content taught in the lesson or respond to a prompt about how they performed or felt about the dances. They write their answer on a slip of paper and place it in a box as they exit the dance space. Following are examples of prompts: "Write the name of your favorite dance you did in class today" and "Write the name of the movement that was the hardest to learn."

❖ **Drawing.** This cognitive and affective assessment reveals students' understanding or feelings about the lesson. Because children take time to complete this assessment, you can ask the classroom teacher if he or she can provide time during the day to complete the assessment. For example, if the assessment asked students to draw one of the body shapes they used in their cloud dance, the students would draw their body shape and add a descriptive word (see figure 6.7 on page 86).

❖ **Peer flash cards.** This psychomotor assessment uses an observer and a performer. Each card represents a symbol that relates to a performance level. For example, a two-card assessment can use one card with a happy face (☺), which means the dancing is fantastic, and a card with a neutral face (the mouth is a straight line), which means the dancing needs more practice. The observer watches the performer and then holds up the card that represents their assessment. Color cards can also be used. Clearly identify the criteria for each card.

❖ **Human graph.** This assessment asks students about their preferences. You set up three signs, attached to a cone, that are lined up side by side. One sign is labeled "Awesome," the second sign is labeled "Okay," and the third sign is labeled "Did not like." You call out a dance movement or a dance completed in the lesson or unit, and the students line up behind the sign that reflects their preference. A human graph appears as students line up based on their preference. The labels can be changed to represent other evaluative terms or dances.

❖ **Journal writing.** Students can use journals for writing or drawing their responses to questions that you ask. The questions can be either cognitive or affective. Collect the journals, read them, and make comments to the students. Following are some sample questions: "What part of the lesson did you like the best?" "How did you work together with your group to create the tornado dance?" "Describe a movement you created for your line dance." "Identify one thing you learned today."

❖ **Dance maps and webs.** This cognitive assessment provides an opportunity for students to draw and write what they learned about creating or learning a dance. The dance map includes a line drawing of the pathways while also noting the movements (see figure 6.16), and the web helps students define terminology or descriptive words about a learned or created dance (see figure 6.17).

❖ **Video recording.** You or the students can use a video recording of a completed dance that they learned or created. Students can learn to use a small video camera to record their own or others' dance performances. You can also set up the video camera at an assessment station where you record students' verbal responses or dance performances.

❖ **Portfolio.** This assessment is a collection of a student's achievement over a period of time. The portfolio contains written tests, drawings, selected journal entries, dance maps, reports on a dance topic, and photographs. In addition to these items, a digital portfolio can contain video of dance learning and performance, student interviews, and verbal explanations of how a student created a dance or their process in learning a dance. Either portfolio type can be used for

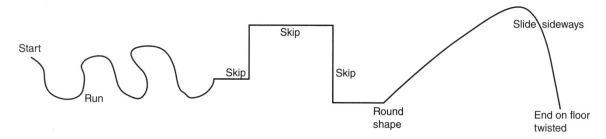

Figure 6.16 Dance map: peer assessment of pathway in partners dance.

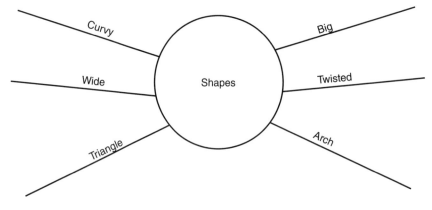

Figure 6.17 Dance web: student self-assessment.

parent conferences or, as Niguidula (2005) says, "As students look through the portfolio and read over their reflections, they recognize how their skills have grown over time and begin to see where they can go next" (p. 46).

❖ **Peer teaching.** As a formative assessment of knowledge and physical ability, one student teaches a dance or a movement to one or more peers. The peer teacher explains how to perform the dance or movements and adds a demonstration. In this way the cognitive understanding and physical ability are integrated. You or the students' peers can develop the criteria for assessing how accurately the peer teacher explains and demonstrates.

❖ **Zone assessment.** This assessment is used in large classes for assessing a student's ability to perform a dance step, sequence of a couple steps, or a completed dance. The class space is organized into three or more zones, and six to eight students are assigned to a space zone. You identify the dance content for assessment and then ask all students in the zone to perform the movements. Use a checklist and note the students who are unable to repeat the movement accurately. Move to the next zone and repeat the assessment with the same or a different move-

ment. This continues until all students in the designated zones are assessed.

SUMMARY

Designing and facilitating assessment in dance can be challenging. However, for dance to be viewed as an important component of the arts or physical education curriculum, it must provide evidence of students' learning. Remember that assessments need definitive criteria and practical rubrics to be effective in helping students understand learning expectations. The content and type of assessment we choose convey a strong message to students about what is important for them to learn. Assessment can be addressed using a variety of approaches. We have discussed four approaches: assessing the teaching effectiveness, students' learning, peer assessment, and student self-assessment. Each assessment instrument provides a strength of its own, and in combination they provide a comprehensive view of what students know and can do. Select an instrument that meets the outcomes and provides meaningful evidence about students' achievement. The value of feasible and relevant assessments is evidenced in increased appreciation and understanding of dance as a language for expression and communication.

 # Questions for Reflection

What type of assessments would you use in evaluating a student's ability to perform a dance with a specific sequence of movements, such as a line dance or cultural dance?

Creativity is frequently included as a criterion for a student-choreographed dance. How would you create a rubric that describes three different creative levels?

Small groups frequently work together to create a dance. What would be criteria for assessing a group's final dance?

Consider how you could use technology in assessing a student's performance.

What type of technology is available for you to use to record observations, journal notes, or reflections at the end of a unit or learning experience?

Including All Children in Dance

All children have the need to express and communicate their feelings and ideas, whether it is through speaking, writing, movement, or the visual and performing arts. Through dance, children with disabilities can discover how movement can be a way to express their emotions, expand their range of movements, engage in social interactions, and explore new ways of knowing themselves and their world. As a dance educator you must be committed to helping each student reach his or her potential. View the child through the lens of ability instead of a lens of limitations. Recognize each child's individuality and avoid viewing the child as a member of a disability category or as a label. All children are respected for their different learning styles, and success is defined with the use of individualized standards. Dance therapist Tortora (2006) notes, "Individuality emerges as individual differences

are supported. Children are encouraged to learn about themselves by feeling and exploring their own existence from a physically and emotionally felt place" (p. 57). Successful educators understand the significance of using multiple strategies to present a concept or skill. What works for one child may not work for another. Creativity, flexibility, empathy, and passion to make a difference are essential characteristics for effective planning and implementation. Cone and Cone (2011) assert, "Each student's uniqueness contributes to everyone's learning experiences. When students learn that there are many variations of a dance and many different ways to perform a movement then acceptance of differences is valued and stereotypes are dismissed" (p. 24). Teach with an open mind and a curious spirit, and know that children enjoy dancing and being part of a group. They also want to experience success.

KNOWING YOUR CHILDREN WITH DISABILITIES

As an educator you will be teaching children with physical, cognitive, emotional, and neurological disabilities. These children all have the ability to learn, create, perform, and respond to dances whether they participate in a full class of children with disabilities or in an inclusive class with their typically developing peers. In either environment, you need to gain information about the student's disabilities and have a strong belief that all children can learn. The list of disabilities is comprehensive, and even if a child is diagnosed with a specific disability, the characteristics are manifested differently in each child. When you teach a child with a disability, understand that each child is unique in ability, personality, interests, and needs. Get to know your students. What is their favorite color, sport team, cartoon character, food, book, or game? (See figure 7.1 for additional questions.) Use this information to motivate students to participate and make the learning meaningful and enjoyable. A student may like the feel of fleece, or the color red, or a poster of Sponge-Bob Squarepants. Each child will have sensory preferences. The music may be disconcerting, the lights may be too bright, or the sound of too many voices may be confusing. Be aware of these preferences, and use them to support the lesson content and avoid other sensory stimuli that can be irritating to the child. In addition, know the child's physical range of motion and strength. Dance movements need to be safe. Be aware of contraindicated movements, especially for students who use wheelchairs, crutches, scooters, or braces to support their mobility. Check with the physical therapist or school nurse for information specific to each student in addition to contacting the student's parents or guardians.

The amount of information about any specific disability, whether available online or in professional journals and texts, is tremendous. Use caution and make sure that your sources are reliable. Accessing information and increasing your knowledge about the causes, characteristics, and teaching strategies and resources are essential to becoming an informed and effective educator. Many organizations dedicated to disabilities provide information on research and fundraising, personal stories, photos, and videos; these organizations also provide access to other sources of information. Another source is the parents or guardians, school administrators, child study team, physical therapists, occupational therapists, school nurses, and other educators in the school who hold valuable information about the child and about teaching children with disabilities. Seek information about laws and regulations regarding the Individuals with Disabilities Education Act 2004 and its definition of the 13 categories of disabilities (http://idea.ed.gov), the operational definition of free appropriate public education and a least restrictive environment, and the child's individualized education program (IEP). Check the student's IEP and incorporate the goals into the dance lessons.

CREATING AN INCLUSIVE ENVIRONMENT

The smile on your face tells a child whether he or she is welcomed into the teaching space and whether you are accepting and eager to help the child learn. This simple facial gesture is significant to any child and especially important to a child with disabilities. The smile also indicates to anyone else in the space, student or adult, that you are caring and willing to make the learning experience meaningful for all. The environment is more than a space; it is an attitude of acceptance that permeates all the activities that occur in a lesson. From the moment the child enters the space, you are there to greet him or her and acknowledge something personal such as a new shirt, a necklace, a toy in the child's hand, or maybe a new haircut. This initial connection

---

What do you want to learn this year in dance?

What are three things I should know about you?

What are your best subjects in school?

What do you like to do in your spare time?

What would you like to do when you grow up?

What did other teachers do to help you be successful?

Do you have any questions for me?

Figure 7.1 Questions to ask children about their personalities and preferences.

provides you with information about how the child is feeling physically and socially on that day. Next, you describe the dance activity and mention how the space and equipment are organized for the lesson and help the child to a place where the lesson will begin. You may say, "Today we are going to dance with the scarves that are in a red basket near the wall. Everyone find a place." If the student with a disability has a paraeducator or a peer buddy, that person will also help the child to the space to begin the lesson. Sometimes, you can play music as the students enter the space to set a calming atmosphere or a signal that this is the dancing space.

The dance teaching space needs to comply with the requirements of the Americans with Disabilities Act for access set forth on their website (www. ada.gov/regs2010/RIA_2010regs/ria_appendix02. htm). Bathrooms, water fountains, and entrances and exits need to be designed for all children to access. The floor should be clean, and the lighting and temperature should be appropriate. Extra equipment such as chairs, bleachers, equipment bins, MP3 players, CD players, and DVD players or computers need to be on carts so they are easily moved when space is needed. The boundaries for dancing need to be clearly marked with tape or painted floor lines or marked with cones. There needs to be space between the end of the boundary and the wall so children can stop without getting hurt. Keep the wall space clear of excess posters and other visual displays to keep distractions to a minimum if appropriate, yet place needed information on the wall.

Simple rules for safety and learning should be posted and reviewed periodically. Develop a strategy about how you will help students who escape out of exit doors, accidently run into equipment, or are resistant to participating in the lesson and roam the space. Provide a rest space that is in the dance space but offers a quiet place for children to rest, calm themselves if they are overstimulated, or need a break from the lesson. Most important, ensure that children dance in a safe space that is comfortable and supports learning.

IMPLEMENTING INCLUSIVE TEACHING STRATEGIES

The goal of dance for children with disabilities is to explore and develop each student's unique movement style. Elin and Boswell (2004) ask educators to embrace the aesthetic of differences, meaning that each student has preferences for music, colors, shapes, movements, textures, and other sensory items. They promote "an approach based not on 'normalizing' the movements of students with disabilities but on perceiving differences associated with disabilities as potential sources of artistic material" (p. 427). This perspective emphasizes the exploration and learning process as the foundation for the dance experience. While a product may emerge, the experience of learning and creating is primary. Teaching children with disabilities, like teaching all children, requires creativity and adaptability. The lessons should be age appropriate, have a sequential progression, accommodate each child's ability, and use effective learning strategies (Apache 2004). One of the most effective strategies for making an accommodation is to ask the student how a movement, prop, space, formation, or complete dance can be changed for their inclusion. They have experience in negotiating their environment and making changes for access to be able to function and participate successfully. Most important, maintain the dignity of students with disabilities. Ensure that they embrace the modifications and maintain a high level of participation (Dunphy and Scott 2003). Following are several strategies that are applicable for teaching dance to all children and can be used in a class for all children with disabilities, an inclusive class, or a class with typically developing children.

❖ Apply the principle of universal design. This strategy reflects the principle of architecture. The premise is that the design accommodates all people. For example, everyone can benefit from using a ramp to enter a building or lever door handles. In dance, the circle formation is inherently inclusive because everyone can be seen and has an equal place in the group. A creative dance about exploring straight and curved shapes is appropriate for all students. The task of finding a way to make a straight shape with a part of your body can be answered in a variety of ways. This strategy is especially applicable to classes where children with disabilities participate with a class that includes typically developing children. Everyone can participate in their own way because multiple answers are encouraged. Another application of universal design is using several sign language gestures with all children to support verbal directions. Teachers frequently use words such as *stop, go, line up, good job, no,* or *look at me*. In this way you use two modes of communication, verbal and gestural, simultaneously to help learners hear and see directions and feedback. Children learn that there are multiple ways to learn and communicate, all equally effective.

❖ **Establish a lesson routine.** This strategy describes a set activity that occurs in the same space and at the same time (at the beginning or end of each dance session). The routine provides a clear, familiar expectation for each child and can help with organization and class management.

❖ **Use designated spots.** Each student has a predetermined place to begin and end the lesson and a place to return to for listening to instructions. The designated place can be marked by plastic poly spots, an X taped to the floor, an identified line, a letter painted on the floor, a hoop, or a taped-down name card.

❖ **Develop dances for beginning and ending the class session.** These dances become part of the lesson routine and emphasize rhythmic patterns and repetition of movement. The same dance can be used throughout the school year or changed monthly. One example that welcomes students and encourages verbal communication combined with rhythm and repetition is the "We Are Glad to See You" dance. In this dance, students are seated in a circle on the floor or in chairs. Everyone repeats the following sequence together, which is accompanied by hand gestures. This is repeated for all students. This dance is best for small groups. A student may need help from you or the paraeducator to move the hands and arms, or you can delete the movements and use only the voice.

- We are (two hand taps on the thighs, one tap on each word)
- Glad to (two hand claps, one clap on each word)
- See you (both hands point to a student in the circle)
- Student's name (hands point to the student)

❖ **Use peer helpers.** The helpers are usually typically developing peers who are in an inclusive class or older or same-age peers who help in a self-contained class. These peers are students you have trained in reinforcing instructions and demonstrations, providing feedback, and increasing practice time. Peers should not manipulate a child's body, move children who are using a wheelchair, or assist with bathroom needs.

❖ **Offer assistance to paraeducators to support learning.** These adults, who are also known as aides, educational assistants, or teaching assistants, may accompany one child or provide support for several children. They may not be familiar with the dance content and not sure how to effectively assist the child. One way is to meet before the lesson and discuss specific strategies for helping, such as reinforcing or reading instructions, providing demonstrations, giving feedback, and helping to keep the child focused on the lesson. You can also send an e-mail or a printed description of the lesson before the class or present a task card upon arrival at the session that describes verbal cues, appropriate feedback strategies, and tactical or visual prompts that help the child learn (see figure 7.2).

❖ **Develop a visual schedule.** This strategy is a pictorial display of the dance lesson showing the order in which the dance tasks or activities will be presented. The schedule can be placed on a wall near the entrance or near where directions

---

DANCE TASK CARD FOR KARA

Warm-up dance: Cue words: "Kara, hands up and down."

Exploring shapes: Cue words: "Kara, round back." "Twist your waist." "Stretch big."

Cloud dance: Help her hold on to the curtain. Use hand over hand if needed.

Feedback: High fives or "Nice job!"

Figure 7.2   Task card for paraeducator.

are presented. A number, the picture, and a word describing the picture are included (see figure 7.3 on page 100). Using the visual schedule allows children to see what will happen in the dance session and helps them feel organized and more secure. After each task or activity, you can return to the schedule and check off what was completed or show what activity is next.

❖ Use person-first language. When referring to someone with a disability, be respectful by using the name of the person or the type of person first and the disability second. For example, use *child who has autism* instead of *an autistic kid*, or the child's name (e.g., *Malik who has an intellectual disability*) instead of *the retarded* or *mentally challenged kid*, or *Jan who uses a wheelchair* instead of *the wheelchair-bound girl*. As an educator, you should always see the child first and understand that the disability is only one of the child's characteristics. Most important, children are not identified by their disabilities; they are viewed as one of the many children you teach who all have their own way of learning and being in the world.

❖ Establish clear stop and start signals. A stop signal is necessary for stopping the dancing and providing additional directions, changing to a new dance, ending the session, or attending to an emergency. The signal can be a verbal command, sound of a percussion instrument, hand signal, or prop held up for all to see. Using a verbal and visual signal is most effective. Be aware of children who are sensitive to certain sounds or need more time to stop to control their bodies. Practice using the stop signal and start signal, and use the signals consistently.

❖ Make feedback meaningful. Responding to a child's action can be affirmative or corrective. Words such as *fantastic*, *great job*, *excellent*, or *you did it* affirm a positive action; however, they will be more effective if the initial phrase is followed by a brief description about what the child did well. For example, the phrase *nice job* is followed by *your arms were raised up very high*. In this way, the child knows what he did well and is more likely to repeat the action. When using a corrective statement, apply the sandwich approach, which begins with a positive statement, follows with the correction, and closes with a positive statement. For example, "Alicia, that turn went

all the way around, but you need to keep your head up so you can keep your balance. I know you can do it." You can also use a positive word wall (Cone and Cone 2011) that has the printed affirmative words listed. You or the student can point to how the child performed the activity.

❖ Set up a personal folder. This strategy helps an individual child focus on the sequence of the dance lesson or expected behaviors. In a folder is a list of the dance activities and a place to check when the activity is completed (see figure 7.4 on page 101). The child, a paraeducator, or you can check the items on the list during the session or at the conclusion.

❖ Change the space, equipment, music, or props. Although many children with disabilities need only minor modifications to a lesson when learning, creating, or performing a dance, some children will need extra modifications to the space, equipment, music, or props that support their way of learning. You can reduce or divide the amount of space for dancing into parts to help children know where to move. Use lines and arrows to mark directions and pathways and formations. You can change the texture of the prop or equipment to make it easier to grip or acceptable to touch, or you can attach props to a wheelchair (check with the school administration before using this approach).

❖ Use mnemonics and key words as cues to identify a dance. Mnemonics is a memory strategy using letters organized into a word that represents a phrase that relates to a specific dance. For example, GET means gather everyone together. This can be called the GET dance, which is a dance that can be performed as part of a beginning routine. Another example of a beginning dance is the HAY dance, or how are you. Key words such as time to go dance or good-bye dance can indicate that this is the dance the class performs at the end of the session.

❖ Provide instructions in chunks. In this strategy, you divide the instructions into smaller pieces of information; you present one instruction at a time in a series. Check for understanding by observing whether a child complies or asking the student to repeat the instruction. Verbal instructions should be accompanied by a demonstration or supported by pictures or objects to provide multiple means of delivering the content.

1	Listening spot	
2	Circle warm-up dance	
3	Shoemaker's dance	
4	Tanko bushi	
5	Listening spot	
6	Line up	

Figure 7.3 Visual schedule.

Date:

Dance activity	Completed
Warm-up dance	
Slow and fast movements	
Learning the cat dance	
Showing the cat dance story	
Sharing time	
My behavior	
I followed instructions.	
I did not yell out in class.	

Figure 7.4   Personal folder checklist.

❖ Wait for a response. After you ask a question or give an instruction, allow a short time for students to process the information and form a response. Some students need time to formulate the words or gestures or use their assistive technology to respond. The waiting time helps everyone think about what and how they want to communicate an answer or make a comment.

❖ Apply closed- and open-skill teaching. Closed-skill teaching means that the movements for the dance are taught in isolation or out of the context of the complete dance. The dance movement is repeated in a predictable way to reinforce cognitive understanding and motor patterns. Then the dance movement can be inserted into an open-skill situation or the whole dance. In the open-skill or whole-dance situation, the movement may take on a variation, or there may be an unpredictable moment where the dancing partners change, the space or tempo is altered, or a spontaneous formation occurs.

INCLUSIVE DANCES

You can modify all dances to include students of various abilities. You know the students' developmental abilities, learning styles, and interests and can make adaptations so that everyone can participate. Some children may not know they like to dance because they have not had the chance to try it or to communicate that they are interested. Others may need additional prompts to stay focused, or they may need time to watch others before they feel confident to join in. Children with hearing loss need to have a clear view of you or the student who is speaking or demonstrating. A child who is blind or has any visual disability needs a clear description of the activity or spatial arrangement, and that child may need help from a peer or paraeducator when moving in the space. Those children with orthopedic disabilities, whether ambulatory or using wheelchairs, crutches, or walkers, can participate in all dances when they have adequate space and time to perform the movements. Dancing benefits all students. Through inclusion, they know that others care about their learning and want them to be part of their group. They increase their experiences in the many ways to move through learning social, cultural, and creative dances as well as experience the benefits of improved fitness, social interaction, decision making, and motor development. All of the inclusive dances in this chapter appear on the CD-ROM.

Cultural and Social Dances

In any cultural or social dance appropriate for elementary-age students, you can change the formation, tempo, skill complexity, and number of movements to meet the learners' abilities. Although these dances have traditional movements and formations, making changes is appropriate without losing the essence of the dance. For example, students can perform the popular chicken dance in a random formation instead of a circle, and the four movements representing the beak, wings, tail, and claps usually repeated quickly four times can be reduced to one repetition. Children can move at random in the space on the second part of this dance instead of all moving in the same direction in a circle. Your role is to be creative in making changes that all children can perform. A child with a disability should not be singled out to do a movement that is completely different from the other children's movements. One example of a social dance is the double circle mixer.

Double Circle Mixer

Students dance with many partners, which promotes positive social interaction and acceptance. The children learn a pattern of movement that is repeated many times, and on each repetition they dance with a new partner.

Organization

Students are assigned a partner. The partners stand side by side facing counterclockwise. This forms the double circle.

Dance Description

All students move forward in the circle formation for 16 counts. Then they stop and turn to face their partners using 8 counts. Next, partners move backward away from each other using 8 counts. They clap their hands 4 times for 8 counts, 2 counts for each clap. Next, they point to the student in the opposite circle who is diagonally to their right for 8 counts. This is their new partner. They move forward toward their new partner and return to the side-by-side position. This takes 8 counts. Now the dance begins again with a new partner. Students can high five or wave to their new partner as they move forward to meet them. The students can walk, skip, jog, gallop, wheel, or be pushed in their wheelchair while traveling the 16 counts in the circle. Students using wheelchairs, crutches, or walkers can easily participate and move forward in the circle for 16 counts while other students are walking. The tempo can be slowed down or any part of the dance eliminated. The goal is to maintain the idea of dancing with a new partner each time the dance is repeated.

Creative Dances

The creative dances described here are examples of dances that the whole class can perform, and allow students to create movements within the dance structure. Accommodations for students with disabilities are included. Additional dance ideas are included in the article *Strategies for Teaching Dancers of All Abilities* by Cone and Cone (2011).

Greet and Meet Dance

This is appropriate for a beginning activity in inclusive and self-contained classes. The children move in toward the center of the circle and out of the circle many times to establish the basic movement pattern for the dance. Different elements of dance are applied in creating movement variations.

Organization

This dance uses a single circle formation with the children facing toward the center of the circle. Children use plastic poly spots or a tape mark to designate their place in the circle.

Dance Description

The music starts and the children clap, bounce in place, step in place, or wave a hand to the beat. Then on your signal everyone moves forward toward the center of the circle. A hoop can be placed in the center to provide a visual cue for the center of the circle. When they arrive at the center, the children can wave to each other or clap their hands. Then everyone is signaled to move back to their place on the circle. They repeat moving forward and back several times to establish a movement pattern. Next, you or the students can suggest movements to express that they are greeting someone, such as a high five, fist bump, or a greeting in another language or sign language. Children using wheelchairs, walkers, or crutches can easily join in this dance and move at an appropriate tempo. Students with visual impairment can hold your elbow or hand or the elbow or hand of a peer or paraeducator. They will need to be told how far they are moving into the circle and how the other children are moving. Depending on their intellectual disability, students can follow others, be prompted with cue words, or hold someone's hand. Children with pervasive developmental disorder and autism spectrum disorder may need to see the whole dance first so they understand what will happen and then either become involved with the rest of the group or dance the same movements outside of the circle. A paraeducator may use cue words such as *move in*, *wave*, and *move back* or use hand over hand where the adult moves the child's hand to show the waving movement. When students are ready, you can suggest a variety of ways to move in and out of the circle and use a variety of directions, pathways, sizes of steps, levels, and tempos. Also, instead of everyone moving in at the same time, you can call for a few students to do the dance. For example, call out categories, such as all boys or all girls, children wearing something blue, or children with birthdays in a certain month. Providing variations can help group members to identify themselves as different and as similar to others in the group (Cone and Cone, 2011).

Freeze Dance

This dance uses locomotor movements or wheelchair movement and still shapes. It can be used in inclusive and self-contained classes. While the music is playing, the children travel through the space using different directions and tempos. When the music stops, they freeze in a still shape. You or the students can decide on the movements for traveling in the space and the type of shapes.

Organization

Students move randomly in the space.

Dance Description

Inform the children that when the music is on, they will move in the dance space, and when the music stops, they will freeze in a shape. Call out a locomotor movement and a direction or tempo, such as "Walk forward slowly." If that is too many concepts for children to comprehend, call only the locomotor movement and add a demonstration. Then stop the music and tell everyone to freeze. A type of frozen shape is called: a round shape or a wide shape or a low shape, among many others. Support the verbal instructions with a printed sign for each locomotor movement and each type of shape. Continue the move-and-freeze pattern several times and then you can add moving with a partner or freezing connected to another student. Children who are deaf or hard of hearing can watch the other children, and you can use a visual stop signal to indicate the music has stopped. Children who are blind or have a visual impairment can hear the music and move in the space while the other children watch to make sure they are not bumping into the child. This dance is also appropriate for children using manual or power wheelchairs, walkers, or crutches. They can use all or parts of the body to make the shapes. Use the paraeducator or peer helper with children when needed to reinforce the directions and cue words.

Shape Get-Together

This group dance requires students to observe other students demonstrating a shape and then reproduce the shapes on their own bodies. All the shapes that each student demonstrates are added together, one at a time, into one dance.

Organization

Students are organized into groups of three to five and form a circle.

Dance Description

Each student in the group is given a number starting from 1 to as many students as are in the group. Each student creates a shape such as big, twisted, round, or any other type. They practice holding the shape for 4 slow beats. The number of beats can vary. The student with the first number demonstrates his or her shape to the group and, in unison, the group members repeat the shape. Next, the second person in the group demonstrates his or her shape and, in unison, the group members repeat the action. Then the group repeats the first shape followed by the second shape. The third person then demonstrates her or his shape and, in unison, the group repeats the shape. Now, the group performs the shapes beginning with the first, then the second, and then the third. This pattern of demonstrating, repeating, and adding the shape to the sequence is repeated until everyone in the group has contributed a shape to the dance sequence. The goal is to remember the sequence, perform in unison, and maintain holding still for 4 beats for each shape. To accommodate students with intellectual disabilities, you or a peer or paraeducator can offer an idea for a shape and use words to describe the shape to support the action with language acquisition. Children who have visual impairment can feel the body of the person making the shape. This is referred to as body brailing. Using descriptive words also helps to support identifying the shape.

Scarf or Streamer Dance

Students use scarves or streamers to form mirroring and shadowing relationships. In the mirroring relationship the leader creates various nonlocomotor movements, and in the shadow relationship the leader uses locomotor movements and still shapes. Students take turns as leaders.

Organization and Equipment Needed

Use a random formation in the space. Students are organized into pairs or groups of three. Each student has a scarf or streamer. The streamers can be paper or plastic. The length is determined by each student's size and range of motion. Streamers range from 1 to 3 feet (.3-1 m).

Dance Description

Each student holds a scarf or a streamer. One partner is the leader and the other is the follower. The leader can choose how he or she wants to slowly move the scarf or streamer, and the follower observes and reproduces the movement at the same time as the leader. The movement needs to be slow to help students with processing and reproducing the observed movements. This dance occurs in a stationary space using primarily nonlocomotor movements. The partners or students in the group take turns being a leader and a follower. Music with a slow tempo will support the slow body movements. The students then change from a mirror relationship to a shadow relationship. One student is the leader and the other is the follower. The leader uses locomotor movements to travel in the space while the follower does the same movements. Students take turns as the leader. The leader can also stop and freeze in a shape and then continue moving in the space. To adapt the dance for students with visual impairment, have a peer or paraeducator use cue words to describe the leader's movements. When they are the leader for the shadow dance, they can hold the elbow of a peer or paraeducator as they move through the space.

Going for a Drive Dance

This dance expresses the actions that drivers use. Students suggest actions such as putting on a seat belt, steering, honking the horn, or pressing the accelerator. An action represents each word or phrase. The actions are repeated several times to form a movement pattern. Students can perform while seated or use locomotor movements.

Organization and Equipment Needed

Use random formations. You will need large chart paper, a poster, or a whiteboard; markers; and pictures of a variety of cars.

Dance Description

Ask the students the following question: "What are some actions a driver uses when driving a car?" Write the students' responses on a poster, chart paper, or whiteboard. You can ask the students to spell the words or write the words. Next, each word is transformed into an action. For example, to create a movement to express steering, ask the stu-dents, "How does a driver's hands and arms move when steering the car?" Students usually pretend to grip a steering wheel and move their hands and arms up and down. To transform this action into a dance, ask the students to do the steering movement slowly and then quickly and then slowly again, developing a pattern based on the dance element of tempo. Students practice the movements and can add upper-body leans to the right and left. Next, select a second word and use the same process: Demonstrate how the body moves to represent the word, repeat the movements several times, add an element of dance, and practice the movement pattern several times. This continues until all the suggested words are transformed into dance movements. Once the students have practiced the movements, you or a student can point to a word or call out a word in any order, and the students respond by performing the movements associated with the word. The caller can determine the duration of the movement before calling another word.

Bandanna Dance

All students are connected by holding bandannas or scarves. They move in circular, spiral, and curvy pathways as one line of students. You can lead the dance, and the students can lead as they move throughout the space.

Organization and Equipment Needed

Students begin in a single circle, change to a spiral formation, and then to a curvy line formation. Each student has a bandanna held in or attached to the right hand. If attaching the bandanna to a wheelchair or walker, tie several bandannas together to make one longer bandanna to allow for more space between the students as they move. Always check with the administrator to ensure that tying the bandanna to a student's mobility device is appropriate and safe.

Dance Description

Students begin in a single circle facing toward the center. Each student holds a scarf with the right hand and then holds the scarf of the student next to them with the left hand. Now everyone is connected in one circle by holding the scarves. The first movement is to lift the scarves up and down three or four times using a slow tempo. Next, the right hand rises up, and while the right hand lowers, the left hand raises up. They repeat this three or four times slowly. Students move forward toward the center of the circle and back to their original places. This is repeated two times. Next you, who are part of the circle, have the student on your right let go of the scarf while everyone else continues to be connected. You, now a leader, move slowly forward inside the circle while the students follow. As you move forward on a spiral pathway, the circle

(continued)

forms a spiral formation. When you arrive at the center of the circle, turn to your right and reverse the spiral pathway. As students follow, they will pass by other students. When the spiral unwinds, lead the students around the space in curvy pathways. The dance ends with you forming a circle of students. The beginning movements, raising and lowering the scarves and moving in and out of the circle, are repeated as the final movements in the dance. Using the scarves provides more space in between students and makes it easier for them to follow the pathway. Also, students who do not like to hold hands can hold the scarves instead. For more space, you can tie two or more scarves together. A variation for this dance is to organize students into groups of five or six and have them form a line instead of a circle. One student at the end of the line is designated as the leader; he or she moves slowly in the space choosing where they want to go while the other students, all connected by bandannas, follow. Each student is provided an opportunity to be a leader.

Olympic Sport Dance

Students observe pictures of athletes participating in Olympic sports and then make their bodies into the same shape as the athletes in the pictures. Three pictures and a variety of locomotor movements are combined to form a five-part dance.

Organization and Equipment Needed

Students use a random formation. Have three laminated photos of athletes in action shapes that represent sports in the Winter or Summer Olympics. You'll also need poster or chart paper and three signs, each with the number 1, 2, or 3.

Dance Description

Adhere the three sport photos to a wall, poster, or chart. Above each picture is one of the number signs to show which picture is first, second, and third. First, the students look at photo 1 and make their bodies into the same shape as the athlete in the photo. They hold the shape for 8 counts. Next, they look at photo 2 and make their bodies into that shape and hold it still for 8 counts. Then they do the same for photo 3. Practice each shape in the three photos several times. Then, in between each still pose, students perform a locomotor movement or move in their wheelchairs for 16 counts. They can choose the pathway, the type of locomotor movement, and the direction. Cue the dance as follows: "Picture 1, hold still 1, 2, 3, 4, 5, 6, 7, 8 and move in the space (count for 16 counts). Picture 2, hold still 1, 2, 3, 4, 5, 6, 7, 8 and move in the space (count for 16 counts). Picture 3, hold still 1, 2, 3, 4, 5, 6, 7, 8."

Olympic sport dance sequence is as follows: photo 1 shape + locomotor movement + photo 2 shape + locomotor movement + photo 3 shape. After repeating the dance several times with your cues, the students can perform the dance on their own time. You can make several variations to this dance. Ask students to change the order of the photos and try a new dance using the same photos in the new order. Another variation is to replace one of the photos with a photo of an athlete in a different sport. Finally, you can add or subtract the number of photos used in the dance.

SUMMARY

Children with disabilities have the right to learn, create, perform, observe, and respond to their own dances and the dances of others. You are responsible for developing an inclusive learning space where every child is respected for his or her distinct abilities. That means involving children with disabilities in all the dancing and making accommodations for meaningful participation when needed. Peers are eager to offer ideas for inclusion and willing to assist when possible. In this way, everyone benefits by learning about acceptance and multiple ways to create and perform a dance. The joy of dancing to music and sharing the dances with friends is the result of a dance program founded on a philosophy that acknowledges the gifts that every child has. When children, all children, dance they learn that a movement, no matter how small, can express powerful ideas, feelings, and ways of knowing the world.

Questions for Reflection

What benefits do children with disabilities gain as a result of participating in dance?

Consider an accommodation for a social dance. Is the accommodation safe for everyone, and does it fully include the student with disabilities?

Think of a topic for a creative dance lesson, such as the water cycle or animal actions. How can you use a visual schedule to support the sequence of activities in the lesson?

What are strategies you can use to help the paraeducator or peer helper be effective when assisting a student with a disability?

Where can you locate information about a child's disability? What resources are available?

How can you include the child's individualized education program (IEP) goals into your dance lesson?

Learning Experiences for Children's Dance

Part II presents 23 exciting dance learning experiences. These ready-to-use experiences are presented in a style that depicts what the experience will be like when a class of children is actively learning. The descriptions provide you with the language for presenting the learning experience initially and then shaping the content to your own style of teaching. Bracketed notes guide you in the process. Although these learning experiences focus on creative dance, we suggest that you use other resources focused on social and cultural dances to present a comprehensive dance program (refer to the suggested readings at the end of the book on pages 201-204).

In this book, the term *learning experience* is used to describe a lesson progression, beginning with an introduction and ending with a culminating dance, that focuses on a set of learning outcomes.

Depending on the amount of time students spend in dance sessions, the learning experience may be presented in one or more sessions.

In part II, you will find two chapters. Chapter 8 contains 12 learning experiences that are appropriate for children in kindergarten through second grade. The content and flow of the learning experience are interesting to and developmentally appropriate for young children. The 11 learning experiences in chapter 9 focus on students in third through fifth grades, who are able to create and learn dances more independently than younger children. Ideas from either chapter, however, can be adapted for all grade levels. For many years, these learning experiences have been part of the physical education and dance program at the Brunswick Acres Elementary School and are now taught in the Teaching Concepts of Dance in Physical Education course at Rowan University. Children as well as college students find the learning experiences enjoyable yet challenging. When a dance unit is announced, the children welcome the opportunity to express themselves through dance and experience the joy of dancing with others.

The learning experiences in part II are organized to help you gain access to the information to make a teaching selection. Each learning experience is formatted as follows:

1. **Name** is the title of the learning experience.

2. **Outcomes** explain what children will gain as a result of participating in the learning experience.

3. **Organization** describes how the children are arranged during the learning experience and specifies whether they will participate individually, in partners, or in small groups.

4. **Equipment needed** is a list of the kinds and amounts of equipment needed for presenting this learning experience to children.

5. **Introduction and warm-up, development, culminating dance, and closure** describe the specific sections of the total learning experience.

6. **Look for** contains key points to keep in mind when informally observing children's progress in the learning experience. These points are related to the outcomes of the learning experience.

7. **How can I change this?** provides ideas for extending the lesson or presenting a variation.

8. **Assessment suggestions** are ideas for developing assessment instruments for student self-assessment, teacher assessment of students' learning, and peer assessment in the psychomotor, cognitive, and affective domains.

9. **Interdisciplinary connections** are suggestions for linking the dance experience with content in other subject areas.

Explore, experiment with, and enjoy using these learning experiences. They are for you and your students to share as you all discover the excitement of creating, performing, and responding to dance. Our hope is that, because of your willingness to teach dance, more children will have the opportunity to learn about this meaningful form of expression. The skills and knowledge they gain will last a lifetime.

eight

Learning Experiences for Kindergarten, First Grade, and Second Grade

Young children delight in dances that use vivid imagery, stories, animals, and familiar characters. Several of the dance experiences in this chapter provide opportunities for children to express their ideas about circus characters, animals, and real or imaginary experiences. As the teacher, you play an important role in planning tasks that are appropriate to the physical, cognitive, emotional, and social needs of a particular age group. In these creative dance experiences, you guide children in creating and expanding their movements within the planned structure of a culminating dance. To facilitate your selection of learning experiences, we have summarized each learning experience in table 8.1.

You will find that each learning experience is outlined in 12 sections that identify outcomes and assessments, equipment and organization, and a detailed description of how to implement the introduction, warm-up, development, culmi-

nating dance, and closure. Additional ideas for varying the learning experience and connecting to other subject areas are included. The description of each learning experience follows this format:

◆ Title
◆ Outcomes
◆ Organization
◆ Equipment needed
◆ Introduction and warm-up
◆ Development
◆ Culminating dance
◆ Closure
◆ Look for
◆ How can I change this?
◆ Assessment suggestions
◆ Interdisciplinary connections

The instructions for each dance learning experience are similar to the dialogue you would use when talking with your students. Any text in brackets indicates suggested instructions that you might use. All of the learning experiences in this chapter appear on the CD-ROM.

Table 8.1 Index of Learning Experiences for Kindergarten, First Grade, and Second Grade

Name of dance learning experience	Description of dance learning experience
Neighborhood Friendship Streamer Dance	Children use colorful streamers in dancing a story about celebrating friendship in a community.
Floating Clouds and Rain Showers	Children explore and express the shapes and movements of clouds in a dance depicting how individual clouds connect and form a huge rain cloud.
Run, Hop, Jump, Skip	A poetic text serves as the accompaniment to four dances that express the words that form a rhythm through rhyme.
The Playground	Children re-create the activities of playing on a slide, the swings, and a seesaw through moving on different levels and in different directions.
Ocean Waves and Swimmers	The dancing space is transformed into an ocean and beach in this dance, which uses the level changes of the waves and actions of swimmers in creating a dance about a day at the beach.
Spaghetti Dance	Are you ready for a bowl of spaghetti? This experience, which focuses on creating straight and curved shapes and pathways while varying levels and tempo, concludes with a dance about the adventure of a box of spaghetti.
Balloon Dance	Inflating, deflating, floating, and popping are the actions explored in a learning experience that uses the image of a balloon in a dance about small and big shapes and movements.
Percussion Instrument Dance	Light and strong forces are the focus of this dance experience that uses the sounds of a drum, a triangle, and maracas in creating three dances that express the quality of the sounds.
The Hungry Cat	In this learning experience, children dance the slow and fast movements of a cat who wakes up, chases and then captures a mouse, and goes back to sleep.
Circus Dance	Welcome to the circus! A suite of dances portrays the actions of four circus acts: the galloping horses, the tightrope walkers, the lions and tigers, and the funny clowns.
Connect the Spots	Children create shapes and locomotor movements as they map out dancing spots in the space. This dance emphasizes sequence memory, body coordination, and balance.
Frog Dance	Did you ever wonder what life was like for a frog that lived one day as a small frog and the next day as a big frog? This dance explores how range is used in changing movements from small to big.

Neighborhood Friendship Streamer Dance

Outcomes

As a result of participating in this learning experience, children will be able to do the following:

1. Create and perform locomotor and nonlocomotor movements that use circular pathways on the floor and in the air. (cognitive and psychomotor)

2. Create and perform four turning movements. (cognitive and psychomotor)

3. Perform circular pathways using a streamer. (psychomotor)

4. Demonstrate understanding of how a community celebrates friendship through dance. (cognitive)

5. Collaborate as a group to dance together. (affective)

6. Perform the complete dance with and without teacher prompts. (psychomotor and cognitive)

Organization

Children begin the lesson by exploring movements individually; then they dance with a small group; finally, all the groups dance together.

Equipment Needed

- MP3 or CD player
- Medium-tempo music for accompaniment that supports a skipping rhythm
- Paper or plastic streamers (1 meter long) equally divided into four colors—blue, green, yellow, and red—with enough streamers for each child to have one
- Four medium to tall cones to mark the corners of the space—one each of red, blue, green, and yellow

Introduction and Warm-Up

Today, we are going to do a friendship dance. The dance uses a lot of circles. You will find ways to travel in the space in a circle, turn in a circle, and use a streamer to make circles in the air. The streamer will be your dancing partner. After I give you a streamer, find a personal space and begin to draw circles in the air.

Find all the places around your body that you can draw a circle with the streamer. Can you draw a circle over your head, on the side of your body, around your waist, in front of you, and in back of your body? Try another way.

Draw the largest circle you can. Reach up high, far out to the side, and down to the floor. Make sure you draw circles with each hand. Can you draw a big circle very slowly? Now, a small circle as fast as you can?

Next, travel in a circle by skipping, galloping, or sliding sideways while making circles with your streamer. Choose one of the ways to travel you didn't select the first time, and make a circle with your streamer in a different way. Now, move the same way you just did, but this time, circle the streamer in another way.

Development

Now, you are going to make circles using your streamer by learning four ways to turn. In your personal space, make a circle with your body by turning on one foot. How can you use your streamer as you do this turn? Next, try a jump turn. This turn can go all the way around or just part of the way. Be sure to land on your feet, and bend your knees as you come down. Now, find a way to turn using a wide stretched shape. On the fourth turn, do it as slowly as you can. Show me how you change levels while you slowly turn. [Children practice each turn several times.]

Next, you are going to practice the four different turns, but now you will add a skip before your turn. Here is the pattern: skip, skip, skip, skip, and turn around. Try this pattern using each turn. [Gallops can be used in place of skips, and you can designate an order for practicing each turn instead of having the children choose the order.]

In the next movement, I want you to toss the streamer high above your head, let it go (making sure not to hit anyone), and watch it fall to the floor. What is the shape of the streamer as it lies on the floor? Is the streamer twisted, folded, straight, or curled?

Find a way to make your body into the same shape as the streamer. Toss your streamer into the air again, let it fall, and see what shape it makes on the floor now. Try out this new shape with your body. Try tossing and making shapes a few more times.

(continued)

Culminating Dance

Now, we're going to combine all the ideas we explored with the streamer into a dance. This is a dance about celebrating friendship in a neighborhood. In this neighborhood, there are four streets. All the children with blue streamers will live on Blue Street in one corner. Children with red streamers will live on Red Street in another corner, yellow streamers on Yellow Street in the third corner, and green streamers on Green Street in the fourth corner of the room. (See figure 8.1.)

Each street group will take turns skipping to the middle of the room, doing a turn, and skipping back to their corner. Red Street group, you will do a one-foot turn, the Blue Street group will do a slow turn moving high and low, the Green Street group will do a jump turn, and the Yellow Street group will do a turn in a wide stretched shape. [Provide time for each group to practice moving together toward the center of the room while skipping and turning.]

Now, I will tell the story about the neighborhood friendship dance as you dance each part. Everyone decided to have a neighborhood friendship dance that lasted for three days. On the first day of the neighborhood dance, the people living on Red Street skipped to the middle of the neighborhood to show everyone their one-foot turn and then they skipped back home. Now, Red Street dancers, show us your skipping and turning. Then, the children

living on Blue Street wanted to show the rest of the neighborhood their slow turn, so they skipped to the middle of the neighborhood, did their slow turn, and skipped back home. Okay, Blue Street, we are ready for you. Next, from the third corner, the children on Green Street skipped to the middle of the neighborhood to show their jumping turn and skipped back home. Okay, ready, Green Street dancers? It's your turn. And the Yellow Street dancers said, "Don't forget us! We want to show our wide stretched turn to the neighborhood." So the Yellow Street dancers skipped to the middle, did a big stretched turn, and skipped back home. It's your turn, Yellow Street dancers.

On the second day of the dance, the children on Red Street looked far across the neighborhood to the children on Blue Street and wondered what it would be like to live over there. At the same time, the children on Blue Street looked across at the children on Red Street and also wondered what it would be like to live on Red Street. Both groups decided to go and visit the other street. The red and blue groups slid sideways, leading with their right side, across the middle of the neighborhood to the opposite street, waving to each other with their streamers as they passed by. [Children slide to the opposite corner, passing the other group on the way.] Then the children on Green Street looked at the children on Yellow Street and wondered what it would be like to live on Yellow Street. And, at the

Green

Red

Blue

Yellow

Figure 8.1 Children with streamers begin the dance in four corners in the room.

same time, the children living on Yellow Street had the same feelings. So both groups slid sideways across the space to the opposite corners, waving their streamers as they passed by the other group. [Children slide to the opposite corner.] Next, the Red Street children became lonely for their street and wanted to go home, and the Blue Street children felt the same way. So both groups slid sideways back to their own corners, waving to each other as they passed by. [Children return to their original corner.] Then the children from Green Street and Yellow Street wanted to go back home. So they slid sideways back across the neighborhood to their own corners, waving to each other as they passed by. [Children return to their original corner.]

On the third day of the party, the Red Street group decided to have their own party and invite the whole neighborhood. [Assign two children to be the leaders for the Red Street group.] Now, Red Street group, skip over to the Green Street group, stop, wave to them, and say, "Hey, come with us." [Red Street group skips to the Green Street group.] Next, everyone in the red and green groups, skip over to the children on Blue Street, stop, wave to them, and say, "Hey, come with us." [Red and Green skip over to Blue, and Blue joins in to make one large group.] And, finally, everyone skip over to the children on Yellow Street, stop, wave to them, and say, "Hey, come with us." [The yellow group joins the others.] Now everyone skip in a big circle around the room, waving your streamers in the air.

Next, the Red Street group leaders stop, face each other, and hold the ends of each other's streamers to make a doorway into the party. Now, each child take turns walking under the doorway and into the party. At the party, everyone is turning and circling their streamers. You can dance by yourself or dance with another person who has a different color streamer. Okay, begin. I see some children turning slowly, some turning very fast, and some children holding hands and skipping. [Children improvise for 1 or 2 minutes.] Now, everyone stop—the party is over. The dance ends with everyone tossing a streamer into the air and making the same shape like we did earlier in the lesson. Ready? Toss. Let the streamer fall to the floor, and now you slowly fall to the floor and make your body into the same shape as the streamer. [You can signal the end of the party, or a child can create a signal that everyone can follow.] Nice job! Let's try the whole dance again. This time perform the dance without my telling the story. Express the story through your dancing.

Closure

That was great fun. What part of the dance did you like the best? What did you like about it? [Ask several children to share their comments.] How do you think the dance showed friendship? [More children respond.] Take your streamer home with you tonight and talk with your family about our dance. You can show them your turn and the shapes you made with the streamers.

Look For

- How children were able to coordinate the skip-and-turn sequence and maintain good balance. Some children may skip too fast and will not be able to change from the skip to the turn without falling.

- Children who need extra help to match their body shapes to the shape of the streamer. Some children will surprise you with their unique interpretations, and others will not be able to match the shape of the streamer with their bodies. You can ask these children to reproduce only a part of the streamer shape.

- Children who bump into others when exchanging corners. Ask the children for suggestions on solving the bumping problem.

How Can I Change This?

- Replace skipping with galloping or walking.

- Ask each street group to collaborate and choose a locomotor movement and a pathway to travel to the middle of the neighborhood. They could move while connected, move low to the floor, or use different directions or tempos.

- Allow children to choose the streamer color. This may lead to uneven groups, but having some groups with more children can make the dance interesting.

- In the section of the culminating dance where two children hold hands to make a door, you can have everyone in the red group hold hands with a partner to make several doors for the other three groups to use as entrances to the party. This strategy will also alleviate waiting in line to enter the party.

Assessment Suggestions

- Teacher assessment—cognitive: Ask students to describe verbally what happens on each day

(continued)

of the friendship streamer dance to assess their recall of the dance sequence. (outcome 6)

- Teacher assessment—psychomotor: Use a checklist to record (yes or no) whether students can perform locomotor and nonlocomotor movements in a circular pathway and whether students can perform the four turning movements. (outcomes 1 and 2)

- Teacher assessment—cognitive: Students can create a vocabulary list of words that describe the shapes of the streamers and their bodies after the toss. They can also make drawings of the shapes. (outcome 2)

- Student self-assessment—psychomotor: Students, organized by their street group, demonstrate to each other the ways they made circles with the streamers. (outcomes 1 and 3)

- Student self-assessment—affective and cognitive: Students can draw a picture of friends dancing together with the streamers. (outcomes 4 and 5)

Interdisciplinary Connections

- Social studies: Use this dance to initiate or conclude a social studies unit on communities or friendship.

- Visual arts: Integrate the dance with visual arts by having the children draw pictures of themselves dancing in circular pathways or doing their turns.

Floating Clouds and Rain Showers

Outcomes

As a result of participating in this learning experience, children will be able to do the following:

1. Create body shapes that represent various cloud shapes. (cognitive)

2. Demonstrate slow and light and fast and strong movements. (psychomotor)

3. Move in different relationships safely—with a partner, in a small group, and in a large group. (psychomotor and cognitive)

4. Use coordination and control when changing shapes and movements. (psychomotor)

Organization

Children dance individually and then with a partner. Next, partners join other sets of partners to form small groups. Finally, the whole class joins together in one formation.

Equipment Needed

- MP3 or CD player
- Slow and fast music for accompaniment, or use a percussion instrument
- Paper and crayons for drawing
- Whiteboard or chart paper

Introduction and Warm-Up

Today, we are going to do a dance called floating clouds and rain showers. This dance is about the shapes and movements of clouds. How can you describe the cloud shapes you have seen? Amy said they are round; Tim said long. I also heard puffy, big, soft, oval, and straight. [Write these shape words on chart paper or a whiteboard.] How do clouds move across the sky? I hear fast, slow, floating, twirling. Yes, sometimes they are still or move up and down. [Write movement words on chart paper or a whiteboard.] Now, we are going to use the cloud shapes and the ways clouds move to create a dance. Find a personal space in the room for our warm-up.

Begin your warm-up following me. I will use slow movements while we are standing in our spaces and then faster movements as we travel in the space. [Slowly move various body parts, bending and stretching in different directions. Then, ask children to walk around the room, followed by galloping, and finally running.]

Development

The cloud-shape words that you described in the beginning of class are on the whiteboard or chart paper. Standing in your personal space, make your body into one of those shapes. Try another one, and now another. Let's try making a round cloud. Can you make the round shape with only your arms? Try making a wide cloud shape, now a long straight shape, and now a small shape. Can you make a cloud shape that uses another body part touching the floor, other than your feet? Meredith has made a long shape on the side of her body, and Tamika is in a wide stretched shape supported by her hands and feet. Try another cloud shape and one more cloud shape.

Choose three cloud shapes and then decide which one you will do first, second, and third. Let's practice changing from the first shape to the second shape and then to the third shape. Ready! Slowly make your first shape, quickly get into your second shape, and slowly make your third shape. Try the three cloud shapes again using the slow, fast, slow tempos. This time try a different tempo sequence for your cloud shapes such as fast, fast, slow or fast, slow, slow. Practice this cloud shape dance a couple times. [Children practice their cloud shapes.]

Choose a cloud shape and find a way to make it travel around general space slowly; now quickly. Choose another cloud shape and decide the speed it will travel. I see round clouds walking slowly, wide clouds sliding sideways, and fast and long straight clouds rolling on the floor.

Feel like your cloud is floating across the sky, changing shapes and tempo as it moves. Be careful to move around the other clouds. [Children practice their cloud movements. Play music or a percussion instrument while children practice.]

Does anyone want to show us your cloud dance? Let's watch and see what shapes the dancers are making and if they change the tempo. [Three or four children demonstrate, and you ask observing children to comment on what they see.]

Now, I will assign you a cloud partner, and I want the two of you to find different ways you can

(continued)

connect your cloud shapes to each other and float across the sky. [Organize the children into partners and provide time for exploration.] What are the body parts you can use to connect to another cloud? I see these two children are using their hands; others are using their feet. I see elbows connected to shoulders, hands connected to a back, and heads connected.

Next, find a way you and your partner can combine your two cloud shapes and make a new cloud shape. Try making three different cloud shapes. Remember to stay connected. What other cloud shapes can you make connected together?

Now, find a way to move your new cloud across the sky. Decide if one person is going to lead or if you are going to take turns as leaders. Can you continue to stay connected as you travel?

Find another cloud and connect together into a larger cloud. What are the body parts you can use to connect to each other? Can you find a way for this cloud to travel across the space? Who will be the leader? What is the shape of your large cloud? When you have a large cloud, move slowly so everyone can move together and stay connected. Let me see how you move slowly in your cloud shape and stay connected. [When children move as connected clouds, you want them to enjoy the challenge of moving with another person and remaining safe. Take this opportunity to discuss cooperation in decision making. Make sure the children agree about how and where they are going to move before they begin. Remind them to move slowly.]

Now, all the small groups of clouds will join together into one really, really big cloud. Before we move, we need to talk about what shape the large cloud will be, how we will be connected to each other, and how the cloud will move. What shape should we use for the large cloud? Carmen suggests a long straight cloud. How will we be connected to each other? Joe suggests holding hands. How will the cloud move? Constantine says that walking will work best. Let's all join hands in a long line with Carmen as the leader and Joe at the end of the line. [Children assemble.] Carmen, begin to lead the cloud around the room as everyone walks slowly. Bring the cloud to the middle of the room to form a circle, and now close the cloud shape by holding Joe's hand. Now, let go of your hands. Let's try it again with a new leader. Can anyone suggest another large-class cloud? [You can try several ideas, with suggestions from the children about the shape and how to move.]

Culminating Dance

Now, we are going to use all the cloud shapes in a dance. The dance will begin with your individual cloud shape and then move into partner or trio cloud shapes. Next, everyone will join together in one giant cloud. Now, each person find a personal space to begin the cloud dance. Begin to slowly make your body into one of your individual cloud shapes and travel in the space. As you move, find another person and connect. Remember to connect with different body parts. Now, find another cloud; connect and travel together across the sky. Move slowly so everyone can stay connected and travel together safely. Now, all the clouds join together by holding hands in a long line with Gary as the leader and Rae at the end of the line. I see everyone is moving slowly and holding hands as you follow Gary around the room. Gary, bring the group into a big circle and join hands with Rae to make a large round cloud. Now, let's try the dance again from the beginning with a new leader.

Closure for Cloud Dance

To end the lesson, lie on the floor and rest while you think about the cloud dance. Pretend you are watching a movie of the cloud dance. Watch yourself make cloud shapes. What shapes are you using? Now you are connecting to another cloud. What body parts did you use to connect? Next, partner clouds are connecting to other partner clouds, and you are all moving across the sky. Are you moving slowly? And, finally, everyone connects into one giant cloud. What is the shape of the giant cloud?

[The learning experience can conclude at this point, or you can continue to add the next section, the rainstorm.]

The next part of the learning experience begins with everyone standing in a large circle like a big round cloud. In this part of the dance, the cloud is going to fill up with rain and burst open. How can we make this cloud become bigger and bigger? I hear from Sari that we can let go of hands and move backward, and Brad suggested that we make big stretching shapes. Let's try both ideas. Let go of hands and move backward 4 steps, growing into a big stretched shape. (See figure 8.2.) Ready! 1, 2, 3, 4. Hold your big shape still. Let's try it again.

Once the cloud is full of rain, it will burst open. What are some other words we can use instead of *burst*? I hear *explode, break open, pop, bust apart*.

How can your body move to show a bursting movement? I hear up, open, stretched, jumping, turning. What kind of force is needed? Yes, strong. Where will you move in space? Okay, up and forward, up and backward, or up and sideward. Create three different bursting movements. Ready! Burst, burst, and burst. Try each burst in a different direction. Burst, burst, and burst. Practice your three bursting movements each in a different direction.

Now, let's combine the cloud filling with rain and the bursting. First, the circle becomes bigger 1, 2, 3, and 4, and now burst, burst, and burst. Let's try that part again: 1, 2, 3, and 4, and burst, burst, and burst. [You can ask several children to demonstrate their bursting movement while the children observe the different directions of the burst.]

After the cloud bursts open, it begins to rain all over the room. What are some ways we can use movement to express the rain? Jennifer suggests that we run all over the room with big leaps in the air, like the wind is pushing the rain all over. Trevor suggests that the rain falls straight down and we should show the falling rain by using our arms, starting high and moving low several times quickly. You may use either of these suggestions or create your own movement for the rain. Will your movement travel around the space or stay in your personal space? Let me see what choices you have made to show the rain. [Children practice being the rain falling while you observe.]

In the last part of this dance, the rainstorm stops and the last drop falls slowly to the ground. Stop

your rain movement and hold your body still. Now slowly, very slowly, fall to the floor. Can you add a turn to your slow falling? Keep your body in control as you fall. What shape will your body be in at the end of the fall? Think about it! Now, combine your rain movement with the stop and slowly fall to the floor ending in a shape. Ready! Rain, rain, rain, rain, rain, rain, rain, rain, and stop. Now slowly fall to the floor, ending in a shape. [Children can practice this sequence several times to coordinate the transitions between movements.]

Now, let's put the whole rainstorm dance together. Begin with everyone holding hands in a large circle. Now, let go as the cloud fills up with rain. Step backward, 1, 2, 3, 4, and make a wide big shape and hold it still, 1, 2, 3. Now, burst and burst and burst; and now, rain, rain, rain, rain, rain, rain, rain, rain, rain, and stop; and slowly fall to the floor and end in a shape. [Note the sequence of movements on a chalkboard or draw picture symbols to indicate the order of the movements.]

Now, let's combine the cloud dance with the rainstorm dance. Ready! Find your personal space to begin your individual cloud. Slowly make your body into the shape of a cloud and begin to travel in the space. Find another cloud and join together. Now, find another cloud and join together to form a bigger cloud. Everyone join in one large, long cloud with Carmen as the leader and Joe at the end. Carmen, lead the cloud around the room and come to the middle of the room to form a circle by taking Joe's hand. Let go of your hands as the cloud fills with rain. Step backward and make a wide stretched shape. Now, burst and burst and burst; and rain, rain, rain, rain, rain, rain, rain, and rain; and stop; and slowly fall to the floor and end in a shape.

Closure for Rainstorm

Ask the children, "What are the types of energy you used to express different parts of the rainstorm? What part of the rainstorm did you enjoy dancing? Why did you like that part?"

Look For

- The shapes the children create. Are they able to represent a variety of cloud shapes with their body shapes?
- How children control their movements in the cloud and rainstorm segments. Specifically, can they coordinate the transitions smoothly between each part of the dance?

Figure 8.2 The cloud becomes bigger and bigger, filling up with rain.

(continued)

- How children use directions for the bursts in the rainstorm. Do you see the whole body or body parts moving in a specific direction?

How Can I Change This?

- Children can create smaller clouds that fill up with rain and burst instead of the one large cloud.
- Add creating a rainbow and a shining sun at the end of the rainstorm. Children can make small-group shapes representing the curved line of the rainbow and the shapes of the sun. Ask them for ideas.

Assessment Suggestions

- Teacher assessment—cognitive: Children can draw and label the shapes they used in the cloud dance. (outcome 1)
- Student self-assessment—cognitive: Partners can write a list of body parts they used to connect to each other in the cloud dance. (outcome 3)
- Student self-assessment—psychomotor: Children use a rating scale to assess their ability to move slowly as a cloud or strong in the rainstorm. Rubric includes the following three levels: I was in control for all movements, I was in control for some of the movements, I did not control any movements. (outcomes 2 and 3)
- Teacher assessment—psychomotor: Record observations to assess whether children can burst in three different directions using control by landing on their feet. (outcome 4)

Interdisciplinary Connections

- Visual arts: Connect to visual arts by having children observe and draw cloud shapes on a large piece of paper.
- Language arts (literature): Integrate children's literature by using the book *Little Cloud* (Carle 1996) as a guide for making cloud shapes and developing a dance to accompany the story.
- Language arts (literature): Integrate children's literature by using the book *Listen to the Rain* (Endicott 1988). The text and illustrations will stimulate ideas for creating dance movements.
- Science: Use this dance to reinforce science concepts about the water cycle, cloud formations, or types of weather.

Outcomes

As a result of participating in this learning experience, children will be able to do the following:

1. Perform four locomotor movements: run, hop, jump, and skip. (psychomotor)

2. Identify how the run, hop, jump, and skip movements are different or similar. (cognitive)

3. Perform a sequence of movements. (psychomotor)

Organization

Children will move individually in their personal space for the run dance, the skip dance, and the hop dance. The jump dance begins individually and ends in a small group.

Equipment Needed

Whiteboard or chart paper listing the four locomotor words and the rhyming words (see figure 8.3).

Introduction and Warm-Up

Today, we are going to dance to words that rhyme with run, hop, jump, and skip. [Words are written on the chart paper or whiteboard.] Can you suggest words that rhyme with *run*, *hop*, *jump*, and *skip*? [Write children's suggestions.] We will use all these words in our warm-up and then select a few words for the dance.

In your personal space, begin to jog in place as we say the words you listed under *run*. *Run, bun, pun, fun, nun, sun*, and *stun*. Now hop on your right foot as we say the words listed under *hop*. Now, repeat the words while you hop on the left foot. *Hop, pop, mop, bop, cop, drop, flop, clop, lop,*

Figure 8.3 Rhyming words listed on whiteboard.

chop, top, plop, stop, and *prop*. Next, jump in place while you say the words listed under *jump. Bump, clump, stump, rump, dump, frump, grump, hump, lump, mump, pump*, and *plump*. The last movement in the warm-up is to skip while saying the words listed under skip. *Blip, clip, sip, dip, flip, drip, grip, slip, lip, nip*, and *rip*.

Development

I have selected a few words from the list to use in the warm-up for the dance. I am going to read the first poem that uses the words *run, fun*, and *sun* and then we will create different ways to move to each word. [Read the run poem.]

> Let's all begin to run
>
> And run, and run, and run.
>
> Everyone stop,
>
> And have some fun
>
> Some fun, some fun, some fun
>
> In the sun, in the sun, in the sun.

First, let's find different ways to run. What are some other ways to run? Let's try Jessica's suggestion to run with tiny steps. Can we think of any other ways to run? Miguel is running with his arms stretched out to the side. [Children try the suggestion.] Now, try your own idea for running. Now, try another idea. [This would be a good time for children to rest and share their running explorations either with the whole class or with a partner.] Think about choosing your favorite way to run for this dance. We will use it in a few minutes.

For the word *fun*, we will create movements that show us doing something fun, like playing ball, jumping rope, petting a dog, roller skating, or playing catch. Think about some other things you do for fun. How can you express them through a movement? Show me now. Exaggerate your movements; make them very big. Choose one you would like to use in this dance. The last rhyming word is *sun*. Create a shape with your arms that is round like the sun. Move your arms from right to left, beginning low on the right side of your body; stretch your round arms high over your head; and end low on the left side of your body. Do you know what this arm movement is like? This movement shows the movement of the sun rising in the morning,

(continued)

moving across the sky, and setting low at night. Try this movement again, starting slowly on the right, reaching up high, and going low to the left. Keep the movement smooth and slow.

This time, as I read the poem, move using the run movement you chose, then the fun movement you selected, and then we will all do the sun movement together. Ready! Do your run movement. "Let's all begin to run, and run, and run, and run." Now use the fun movement. "Everyone stop and have some fun, some fun, some fun, some fun." What are your fun movements? Everyone does the sun movement all together. "In the sun, in the sun, in the sun." Try it again, but I'm not going to tell you when to do things. [Read the poem again while the children perform their dance.]

Our next dance uses words that rhyme with *hop.* I will read the poem, and you listen carefully for the words that rhyme with *hop.*

One day we all went out for a hop

With our hands placed on our top.

Then someone came by and yelled "stop!"

We then did a pop and a drop.

What were the words that rhymed with *hop?* Yes, *drop, stop, top,* and *pop.* Good listening!

Let's begin with the word *hop.* What are the directions you can use for your hop? I see some children hopping forward, some backward, and others sideward. When you hop, remember that one foot is doing the hopping and the other foot is up off the floor. While you are hopping, can you place the leg that is off the floor in front of your body? What about stretched in back of your body? Out to the side? Give each leg a turn to hop.

The next word is *top.* Create different shapes with your hands when they are on the top of your head. Pretend your hands are like a hat on top of your head. I see some pointed hats, round hats, flat hats, hats that look like horns, and some that look like a crown. Do you think you can hop with your hands on your top? Choose a hat shape and a way to hop, and give it a try.

The third word is *stop.* Create a still shape. Make a round shape, a twisted shape, a stretched shape, and a shape with many angles in the body. Each time I clap my hands I want you to make a different still shape and freeze. Ready! [Clap 6 to 8 times.] Remember your still shapes; we will use them when we dance to the poem.

The fourth word is *pop.* We are going to explore ways to pop up in the air. It's like a jump. Make sure you land on your feet with your knees bent. Can you pop in the air and make a stretched shape? Can you take off on two feet and land on one foot? Can you add a turn to your pop? Try a pop where you jump high into the air and a pop that does not go very high.

The last rhyming word is *drop.* I want you to be safe and drop slowly as if you are melting to the floor. Show me how you can slowly lower your body to the floor very carefully. Use your hands to help you as you become lower and lower. Can you add a turn as you drop? Let's practice combining the pop and drop. Ready and pop! And now drop very slowly. I see you can change from a strong, fast movement to a light, slow movement.

Now, I will read the whole poem, and as I say the words I want you to dance the movements you created. Here's the poem: "One day we all went out for a hop with our hands on our top." [Children hop with hands on the top of their head in a hat shape.] "Someone came by and yelled 'stop!'" [Children freeze in a shape.] "We then did a pop and a drop." [Children jump into the air for the pop, and slowly drop to the floor.] Try the dance again as I read the poem. [Repeat the poem again.]

Our next dance uses words that rhyme with *jump.* Here's the poem:

We all went out to jump

And jump and jump and jump.

We jumped so close together

We all started to gently bump

And bump and bump and bump

And slowly fell into a clump.

What words rhymed with *jump?* Good, Alyssa, one is *clump.* Yes, Min-Su, another one is *bump.* The first word we will use is *jump.* When I say go, I want you to find a space and try different ways to jump in place. Go! Can you jump so your feet move together and apart? What are the shapes you can make with your arms as you are jumping? Try jumping forward in a zigzag pathway. Find a way to take small jumps and then large jumps, first moving forward, then backward, and finally sideward. As I read the first part of the poem, choose your favorite way to jump. [Read the first two lines of the poem while the children jump.]

The next word is *bump.* We are going to use different body parts to lightly bump against another person. As you walk around the room and come close to another person, lightly bump them with your arm. I want Curtis and Tamika to demonstrate a light bump with their arms. [Children demonstrate.] They are using a soft touch for the bump. Now, everyone try the soft bump with your classmates. Try bumping with another body part, like maybe your foot, knee, elbow, hand, shoulder, hip, back, or finger. The bumping will be a big change of force from the jumping. Let's combine the jumping with the bumping. Make sure you have a place in the room where you have lots of space around you. I will read the poem, and I want to see how you change from the strong force used in the jumping to the light force used for the bumping. Get ready to move! [Read the first five lines of the poem while children jump and bump.]

The last word in this poem is *clump.* What is a clump? Ryan says it is a lot of things bunched up together. We are going to be a clump of children at the end of the poem. To make the clump we will slowly fall to the floor and end in a round shape. In your own space, try slowly falling to the floor in a round shape. Now, I want two, three, or four people to get together in a group and together, using a slow tempo, fall to the floor. Can all of you stay together in a small space and fall slowly at the same time? Try it again.

Now, I will read the whole poem. I want you to end the dance in the clump with the same people you were just with. Start the dance far apart from each other and move toward each other on the jumps, then gently bump the people in your group, and then slowly fall into a clump. [Read the whole poem as the children dance.] Nice job jumping, bumping, and clumping!

This last dance rhymes three words with the word *skip.* Listen to the poem for the words that sound like skip.

We all began to skip

And skip and skip and skip.

Then tried to do a flip

A flip, a flip, a flip.

Instead we began to trip

And fell upon our hip.

Begin the dance with exploring pathways for skipping. First try skipping in a straight path. Now,

try a curved pathway. Can you skip backward on the straight or curved pathway? Try different ways to move or make shapes with your arms as you skip. I will assign you a partner, and I want you to show each other your favorite pathway to use in the skip. Tell your partner what kind of pathway you observed while they skipped. Now, I will read the first two lines of the poem and you can skip using your pathway or the pathway your partner used. [Read the first two lines as the children skip.]

The second rhyming word in the poem is *flip.* We are not going to really do a flip. That would be too dangerous; but we are going to create a turn that changes levels. Find a way to turn on one foot or two feet so your turn starts on a high level, changes to a low level, and ends on a high level. [Children practice turning while you cue the movements.] Ready! Turn high, low, and high. Try another turn using high, low, high levels. As I read the third and fourth lines of the poem, try your flip turns that change levels. [Read the poem.]

The third word is *trip.* We are going to slowly fall to the floor using your hands to help you lower your body to the floor. Can you add a turn to your slow fall? [Children practice slowly falling to the floor.]

The last word in the poem is *hip.* Point to your hips. Can you lie down with your right hip touching the floor? Now try your left hip. Find another way to lie down with your hips touching the floor. Try one more way. Now, let's combine slowly falling to the floor and ending the fall in one of the ways you created to lie on your hips. Ready? Slowly fall and have your hips on the floor. Now, as I read the last two lines of the poem, do the falling movements ending on your hips. [Read the last two lines of the poem.]

This time, as I read the whole poem, perform the movements you created to represent the words *skip, flip, trip,* and *hip.* Let's review all the movements first. Here's the first line: "We all began to skip, and skip and skip and skip." Show me the pathway you chose for your skip. "Then we tried to do a flip, a flip, a flip, a flip." Now, do your high, low, high turn. "Instead we began to trip." Slowly fall to the floor. "And fell upon our hip." End in a shape with your hip touching the floor. I will read the poem again. I want you to dance the movements you created as you hear the rhyming words, but I'm not going to tell you what to do. Ready? [Repeat the poem.]

Culminating Dance

Each of these poems can be performed individually as a culminating dance, or you can combine two,

(continued)

three, or all four poems to form a longer sequence as the culminating dance.

Closure

Ask the children, "What was your favorite poem? Raise your hand when I call out the one you liked the best. The run poem. The hop poem. The jump poem. The skip poem. Does anyone have another movement that we could use to create a poem dance?"

Look For

- Children who are not ready to perform the skip. You can substitute a gallop or present the dance when everyone has learned how to skip.
- Children who tire easily when performing many repetitions of locomotor movements that require strength and balance. Provide more opportunities to rest.
- Changes in the children's use of force in all four dances. All dances begin with strong force and end using light force.

How Can I Change This?

- Children can choose their favorite poem (run, skip, hop, jump) and perform the dance while other children accompany the dancing by playing percussion instruments.
- Use other locomotor or nonlocomotor movements as the inspiration for rhyming words and creating movements.

Assessment Suggestions

- Peer assessment—psychomotor and cognitive: Students organized into partners or small groups select two of the poems, practice the movements, and perform the poems for another set of partners or another group. The observing student identifies the selected movements. (outcomes 1 and 2)
- Teacher assessment—psychomotor: Use a checklist to note how well each child performs the locomotor movements in the poem dances. Also, use the checklist format to assess how well children can change from one movement to another in the dance sequence. (outcomes 1 and 3)

Interdisciplinary Connections

- Language arts (vocabulary): Ask the classroom teacher about vocabulary words children are learning that could be used for rhyming dances.
- Language arts (writing): Children can write poems using action verbs and then create movements to express the words.
- Language arts (reading and writing): This dance supports language arts content focused on rhyming.
- Language arts (reading): Add children's books that use locomotor movements as content, such as *Hop Jump* (Walsh 1993); *Jump, Frog, Jump* (Kalan and Barton 1981); or *In the Small, Small Pond* (Fleming 1993).

The Playground

Outcomes

As a result of participating in this learning experience, children will be able to do the following:

1. Perform the three swinging arm movements to represent the playground swings. (psychomotor)

2. Coordinate changing levels with a partner to represent the seesaw. (psychomotor and affective)

3. Remember and demonstrate the movement sequence for the slide. (psychomotor and cognitive)

Organization

Children move individually, in partners, and with a large group as they visit the various imaginary playground spaces.

Equipment Needed

- MP3 or CD player
- Lively music for accompaniment
- Signs indicating the playground spaces
- Tape

Introduction and Warm-Up

Today, we are going to create a dance about the playground. Pretend this room is a playground. What are the ways you play at the playground? I hear sliding down the slide, going on the seesaw, swinging on the swings, playing on the climbing bars (monkey bars). Let's choose three areas to visit on the playground today: the seesaw, the sliding board, and the swings. I have a sign for each of these areas, and I will place the signs on the walls. The slide will be at this end of the room [place sign on wall], the seesaw will be in this corner [place sign], and the swings will be in the middle of the room around the center circle [place sign on the floor].

For our warm-up, we are going to find ways to travel to the playground. Let's pretend we are walking to the playground. Try walking fast in a curvy pathway; now walk backward slowly. Can you pretend to be riding a bicycle, steering to the right and to the left? Next, let's warm up our arms by swinging them forward and backward, now side to side. Start with small swings and make them bigger

and bigger and as big as you can, then smaller and smaller and as small as you can.

Development

Now that we have arrived at the playground, let's go on the slide first. Everyone begin on one end of the room. Pretend the space in front of you is a giant slide. Let's start by using our arms and legs to climb up the ladder using 8 counts. Begin low and reach higher on each count: 1, 2, 3, 4, 5, 6, 7, 8. [Demonstrate while counting to 8.] Now, let's try climbing to the 8 counts all together. Begin in a squat position low to the floor and climb a little higher on each count. [Children practice the imaginary climb while counting to 8.] Now, let's pretend to slide down the slide. Lower your body to the floor, and find a way to move forward as if you were going down a slide. I see some children on the front of their bodies pulling themselves with their hands along the floor, others are sitting and using their arms and legs to push and pull, and others are moving forward walking on their hands and feet. When you arrive at the other end of the room, go back to where you started. Climb up the ladder for 8 counts, and try another way to move down the slide. Can you travel sideward down the slide?

Next, let's go to the swings. In this dance, we all move in unison. That means we all do the same movement at the same time. I want everyone to join together and make a circle. Now, swing your arms forward and backward, forward and backward, using 4 counts. Let's try it all together: forward, backward, forward, backward, or 1, 2, 3, 4. [Lead the unison practice with the children.] Now, place one foot forward. Rock forward toward the front foot and then rock backward, shifting the weight to the back foot. Add the arms we just practiced to the rocking feet. All together, swing forward, backward, forward, backward. [Lead the unison practice.]

Let's add a second part to this dance. This time make a giant arm swing forward, walk forward 4 big steps, and stretch up on the fourth step. [Demonstrate the walk and stretch.] Ready, all together with me. Swing your arms forward and step, step, step, step, and stretch. (See figure 8.4 on page 126.) What happens to the circle when we do this at the same time? Yes, it gets smaller. Now, swing the arms backward and take 4 steps back. Let's try the swing and walk several times. Ready? Swing forward

(continued)

1, 2, 3, and 4; swing backward 1, 2, 3, and 4. [You and the children practice the swinging forward and backward in unison several times.]

Let's combine the first and second parts of the swing dance. Remember, 4 swings with the arms (4 counts), 4 swings with rocking feet (4 counts), swing walking forward (4 counts), and swing walking backward (4 counts). The whole dance is 16 counts long. Let's try it all together three times.

Now, let's move over to the seesaws. I will assign you a partner or make groups of three. Can someone tell us how seesaws move? Marcos suggests that when one side is up the other side is down and they keep changing. Face your partners and find a way for one person to start low and the other start high and then change at the same time. Can you hold hands and do the seesaw movement? Can you connect with another body part? Find a way to do the up-and-down seesaw movement while sitting on the floor. You and your partner create three different ways to move in opposition to show the seesaw movement. Practice each of the ways three times. Show me how you can change smoothly from the first way to the second and then to the third.

Culminating Dance

Now, we are going to combine the three short dances into one big dance. The first time we do

Figure 8.4 Swing dance part of the playground dance.

the dance we will all go to the same place in the same order. The second time you perform the dance you can choose the order for your dance. Ready! Let's all travel to the playground by riding our bikes. Here we go. [Children can follow you or choose their own pathway and meet at the slides.] Well, here we are at the playground. Let's all go on the slide first. Ready to climb? Start low: 1, 2, 3, 4, 5, 6, 7, 8, and slide down forward or backward. Go back to the other side of the room and try the counting and climbing again, and this time, choose another way to slide.

Now, let's go over to the swings. Make a big circle. Everyone ready? Let's do this dance together. Arm swings, 1, 2, 3, 4; rocking swings, 1, 2, 3, 4; swing walk forward, 1, 2, 3, 4; swing walk backward, 1, 2, 3, 4.

Now, let's go to the third area, the seesaw. Find your partner and do the seesaw movement, either standing high and low or sitting high and low. Count to 12, and then meet me near the chalkboard.

You now can do the dance by yourselves while I play the music. This time you choose what area of the playground you are going to play in first, second, and third. Perform the movements we practiced at each area. Start when the music begins, and meet me by the chalkboard when you are finished. [Start the music.] I see Danielle is on the slide—I can hear her counting to 8 as she climbs—and Hector is on the swings moving forward and backward, and Theresa and Steve are at the seesaw moving opposite each other going high and low.

Closure

Everyone show me your favorite movement of the dance. Next, show me the movement that was the hardest for you to perform. Can you think of another piece of playground equipment we could add to this dance? How would you create a dance about that piece?

Look For

- How children perform the skills based on their motor development and fitness level. Can children alternate hands and feet as they represent climbing? Do children demonstrate adequate strength to travel low to the floor as needed in the playground slide? On the seesaw, are the children able to coordinate their muscles to move up and down with even rhythm?

- Children who may need help to make a decision about which playground area to play in during the second part of the culminating dance. These children may need to follow other children.

How Can I Change This?

- Children can make shapes with their bodies either individually or with others that represent the shape of the swings, the slide, and the seesaw.
- Children can draw pictures of the areas of the playground and place them under the signs.
- Children can suggest other pieces of playground equipment for the dance.
- Take time before children try the second part of the culminating dance to have them plan the order, and write or draw pictures of which playground area they will go to first, second, and third.

Assessment Suggestions

- Teacher assessment—psychomotor: Use a rating scale to record how well students can complete the swinging arm sequence. The rating scale uses the following rubric: A = student accurately completes all 3 parts, B = student accurately completes two of the three parts, C = student completes one of the three parts. Note the uncompleted parts. (outcome 1)
- Student self-assessment—psychomotor and affective: Assess using a verbal response to these questions: Can you and your partner perform the seesaw dance with one person up while the other is down and be able to switch? How did you work together to perform the seesaw movements? (outcome 2)
- Teacher assessment—psychomotor and cognitive: Use a checklist to record whether students remember and perform the sequence of climbing up and moving down the slide. The checklist uses the following rubric: yes = student can remember and perform both parts, no = student remembers and performs only one part (outcome 3)

Interdisciplinary Connections

- Math: The dance sequences reinforce math concepts of counting and patterns.
- Social studies and math: Children can use mapping skills to draw a playground map, arranging the playground equipment in different spaces to correspond to the dance or create a new playground map.

Ocean Waves and Swimmers

Outcomes

As a result of participating in this learning experience, children will be able to do the following:

1. Coordinate arm and leg movements to express the swimmer's movements. (psychomotor)

2. Remember the three movements used to represent the ocean part of the dance. (psychomotor and cognitive)

3. Describe whether they prefer the role of the ocean or the swimmer in the dance. (affective)

Organization

Children explore movements individually using levels, pathways, and directions, and in two large groups they perform the culminating dance.

Equipment Needed

- MP3 or CD player
- Music with the sound of ocean waves
- Pictures or video of waves or swimmers
- Drum or other percussion instruments

Introduction and Warm-Up

Today, we are going to the beach. Did you bring your swimsuit and towel? The ocean will be in this half of the room, and the beach will be in the other half. (See figure 8.5.) In this dance, we will move high and low and use different pathways and directions. Has anyone been to the beach? Can you describe how the waves move? Now, let's do our warm-up so we are ready for a day of fun at the beach.

Begin the warm-up by walking in the space. Let's pretend we are walking to the beach. I will play the drum with an even, steady beat. As you walk, match the tempo of the drumbeat with each step. Swing your arms as you walk. Can you walk and change levels, reaching up high and bending down low? Now change the walk to a skip or a gallop as I change the drumbeat. Keep swinging your arms.

Development

In your personal space, let's first create some movements about the ocean waves. Using your hands and arms, show me how an ocean wave moves. I can see that your hands and arms are moving up and down. Make the up movement bigger and higher, and reach the down movement low to the floor. Try both arms at the same time. Now, add your whole body when you reach up high with your arms, and then bend your whole body as you reach down low with your arms. Let your head follow the up-and-down movement too. Add these 4 up counts and 4 down counts to the movement as I play the drum. Take all 4 counts to move up and all 4 counts to move down. Up-up-up-up and down-down-down-down, and up-up-up-up and down-down-down-down.

This time, find a way to walk forward in the space and move your body high and low. Add the counts up-up-up-up and down-down-down-down. Remember these walks; we will use them later in the dance to represent the movement of the ocean waves.

Now, let's create movements that feel like the splashes of the ocean waves as they hit the beach. Keeping your body low to the floor, how can you use your arms and legs to show the movement of a splash? Where do your arms and legs move in the space? What kind of force will you choose? Can you splash in different directions?

What happens to the wave after it hits the beach and splashes? Yes, it rolls back into the ocean. Show me how you can roll your body sideways as if you are a wave going back into the ocean. Add some of your splashing movements as you roll.

Now, let's combine the three different ways the wave can move. First, in your self-space, do the rising up-and-down movement of the waves. Ready! Up-up-up-up and down-down-down-down. Do it again. Now, add walking forward, up-up-up-up and down-down-down-down, and end down on the floor. Let's repeat this from the beginning: in place, up-up-up-up and down-down-down-down, and, again in place, up-up-up-up and down-down-down-down; now walking forward, up-up-up-up and down-down-down-down, and end on the floor.

Now, add the splashing movements in your self-space on the floor. Ready! Splashing, and splashing, and splashing, and splashing. You really have to use lots of force in your arms and legs. Now, splash in different directions.

The third wave movement is rolling back to the ocean with little splashes of your arms and legs. Ready! Roll, and roll, and roll, and roll, and add splashes each time you roll onto your back.

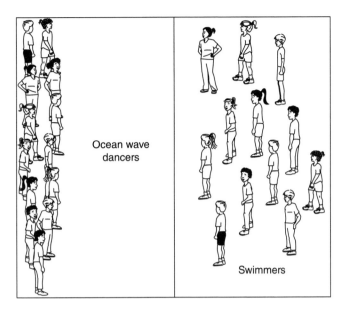

Figure 8.5 Beginning places for the ocean waves and swimmers.

Remember the three movements of the ocean. We will use them later in our dance. Now, let's create movements for the swimmers. What are the ways your arms move when you are swimming? I see arms moving forward, backward, sideways. Try a movement in which you alternate your arms. Try another way to move your arms so they move together, then apart, and together and apart. Now, add walking to your swimming arm movements. Use forward, backward, and sideward directions in the walking and in the arm movements. Swim all over the room using curvy pathways, as if you are swimming in all parts of the ocean.

I will divide the class into two groups. One group will be the ocean waves, and the other group will be the swimmers. Each child will have a chance to dance as the waves and swimmers today. The swimmers and waves will begin the dance on opposite sides of the room.

Culminating Dance

[At this point you tell the story, and the children listen without dancing.] This is a story about the ocean waves and the swimmers. Listen to the whole story first before we begin the dance. First, the swimmers put on their swimsuits; grab their towels; and walk, skip, or gallop to the beach. They move on the beach side of the room. Next, they find a spot on the beach and pretend to place the towels down by using a swinging arm movement. They lie down on the towel to feel the sun. Think about what shape you will use when you lie down on the towel. It is a very hot day, and the swimmers decide to go for a swim. They stand up on their towels and look toward the ocean. While the swimmers are standing and watching, the ocean waves begin to rise up and down and then move forward and splash. The swimmers walk in between the splashing waves, using their swimming arm movements. Some swimmers are swimming backward, some are swimming forward, and others are swimming sideward. Everyone is using different arm movements for the swimming. Some swimmers may be surfing. Then, the swimmers walk back to the beach for a rest and sit down on their towels, and the ocean waves roll back into the ocean. The ocean waves splash a little as they roll back. This is the end of the dance. Then the ocean waves and the swimmers change places.

Let's begin the dance. This time when I tell the story, you will dance. [Assign each group, and the children go to the designated space. Children are assigned roles, and you tell the story again as the children move. This process helps the children remember the sequence of movements and clarifies how the ocean waves and swimmers interact with one another.] Ready, swimmers move first. [Relate the swimmers' part of the story.] Now, the ocean waves begin to move. Remember to count, up-up-up-up and down-down-down-down and up-up-up-up and down-down-down-down. Now, walk forward up-up-up-up and down-down-down-down, and

(continued)

move to the floor for the splash. Be sure to have a big space around your body, so the swimmers will be able to move around you. Now, the swimmers move around and between the ocean waves. Swimmers return to their towels, and the ocean waves roll back into the ocean. [Cue children for the movement when needed.] Now, switch roles. Can you do the dance by yourself without my telling you the story? Try it to the sounds of the ocean waves.

Closure

Ask the children the following: "If you liked to dance the part of the ocean waves, show me one of the three ocean movements. If you like to dance the part of the swimmers, show me how you used your arms while swimming."

Look For

- Children to exaggerate stretching up and bending low for the ocean waves. Are they doing the ocean movement with a big change of level?
- How well children can coordinate up-and-down wave movements and counts. Can they move using all 4 counts to stretch up and all 4 counts to move down?
- The ability of the swimmers to keep the arm movements continuous as they walk between the spaces of the splashing waves. Can the swimmers use different directions?
- How well children can use personal space when they perform the splashing waves. Discuss with children why this safety concern is important.

How Can I Change This?

- You can elaborate on the story by adding playing in the sand before children go in for a swim. You could have swimmers lie on beach towels on the front, side, and back of their bodies, and have the swimmers dry off different body parts after the swim.
- Use real towels or towel-size pieces of plastic for the swimmers' props. The ocean wave dancers can hold blue streamers as props and move them up and down to emphasize the ocean waves.

- Children can perform the ocean waves by dancing in partners and moving in unison. Also assign partners so that the swimmers can move together.
- You can give children the choice of performing the dance sequence without your cues. Discuss with the children how they will know when to initiate the different parts of the sequence.
- You can emphasize the concept of unison movement with the waves in the up-and-down wave movements. Talk about what unison means and how children will be able to use it in the dance.
- Add ocean fish, crustaceans, and birds as characters living in the ocean (e.g., pelicans, dolphins, crabs, seagulls, lobsters, clams).

Assessment Suggestions

- Student self-assessment—affective: The children draw a picture of themselves performing the dance they preferred (either the swimmers or the ocean waves). They can label the picture or write a sentence about what is happening in the picture. (outcome 3)
- Teacher assessment—psychomotor and cognitive: Observe how many students remember all three parts of the ocean dance. Based on the observation, you can review the sequence and add additional practice. (outcome 2)
- Teacher assessment—psychomotor: Observe the swimmers' movements as they move around and between the ocean waves to see if the children can continue to move their arms in a swimming motion as they walk. (outcome 1)

Interdisciplinary Connections

- Science: Connect this dance to science concepts focused on water forms or ocean study.
- Music: Connect to music when songs and music compositions about the beach or ocean are added as accompaniment to the dance.
- Language arts (literature): Introduce the dance using poetry or stories focused on ocean life or experiences at the beach.

Outcomes

As a result of participating in this learning experience, children will be able to do the following:

1. Move their arms, legs, and whole bodies to create straight and curved shapes. (psychomotor)

2. Travel in space using straight and curved shapes and pathways. (psychomotor)

3. Change from a straight shape to a curved shape. (psychomotor)

4. Reflect on their dance performances and describe the improvements they made from the first performance to the second. (cognitive)

5. Identify their body shape as straight or curved. (cognitive)

Organization

Children move individually in their personal space for the introduction and development sections of the experience. In the culminating dance, children begin in small groups and then dance as part of a large group.

Equipment Needed

- MP3 or CD player
- Music with a steady beat
- Drum or wood block

Introduction and Warm-Up

Today, we are going to dance about straight and curved lines. Look at your clothes. Does anyone have any straight and curved lines on their clothes? I see Becka has straight lines on her shirt, and Michael is showing us the straight lines on his pants. Sydney has found lots of curvy lines on her shirt, and Tinesha is pointing to her belt that makes a curved line around her waist.

For our warm-up, let's go on a trip around the room and find all the straight lines. As you walk around the room, I want you to look for straight lines on the ceiling, the walls, the floor, and the objects in the space. When you see a straight line, stop and make your body into a straight shape. I see Kelly has made a straight shape lying next to a line on the floor. Fernando is standing in a straight shape near the door. Now go to another place, and find more straight lines.

Try making curved lines where you see a curve in the room. Lana has found the round clock and is making a round curved shape on the floor, and Mario is standing with his back curved to the side next to a chair with a curved back. Go and find other places to make curved shapes.

Development

Now, you are going to make straight shapes with your arms, legs, and then your whole body. Stand in your personal space. Make a straight shape with your arm. Find another way to make a straight shape with your arm, now with both arms. Each time I beat the drum, make your arms into a different straight shape. [Beat the drum 8 times.] Try making straight shapes with your legs on each of the 8 drumbeats. Now make your whole body straight. Use your legs, your arms, and your back. Make a straight shape on each drumbeat. [Beat the drum 8 times.]

This time I want you to make a curved shape with your arms. Use all 4 drumbeats to make the curve. [Play 4 beats on the drum as the children slowly make the arm shape.] Now, make a different curved arm shape and another and one more different curved shape. Now, use the whole body to make a curved shape. Make the shapes at different levels—some high, some medium, and some low to the floor. Ready and begin. Make a whole-body curved shape, now another, and another, and one more curved shape. [Play 4 beats on the drum each time as the children slowly make the whole-body shape.]

Now, I am going to ask you to change your body from a straight shape to a curved shape using this sequence: Make 4 straight shapes with a body part or the whole body and then one curved shape. The first 4 drumbeats are for the 4 straight shapes and the second 4 drumbeats are for the one slow, curved shape. The straight shapes will be quick and sharp, and the curved shape will be slow and smooth. Ready? Straight-straight-straight-straight and curved. Let's repeat it again using different shapes at different levels.

Now, we will explore moving our shapes on straight and curved pathways. This time I want you to find a way to keep most of your body parts straight and walk using a straight pathway. Can you

(continued)

keep your straight shape and change the direction to backward? Try another straight shape and travel sideways. Can you find another way to travel that is different from walking? Remember to use straight pathways.

Let's create different ways to travel in a curved shape on a curved pathway. Can you travel forward, backward, and sideward? Now, try making many different curved shapes as you travel, sometimes reaching high in your curved shape and sometimes letting the curved shape take you low. Keep the body moving into various curved shapes. Change the speed and run and jump into the air as you make curved shapes with your body. See if you can keep your body curved as you jump into the air. This movement looks like someone tossed a rope into the air.

Culminating Dance

We are going to use all the movements you created in a dance about spaghetti. First, let me tell you what happens to the spaghetti in this dance. The dance begins with the spaghetti in a box. This is straight spaghetti. The box is opened and the spaghetti jumps out and travels from the box to a big round pot of boiling water in the middle of the kitchen. The spaghetti jumps into the water and begins to cook. It changes from a straight shape to a curved shape and travels in curved shapes through the pot of water. Then slowly a big bubble appears in the center of the pot. It becomes bigger and bigger, pushing the spaghetti pieces to the edges of the pot until they jump out of the pot and fly all over the kitchen. The spaghetti gets stuck to the wall in a curved shape and then slowly falls from the wall back to the middle of the kitchen and onto the dinner plate.

In this dance, you will be the straight and curved spaghetti. The dance begins with four boxes of spaghetti, one in each corner of the room. (See figure 8.6.) I will assign you a box of spaghetti for the beginning of the dance. When you get to the corner, organize the group into a line. Everyone is standing in a straight shape. On my signal, the first piece of spaghetti from each box travels from the box to the giant pot of water—the taped or painted circle in the middle of the room—keeping its body in a straight shape moving on a straight pathway. As soon as the first person begins, the next person can start until everyone is standing around the circle.

Next, the spaghetti will take a small jump into the pot when I hit the drum. Ready and jump! Very slowly begin to change your straight shape into a curved shape beginning with your feet; then your legs; waist; back; arms; and, finally, your head. Travel slowly in the circle, moving in between each other without touching. Keep changing into many different curved shapes. Use high and low levels as if you are swimming all through the pot of water. I see Krista is really curving her back in various ways as she cooks in the water. Theo is moving high and low as he changes curved shapes.

Now, just listen as I explain how we will add the part where the giant bubble appears. I will be a slow bubble that begins to grow in the middle of the pot. I will start low in a curved shape in the middle of the pot, then begin to make my shape bigger and bigger until I am stretched out in a wide shape. [Demonstrate how you will perform the bubble movements.] The spaghetti will begin to move to the edges of the pot until I wave my arms at you as if I am pushing you out of the pot. When you get to the edge, jump out. When everyone is out, the bubble spins around and the spaghetti runs and jumps as it flies around the kitchen. Everyone needs to run and jump in one direction around the circle. Remember to keep your curved shapes as you move around. Ready? Let's try the bubble. I want you to keep cooking as the bubble begins to grow. I am beginning to grow bigger and bigger, and now I stretch out into a wide shape. Begin to move to the edges of the pot and as I wave my arms, jump out. First, these pieces of spaghetti jump out, now these pieces, and these pieces over here. Oh, I cannot forget these pieces! Now everyone is out, and I begin to spin around. You begin to run and jump in curved shapes.

Now, the spaghetti becomes stuck to the wall. On the drumbeat, I want you to find a place to stick to the wall in a curved shape. What body part will you use to connect to the wall? Great, look at Andrew. He is standing on one foot in a curved shape and his arm is stuck to the wall. Find another way to stick to the wall and keep your curved shape. Now, very, very slowly find a way to keep your curved shape and travel from the wall to the center of the room, where the pot of water has now become the dinner plate. Slowly fall to the floor onto the plate and end in a curved shape. And that is how the dance ends. [You can repeat this section for additional practice.]

Let's go back to the beginning of the dance and try all the parts together. [Conduct a review by asking the following questions.] Who can tell me how the dance begins? What shape are you in? What happens next? When does the spaghetti change from a straight to a curved shape? How can you

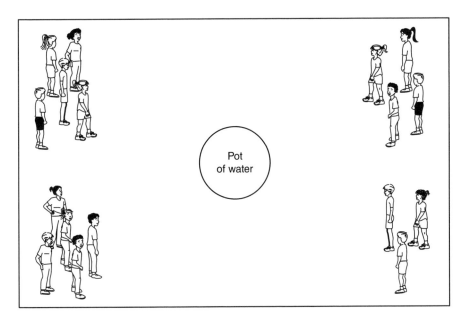

Figure 8.6 Children begin the dance pretending they are uncooked spaghetti standing in four boxes.

move in the pot of water and not bump into your friends? What happens to the spaghetti when the bubble appears? What movements do you use when you are flying around the kitchen? When you hear the drum, what happens? What shapes are you in? How will you move from the wall to the plate? What shape will you be in for the end of the dance? This dance starts slowly, becomes a little faster, then very fast, stops, and ends slowly. Any questions? Ready?

Let's try it from the beginning. The first time I will tell the story as you move, and the next time you can do the dance without my directions. [Children dance the story while you provide needed cues.]

Closure

Ask the children to identify which parts of the dance use light force, strong force, large movements, small movements, slow tempo, and fast tempo. Ask children to talk to another child about their favorite part of the dance. This partner discussion is referred to as pair-share.

Look For

- The many ways children create curved and straight shapes.
- How children move between one another when they are cooking in the pot of water. Can they do it without bumping into others?
- The transition from a straight shape to curved shapes. Does this change occur gradually or all at once?

How Can I Change This?

- Use two or three pots of water in the culminating dance, and the children can choose which one they want to use for their dance. You can also use two or three plates at the end of the dance.
- Repeat the section of the culminating dance where the spaghetti flies around the kitchen and sticks to the wall several times, instead of only once, so the children can find different places to stick to the wall.
- Children can travel to the pot of water connected. They can also stick to each other instead of the wall and then travel connected from the wall to the plate.
- Three or four children can dance the part of the bubble instead of you.
- Introduce the dance by reading the poem "Spaghetti" by Shel Silverstein (1974).
- Bring in a box of uncooked spaghetti and a pot of cooked spaghetti to use when you are telling the story.

Assessment Suggestions

- Student self-assessment—psychomotor and cognitive: Record a video of the class performing the dance, then show the video to the children and ask them to observe and describe how they each performed the straight and curved shapes. (outcomes 1, 2, 3, and 5)

(continued)

Spaghetti Dance *(continued)*

- Teacher assessment—psychomotor: Observe whether children can change from a straight to a curved shape as they jump into the pot of water and begin to cook. Record the observation on a checklist. (outcome 3)

- Student self-assessment—cognitive: The children recall their performance and choose a part they would like to improve and then perform the dance again and talk about what changes they made and how those changes improved their performance. (outcome 4)

- Student self-assessment—cognitive: Children draw themselves in a straight or curved shape that they used in the dance and label the drawing. (outcome 5)

Interdisciplinary Connections

- Language arts (literature): Introduce the dance using the humorous poem "Spaghetti" (Silverstein 1974).

- Visual art: Connect to visual arts concepts on how straight and curved lines appear in paintings and sculptures.

- Social studies: Include social studies concepts that discuss how noodles are part of the cuisine in a variety of cultures.

- Language arts (reading): Read from the book *Noodles* (Weeks and Carter 1996) as an introduction to the dance.

Balloon Dance

Outcomes

As a result of participating in this learning experience, children will be able to do the following:

1. Identify how they used their bodies to change their movements from small to big and big to small. (cognitive)

2. Collaborate with others in a group to create and practice a dance. (affective)

3. Perform the balloon dance in unison and demonstrate a slow change in movements from small to big. (psychomotor)

Organization

Children dance individually, with a partner, and in small groups.

Equipment Needed

- Balloon
- MP3 or CD player
- Slow music for accompaniment
- Drum

Introduction and Warm-Up

Today, we are going to dance using small movements that become bigger and bigger. What are some things that start small and become bigger? Our warm-up includes movements that are small and big. Find a personal space and make small movements with your fingers that open and close. Now, make the movement bigger by opening and closing your whole hand several times. Now, the open-and-close movement is bigger and uses your arms. Try the open-and-close movement jumping with your feet apart and then together. First, start with a few small jumps; then make your jumps wider and wider. The last part of the warm-up uses running, skipping, or galloping. Choose one of these three ways to travel in the space. Take 10 small steps, 10 medium-sized steps, and 10 giant steps. Now, do those 30 steps again. [Instruct the children to repeat the warm-up movements several times.]

Development

Sit on the floor and make a small round shape using your whole body. Great! I see that you have rounded your back, legs, arms, and head to make the shape. I am going to beat on the drum 8 times. On each count, make your shape bigger: 1, 2, 3, 4, 5, 6, 7, 8. [Play the drum and counts aloud as the children move.] Now, go back to your small round shape in 4 counts, becoming smaller and smaller: 1, 2, 3, 4. Let's try making the round shape big and small again. Ready to become bigger on each count? Now, make a different small shape. Choose a high, medium, or low level as you get smaller. As I play the drum, make your shape grow bigger in 8 counts and then smaller in 4 counts. Ready! Big 1, 2, 3, 4, 5, 6, 7, 8, and small 1, 2, 3, 4. This time, make your shape grow big in 4 counts and smaller in 2 counts. This will feel faster. Ready! Big 1, 2, 3, 4, and small 1, 2. Can you suggest a number of counts for becoming bigger and smaller? Sanam says to use 3 counts to get bigger and 13 counts to get smaller. Let's try it. I will beat the counts on the drum.

We are now going to explore small and big movements with one or more partners. You will face your partners and mirror each other's movements. One partner is the first leader, and then the others will take a turn as the leader. Brian and I will demonstrate. I will be the first leader, and Brian will mirror my movements. As the first partner, I will create movements that start low and small and become big and high. Be sure to go slowly so your partner can follow. [Demonstrate with a child.] Then, the next partner will create movements that start big and high and change to small and low. I will tell you when to switch partners. [Use slow music to accompany this exploration.] I will assign you a partner, and you can choose who will go first. Then begin when the music starts and change leaders when the music stops.

Now, I will organize you into groups of four or five children and you will stand in a circle. I want you to work together to find a way to make your circle become bigger and smaller. See if you can all move at the same time, as you did when you were mirroring your partner. Select a leader in the group who will tell the group when to begin moving and when to stop. Make sure you listen to everyone's ideas, then try the ideas out, and choose how your circle will move from small to big and back to small. After each group has practiced, we will share our dance with another group.

(continued)

Culminating Dance

For this next part, you'll stay in your small groups. You are going to create a dance about a balloon that inflates and deflates and, when it is fully inflated, all the air fizzles out. Your dance will be like this balloon I am going to blow up. [Blow up a balloon using the following sequence.] First, I blow just a little air into the balloon and then let the air out while holding onto the balloon. The second time, I blow more air into the balloon so it is bigger and then let all the air out. Then, I blow the balloon up a third time so it is bigger than the first two times and, again, let the air out. Then, the fourth time I inflate the balloon to its fullest and let it go so it flies around as the air comes out. Watch to see how it flies around in the air. How does it move? Show me with your hand. [Let go of the fully inflated balloon.]

Use this sequence for your group dance. Your group will need to decide what movements you are going to use to show the balloon inflating and deflating four times, with the balloon becoming bigger each time before the air goes out. Then, choose what movements you will use to show the balloon flying around as the air comes out. How will the balloon land on the floor? Listen to each person's ideas for the dance, try them out, and choose the movements for the group. One person will need to be the leader to tell the group when to inflate and deflate and when to let all the air out and fall to the floor. I will come by each group to see if you need any help. Practice your sequence several times to make sure everyone is moving together. Can you add any voice accompaniment to your dance? When you are ready we will stop and show the dances to the other groups. [Visit all the groups as they create their dances.]

Each group will share their balloon dance with the class. Before you perform, tell the class how your group chose the movements for the dance. The observers need to look for the pathway of the fizzle movement.

Closure

I want your group to sit together and talk about how you worked together to create the dance. Each person needs to say something about the dance. Then, make up a name for your balloon dance. [Children spend a few minutes talking, and then they are asked to share some of the comments and tell the rest of the class the name of their dance.]

Look For

- How children perform the mirroring activity. Are the movements too fast to follow, or are children moving slowly?

- How well the children use unison movements in the small group as children find a way to move from small to big. Can they all make their movements grow bigger at the same time?

- How well the groups work together sharing ideas.

How Can I Change This?

- The dance can be taught as a full-class experience with everyone as part of one balloon circle. Working as a single large group may be more appropriate for young children.

- The children can add a floating part to the dance after the balloon is fully inflated and before the air fizzles out. They can move slowly up and down like they are floating in the air.

- The dance can end with the balloon popping instead of the air fizzling out.

Assessment Suggestions

- Teacher assessment—affective: During the time when students are creating their dances, observe how each group collaborates. Does each person have an opportunity to voice his or her idea? Does the group try different ideas and then choose one or more for the dance? Are they using the time to practice the dance moving in unison? (outcome 2)

- Teacher assessment—cognitive: As the groups are involved in the closure discussion, visit each group and ask this question: How did you change your movements to show that the balloon was getting bigger each time it inflated? (outcome 1)

- Teacher assessment—psychomotor: Assess the students' ability to move in unison as a group and slowly show how the body shapes change from small to big (see figure 8.7). (outcome 3)

Interdisciplinary Connections

- Language arts (poetry): Introduce the dance by reading aloud the poems "Eight Balloons" (Silverstein 1981) or "Balloons" (Chandra 1993).

- Science: Connect to science concepts on air currents, flight, or force.

- Social studies: Include a discussion on how people use balloons to celebrate events to connect with social studies concepts on celebrations and traditions.

Groups for balloon dance	Rubric: Excellent Criteria: All students performed the dance in unison, and the movements clearly demonstrated a slow change in tempo from small to big.	Rubric: Good Criteria: Only two or three students were in unison and the change from small to big demonstrated different tempos.
Group A: John, Sasha, Steph, Arthur	X	
Group B: Chelsea, Nijah, Joe, Carly		X Joe jumped too fast. Carly did not move at all.
Group C: Al, Mora, Ken, Meaghan	X	
Group D: Alexa, Jermaine, Kendra, Rob	X	

Figure 8.7 Assessment instrument for balloon dance.

Outcomes

As a result of participating in this learning experience, children will be able to do the following:

1. Match the quality and tempo of their movements to the sound of a drum, a triangle, and a set of maracas. (psychomotor and cognitive)

2. Move using contrasting light and strong forces and fast and slow tempos. (psychomotor)

3. Balance while moving and while holding still shapes. (psychomotor)

Organization

Children begin the lesson moving individually and then divide into three groups for the culminating dance. The room is set up with each instrument in a different space (see figure 8.8).

Equipment Needed

- Drum
- Triangle
- Set of maracas

Introduction and Warm-Up

Today, we are going to create movements to the sound of a drum, a triangle, and the maracas. I will show you the instruments and then demonstrate the different sounds each one can make. [Play each instrument to demonstrate the sounds it makes. First, a light drumbeat is played 8 times and then a strong drumbeat 8 times. Next, the triangle is tapped once, and then after the sound ends, it is tapped again. Next, the triangle is played lightly and rapidly. Finally, the maracas are shaken slowly and lightly and then strongly and rapidly.]

We will use each instrument in our warm-up. First, we are going to begin with the sound of the drum. As I play slowly and lightly, lie on the floor and slowly stretch your arms and legs as if you are just waking up. Now, sit and stretch, and then slowly rise to standing and continue to stretch. Let's repeat the stretching with the drum. Now, I am going to play the drum strongly and quickly, and I want you to reach in different directions on each beat. Next, we'll do the triangle. On each tap of the triangle, take one giant slow step forward. [Tap the triangle 8 times.] This time go backward as I tap the triangle. As I shake the maracas, I want you to take small running steps in the space. When you hear the maracas stop, freeze in a shape. [Play and stop the maracas several times.]

Development

Everyone move to the space where the drum is placed. We will begin to explore movement using the light and strong beats of the drum. Begin standing in a frozen shape. When I play the drum lightly, you will find a way to do small light leaps, hops, or jumps in different directions and stop when the drum stops. [Play the 8 light beats in a medium tempo, and the children explore light leaps, hops, and jumps.] Let's try this a few more times. Can you change your movement and the direction?

Next, I will play 8 strong drumbeats, and on each beat I want you to take a big strong leap,

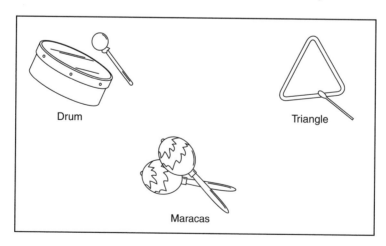

Figure 8.8 Instruments are placed in three spaces in the room.

hop, or jump and then freeze in a shape. [Give the ready cue and then play the 8 strong beats at a medium tempo.] Let's try this again. This time mix up the leaps, hops, and jumps while you move to the 8 beats. Remember to make the frozen shapes when you land. [Play the 8 strong beats.] Let's try this again.

Now, I will play 8 light drumbeats, then 8 strong drumbeats. Take small light leaps, hops, or jumps, then big strong leaps, hops, or jumps adding the frozen shapes. [Play 8 light beats then 8 strong beats.] Now, let's try this with 6 light beats and 6 strong beats. Now, move using 4 light and 4 strong beats. Finally, move with only 2 light and then 2 strong beats. This is the drum dance. Let's put it all together, first using 8 light and strong, then 6, then 4, and then 2. Can you do it? [Play the drum while the children perform.]

Now, everyone walk over to the triangle. Listen to how long the sound lasts after each tap. Sit on the floor, move your arms slowly, and keep them moving until you can no longer hear the triangle after the first tap. [Tap the triangle.] Let's try again. Now, stand up and take one step each time you hear me tap the triangle. [Make 4 taps.] Step-step-step-step. Try taking the steps backward or sideward this time. [Tap the triangle.] Step-step-step-step. This time, combine the steps and the slow arm movement for 4 beats. [Tap the triangle.] Now, as I play the triangle faster, find a way to turn your body around quickly; you can choose any level. [Tap the triangle quickly 8 times.] Try a different turn. [Quickly tap the triangle 8 times.] Now, combine the 4 slow steps using the arms with the 8 fast taps for turning. [Play 4 slow taps, then 8 quick taps.] Let's repeat this triangle dance again. Remember to take 4 slow steps and then do your quick turns.

Let's move to the third space where we will dance to a set of two maracas. Listen to how the sound changes when I shake them lightly and then strongly. I will start with a light shake as I move the maracas just a little. [Play the maracas to demonstrate the different sounds.] Begin a small shaking movement in your fingertips as I shake the maracas lightly. Keep the movement small and light. Now, let the shaking go to your hands, forearms, elbows, and all the way up your arms to the shoulders. Now, try the shaking beginning with your toe, then your whole foot, your leg, and then up to your hips. Is there another body part where you can begin shaking and then let it move to other parts of your body? I see Cole and Jenny have chosen their heads, others are beginning

the shaking in their bellies, and Carmen chose to start in her shoulder. This time, listen as I change the sound from light to strong and show that change of force in the shaking of your arm. Begin the shaking small and light and let it become strong and big as the maracas become louder. [Shake maracas.] Try light-to-strong shaking in your legs, starting with your toes and going all the way up to your hips. Now, begin shaking your whole body, going from light and small to strong and big. Try this lying on the floor, then sitting, and now standing. Each time I play the maracas from light to strong, start the shaking with a different body part. Also, choose if you will be lying down, sitting, or standing. [Shake the maracas for about 10 to 15 seconds.] Find a way to travel with the shaking movement, beginning with light and small movements and increasing the movements to strong and big. Can you take the strong shaking up off the floor into a jump? [Shake maracas for 10 to 15 seconds.]

Now, let's combine the light and strong shaking into a dance. Ready? [Children move as you tell the story.] The children are sleeping on the floor. They wake up slowly by shaking lightly. Then they stand up and continue to lightly shake. The shaking begins in one body part, and then more body parts begin to shake until the whole body is shaking. The children go out to play. The shaking grows stronger and the children shake with big and strong movements as they travel in the space. The shaking suddenly stops, and the children freeze in a shape. The children resume the shaking as they return home and slowly fall to the floor and go back to sleep.

Culminating Dance

Now, when you perform the three dances, you may choose which one you want to dance to first, second, and third. Think about your order for the dances. Now, everyone who wants to dance first to the drum go over to the drum space. Those who are dancing to the triangle first go to the triangle place. And those who are dancing first to the maracas go to where the maracas are placed. Only one group will dance at a time while the other two groups sit and observe.

I will play the drum first. Ready, drum dancers? Remember to make clear changes between the light and strong movements as I play the light and strong drumbeats. [Play the sequence of beats while the children dance.]

Now, I will play for the triangle dancers. Who can tell us what type of dance goes with the triangle?

(continued)

Juwon explains, "You take four slow steps on each tap, then fast turns on the fast taps." Okay, ready, everyone? Let's try it all together. [Play the triangle sequence while the children dance.]

The third dance is the maracas. Here, the dancers perform a story about waking up, going out to play, and then going back to sleep—all through shaking movements. Observing children, watch how the shaking starts small and light and becomes bigger and stronger. I will tell the story as I play the maracas. The dancers begin to wake up by lightly shaking. Now, they stand up and begin the light shaking in one body part and now more body parts begin to lightly shake. Next, they go out to play as the shaking becomes bigger and stronger. They begin to travel in the space shaking and shaking, sometimes jumping into the air. The maracas suddenly stop, the dancers freeze, and then they lose their strong shaking energy and lightly shake all the way home and go back to sleep.

Now, I want everyone to point to the next instrument you want to dance to and walk to that place. [Remind the children to walk as they change from one instrument area to another. Excited children will tend to begin running to an area.] I will play the instruments in the same way, beginning with the drum dance, and then the triangle dance, and ending with the maraca dance. When you are not dancing, I want you to notice how your classmates are showing light and strong force as they dance. [Children perform their second dance and then move to the third instrument to perform their third dance.]

Closure

I will assign partners, and I want you to tell each other the order of your dances and your favorite dance. [Children spend a few minutes sharing their experiences with each other.] Now, I would like to hear about your favorite dance. [Ask a few children to talk about their favorite dance.]

Look For

- How children perform strong and light movements. Are they able to clearly demonstrate the difference in the force?

- What dances the children choose first, second, and third. You may want to discuss with them why they chose a certain order. Which dances did they like to perform or which one did they least prefer?

How Can I Change This?

- Play different instruments.
- Use more or fewer instruments.
- Add a specific rhythm to each instrument instead of playing the regular beats.
- The children can develop their own stories to accompany the instruments for their dances.
- Ask the children to play the instruments.

Assessment Suggestions

- Student self-assessment—cognitive: Students draw a picture of the instruments or themselves dancing to one of the instruments and add words to describe how they moved their body. (outcome 1)

- Peer assessment—psychomotor: Students organized in partners as observers and performers. One partner assigned as the performer dances the movements connected with the instrument while the other partner observes. After the performance, the observer tells the performer if their movements corresponded to the instrument. Partners reverse roles. (outcome 1)

- Teacher assessment—psychomotor: Record anecdotal notes about children who demonstrate difficulty with balance in the slow movements and frozen shapes. For example, Shanida was unable to hold the frozen shapes still, and she lost her balance three times. (outcome 3)

- Teacher assessment—psychomotor: Use a checklist to note whether the children can demonstrate strong and light and fast and slow movements. At the end of the learning experience, ask four students at a time to perform a strong movement, then a light movement, then a fast movement and then a slow movement. This procedure continues until all children in the class have had an opportunity to perform. (outcome 2)

Interdisciplinary Connections

- Music: Connect to music concepts focused on types of percussion instruments, timbre, and tempo.

- Language arts (writing): Children write stories inspired by the dance sequences or write stories and then express them through dance and percussion instruments.

The Hungry Cat

Outcomes

As a result of participating in this learning experience, children will be able to do the following:

1. Perform movements using fast and slow tempos. (psychomotor)
2. Move a body part in isolation. (psychomotor)
3. Remember the dance sequence and perform a dance without teacher cues. (psychomotor and cognitive)

Organization

Children will dance individually throughout the entire learning experience.

Equipment Needed

Percussion instruments—a drum and a triangle

Introduction and Warm-Up

In this dance learning experience, we are going to find different ways to move fast and slow. We will then do a dance about a hungry cat who moves fast and slow. We'll start with a warm-up using slow and fast movements.

When I say go, find a personal space and run in place as fast as you can. Go! Now run in place as slowly as you can. Now find a different way to travel through general space as fast as you can. Find another way. What are some of the ways you traveled fast? [Children share their answers with the class.] Now move through space as slowly as you can, taking a long time for each step. Find another slow way to move. How slow can you go? Can someone show the class how slow they can travel in the space? [Select several children to demonstrate moving slowly.]

Think of some things that you do to get ready for school in the morning. [Children answer with morning routines such as brushing teeth, getting dressed, eating cereal.] We are going to pretend to do some of these slow and then fast. Ready? Let's all do the movement of brushing our teeth as fast as we can, now as slowly as we can. Now, try slowly putting on your clothes; now, get dressed as fast as you can. The third movement is about eating a bowl of cereal very slowly. Shake the cereal into the bowl slowly, pour the milk slowly, take your spoon and scoop up the cereal slowly, and put it in your mouth slowly. Now, eat the cereal as fast as you can. Feel the difference in your muscles when you move fast and slow. Can someone tell us what that feels like?

Development

Today, I am going to play a triangle for all of our slow movements. Listen to how long the sound lasts after I hit the triangle. Now, begin to move your arms when I hit the triangle and continue to keep them moving until you do not hear the triangle. [Tap the triangle once.] Keep your movement smooth and slow. Feel your arm moving for a long time. Can you keep the movement going? Now, try this with another body part. I want to see if you can listen to the sound and move one body part slowly until the sound of the triangle stops. I see that some of you are moving your arms forward and backward, some are moving their arms together and apart, and some are moving one arm and then the other. Some children are moving their shoulders, their legs, and their whole bodies. Notice how each movement takes a long time when you move slowly.

I will play fast drumbeats to accompany the fast movement. See if you can move your arms as fast as you can until you hear the drum stop. [Play fast drumbeats for a few seconds.] Try moving your arms high and low, forward and backward, together and apart. [Again play fast drumbeats for a few seconds.] This time, point with your arm to a different corner of the room as fast as you can on each of the 4 drumbeats. [Play 4 drumbeats as the children point.] Try pointing with the other arm. [Again, play 4 drumbeats as the children point.] We will use this movement in our cat dance.

This time, run as fast as you can and stop when you no longer hear the drum. [Play fast drumbeats for 10 seconds.] This time, add a leap or jump to the run as I play the fast drumbeats. [Play fast drumbeats for 10 seconds.] Try this again and make sure you land on your feet with your knees bent at the end of the jump or leap. [Play fast drumbeats for 10 seconds. Children practice this movement several times.]

Culminating Dance

Now, it is time for the hungry cat dance. Everyone find a personal space and lie on the floor. We are going to practice each part of the dance first and then put them all together. In the first part, the

(continued)

cat is sleeping. What are the different shapes a cat uses for sleeping? Yes, curved, perhaps stretched. Find another sleeping cat shape and another. I see many of you in round curled shapes, some of you are on your backs, others are sleeping on their sides. (See figure 8.9.) Change slowly from one sleeping shape to another each time you hear the triangle sound. I will tap the triangle four times. Ready? [Make four taps on the triangle.] Make your first sleeping shape, now slowly change to your second shape, now take a third shape, and finish by moving slowly into the fourth and last shape. That was great! You used four different sleeping shapes and moved very slowly into each shape.

Next, still lying on the floor, the cat begins to wake up and stretch slowly. On each tap of the triangle, I will tell you a body part to stretch. [Make one tap on the triangle.] The cat stretches one arm reaching high with its paw. [Make a second tap on the triangle.] Now, the other arm stretches high. [Make a third tap on the triangle.] Now, the cat stretches one leg up high reaching with its foot. [Make a fourth tap on the triangle.] Then the cat stretches up the other leg. The cat sits up and slowly moves its head, then its back, and then its shoulders. [Make three taps on the triangle: one each for the head, back, and shoulders.] The cat stands up slowly onto two feet. Make sure you take your time as you stretch each part of your body as you wake up. This is the beginning of the dance. All the movements are smooth and slow. Let's practice this part again.

Now, in the second part, we will change to make fast sudden movements on each drumbeat. The cat will move fast when it suddenly sees and points to a mouse. Move your arm quickly to point to a corner of the room. The cat sees a mouse over there! Now, the

mouse has moved to another corner; point to that one. Oh, no, the mouse moved to another corner! Point to it! And now point to the last corner as the mouse moves one last time. Make your pointing movements strong and fast. I will beat the drum once for each pointing movement. Ready? Point, point, point, point. [Beat the drum.]

In the third part, the cat chases the mouse around the room. I will beat the drum very fast, and you will run adding leaps and jumps. Ready? [Beat the drum fast for about 10 seconds while the children run after the imaginary mouse.]

In the next part, the cat catches the mouse by taking one big jump. The cat slowly bends forward to pick up the mouse by the tail, opens its mouth, and drops the mouse in. Now, the cat is so tired after chasing and eating the mouse that it slowly moves back to the place where it was sleeping. I will play one loud drumbeat to cue the jump. [Play one loud drumbeat.] Then, I will play the triangle to accompany the slow movements as you pretend to pick up the mouse, eat it, and go back to sleep. Let's try this part of the cat story. Begin with a jump and bend down slowly to pick up the mouse; pretend to drop it in your mouth, and add a stretch and yawn to show you are tired before you slowly go back to sleep. [Play the drum and triangle as the children dance the sequence of movements.] Let's try this part again.

Now, let's put all the story parts together into one big dance. I will play the instruments while I tell the story. Then, the second time you will do the dance by yourself. [Play the instruments and tell the story while the children dance.] Now, I will play the instruments and not tell you the story. You can dance the story because you have practiced it now a few

Figure 8.9   In the beginning of the hungry cat dance, the cats are sleeping.

times. Before we begin, can someone describe the dance? [One or more children describe all or part of the dance.] Be clear about making the slow movements slow and the fast movements fast. Feel the difference in tempo as you dance.

Closure

Can anyone suggest any new parts we could add to this cat dance? Are there any parts we should take out of the dance?

Look For

- How well children can change from fast to slow movements. Is the difference clear?
- How effectively children can move in the space without bumping into each other during the mouse chase.

How Can I Change This?

- During the development section, you can divide the room into two zones: the fast zone, where the children can perform the fast movements, and the slow zone, where the slow movements are performed.
- Develop short movement sequences that combine fast and slow movements. For example, children choose a movement and perform it using this sequence: slow-fast-slow or fast-slow-fast. Try different combinations with nonlocomotor and locomotor movements.
- Children are organized into partners. One partner does a fast or slow movement, and the other partner responds doing the same movement in the opposite tempo. For example, partner 1 touches the head with the hands, turns around, and makes a stretched shape using a

fast tempo. Partner 2 responds by doing the same three movements using a slow tempo.

Assessment Suggestions

- Peer assessment—psychomotor: Students are organized into partners. One partner calls out a nonlocomotor movement and chooses a fast or slow tempo, and the other partner performs the movements. For example, "Wiggle your whole body fast," or "Twist slow." Students take turns. Repeat this activity using locomotor movements. (outcome 1)
- Teacher assessment—psychomotor: Use a checklist to observe whether children can isolate body parts in the part of the dance where the cat wakes up. You can assess this part of the dance while the children are dancing. (outcome 2)
- Teacher assessment—psychomotor and cognitive: Record a video of half of the class performing the dance without teacher cues and then record the other half. Later review the video to assess whether children remember the sequence and clearly demonstrate the fast and slow movements. (outcome 3)

Interdisciplinary Connections

- Language arts (reading): Introduce the cat dance by reading stories or poems about cat adventures.
- Science: Integrate this dance with science concepts focused on animal life.
- Visual arts: Add visual arts and music through creating cat and mouse masks and using music with an emphasis on slow and fast tempos.

Circus Dance

Outcomes

As a result of participating in this learning experience, children will be able to do the following:

1. Identify and perform locomotor and nonlocomotor movements at different levels that relate to the circus animals and performers. (cognitive and psychomotor)
2. Perform one of the four circus dances. (psychomotor)
3. Balance while traveling and holding still shapes. (psychomotor)
4. Choose a favorite character or animal that they performed in the circus dance. (affective)

Organization

This learning experience includes four dances: the galloping horses, the tightrope walkers, the lions and tigers, and the funny clowns. Three of the dances require children to dance individually, and one dance, the funny clowns, uses partners or small groups.

Equipment Needed

- MP3 or CD player
- Circus-type music or lively music
- A stick with multiple streamers taped to the end to be used by the circus leader
- Three hoops for the lions and tigers
- Painted, chalked, or taped lines on the floor for the tightrope walkers
- Whiteboard or poster to write the order of the circus dances

Introduction and Warm-Up

Has anyone been to the circus? What did you see? [Children share their experiences.] Today, we are going to turn our room into a circus with galloping horses, tightrope walkers, lions and tigers, and funny clowns. You are going to be the circus performers, and I will be the circus ringleader. [You can share books or pictures about the circus.]

For our warm-up today, we will practice moving high and low and forward, backward, and sideward. I will organize you into groups of four or five, and each person in the group will have a number from 1 to 4 or 5. Then, when I play the music, person 1 will step into the center of the circle and create a movement that moves high and low. You can use your whole body or only one body part. Everyone in the group follows the leader and does the same movement. Then, I will say "change" and person 2 will do a different high and low movement and everyone will follow. Everyone will have a turn to create a movement. [Play the music and call "change" after 15 seconds until everyone has had a turn as the leader.] The second part of the warm-up is just like the first except your movements will be forward and backward or side to side. Let's begin this time with person 5 and end with person 1. [Play the music and call "change" after 15 seconds until everyone has had a turn as the leader.]

Development

This learning experience is composed of four short dances about the circus. The first dance is about the galloping horses. Let's explore different ways to gallop. First, make a shape with your hands and arms that are like two front hooves. Your hands can be close together, wide apart, or one high and one low. Keep the hand and arm shape as you gallop forward. Can you gallop in a large circle pathway? Now try a small circle. Can you pretend you are a horse leaping into the air as you gallop? Can two or three horses gallop in the space with one horse as the leader? Now change leaders and the pathway. [Play the music while the children practice.]

Next are the tightrope walkers. For this circus act, you will use the lines on the floor as the tightropes. Find a line and begin to walk forward. Can you change your level to low and high as you walk? How about walking backward? Can you walk and turn or hop or jump and stay on the line? Find a way to balance on one foot. Be still and count to 5. Can you find another way to make a still, balanced shape? How about another balanced shape? Now, you will choose three tricks for your tightrope act. You will need a locomotor movement, a still balance, and a turn. You can change levels and directions but keep the movements slow. Now, practice your tightrope act. [Play the music while the children practice. Also, you can write the three components of the tightrope act on the chalkboard or on chart paper.]

Our next circus performers are the lions and tigers. In this circus act, the lions and tigers will stay low to the floor and walk on their hands and feet, stretch up as they let out a loud roar, jump through a hoop, and roll on the floor. Let's practice the walking on hands and feet. Show me how you can walk on your hands and feet using small steps, now big steps. [Children may need a brief rest due to the strength involved in using the arms to support the body weight.] Now, let's practice the lion and tiger roar. Kneel down and sit back on your heels with your hands touching the floor. This is the waiting shape. [You are holding a stick with streamers attached, and when you raise the stick the children stretch up and use their voices to make a loud roaring sound.] When I raise the stick, this is the signal for the lions and tigers to stretch their front paws and let out a loud roar. When I move the stick down, the lions and tigers stop the roar and return to the waiting shape. Let's try this a couple times. How high can you stretch your arms and how loud can you roar? [Move the stick up and down a few times and the children follow the signal.] In the next trick, the lions and tigers jump through the hoop and roll on the floor while reaching with their paws. [You or several children can hold hoops vertically as the children jump through the hoop and then do a sideward roll, similar to a log roll. The hoops can be held at different places in the space. Also, play the music while the children practice.]

The final act of the circus is the funny juggling clowns. You are going to pretend that you are juggling. Let's create many ways to juggle. [A light juggling scarf can be added as a prop.] First, put a big smile on your face and move your arms and hands to show a juggling movement. Can you juggle while walking forward or backward? Try juggling lying on your back, kneeling, sitting, standing on one foot. What other ways can you juggle? Turn and face another person and pretend you are juggling together. Can you move high and low at the same time or opposite each other? Can you move apart and then together while you juggle? Select three juggling ideas, choose the order, and practice the first idea, the second, and the third without stopping. [Play the music while the children practice.]

Culminating Dance

Welcome to the circus! Now, we will combine the four dances into one dance. The first time we per-

form the dance, everyone will do all the dances in the order we learned them. The second time, you may choose which dances you would like to perform. When you are not performing, you will be the audience. On the whiteboard I have drawn a picture of each circus act in the order we will perform them. (See figure 8.10.)

The galloping horses will start. I want everyone to make one line. When I introduce the galloping horses, you will gallop in a large circle. Then, listen for my instructions to show your horse tricks. Here we go! And now for the talented galloping horses! [Use the stick with streamers to direct the first child in line to lead the gallop. This is also a good time to play the music.] Watch them as they gallop together in a big circle. Now, for their first trick, horses take small gallops in their own small circle. Can you gallop in the other direction? Next, gallop and jump or leap into the air. Horses stop, turn in place, and take a bow.

In our next circus act, I ask you to look high above the crowd to see the amazing tightrope walkers. [Ask everyone to take his or her starting place on a line.] The tightrope walkers will do three tricks today: traveling forward and backward, a still balance, and a turn. Here they go. [Play the music while the children perform their movements.] Everyone is staying on the line—great balance and control! What a great group of performers. Amazing! Tightrope walkers, take a bow.

Figure 8.10 Children can refer to the drawings on the whiteboard or poster to see the order of the circus acts.

(continued)

The third circus act introduces the fabulous lions and tigers. I want everyone to sit side by side, on a line, facing me. When I introduce the lions and tigers, I want you to walk forward on your hands and feet taking 10 steps and then kneel down in the waiting shape. We will do the roaring stretch three times, jump through the hoops, and roll back to the line where you started. [Assign three children to hold the hoops. One-third of the performers are assigned to each hoop.] And now for the fabulous lions and tigers—here they come! Don't be afraid—they are friendly. Now, watch them roar when I lift my stick. And roar! [Lift the stick up and down three times.] Now, watch how skillfully they jump through the hoops and roll. Will my assistants please hold the hoops? [The children make three lines and jump through their assigned hoop. The jumping may be repeated several times.] Okay, lions and tigers, take a bow.

Our final circus act is the funny juggling clowns. They will perform their many juggling tricks. [Children stand around the perimeter of the room and begin their imaginary juggling when the music starts.] Some are juggling low to the floor, some are moving backward, and some are juggling with other clowns. Wow! Look at all the super juggling! That was great! Now, take a bow.

This time, I will introduce the circus act and you may choose to perform or be in the audience.

Closure

Each child shows one movement from any one of the dances and the rest of the group will guess which circus act the movement represents.

Look For

- Ways to encourage leadership in the dances by assigning children a specific role or asking children to take responsibility for leading a small group or the whole class.
- Children who may need help structuring their sequences in the tightrope and clown dances. They can write or draw the sequence to help them organize and remember their dance.

How Can I Change This?

- Use different circus acts such as the balancing elephants, swinging trapeze performers, dancing bears, jumping and turning seals, or galloping equestrians.

- Children can work in small groups to create their own galloping horse dance using circle pathways moving right and left and forward and backward.
- Tightrope walkers can perform in partners using a leading-and-following relationship.
- Lions and tigers can create different ways to jump through the hoops using different directions or shapes.
- The juggling clowns can create funny bows at the end of their act.
- Props and costumes can be added, such as scarves and streamers.
- Use a different piece of music for each circus act. Use popular music or look for music that traditionally accompanies a circus.
- The culminating dance can include a circus parade with the children choosing a character for the parade.

Assessment Suggestions

- Student self-assessment—affective: Students draw a picture of their favorite part of the circus. They can include a movement they performed or draw the circus character. (outcome 4)
- Teacher assessment—psychomotor: Complete a checklist that records whether students can perform the locomotor and nonlocomotor movements in correct order representing the animals or performers in one of the four circus dances. (outcomes 1 and 2)
- Teacher assessment—cognitive: Students write a list of the locomotor movements they used in each of the dances. Review the list to note students' accuracy in identifying locomotor movements. (outcome 1)
- Peer assessment—psychomotor: Students are organized into groups of three or four and show each other the different balances they performed in the tightrope walkers' dance. Peers comment on how well the performers held their shape still. (outcome 3)

Interdisciplinary Connections

- Language arts (literature): Connect to children's literature using the illustrations in *Circus* (Wildsmith 1970) or *Circus 1-2-3* (Halsey 2000).

- Social studies or science: Integrate the circus dance with a unit in social studies or science focused on animal characteristics or how people interact with animals.
- Language arts (writing): Use the dance to initiate writing stories about the circus acts.

- Language arts (vocabulary): Create vocabulary lists based on words connected to the dance, such as *tightrope walkers, galloping, lions, tigers, rolling, balance, hooves, clowns, juggling,* or *roar.*

Connect the Spots

Outcomes

As a result of participating in this learning experience, children will be able to do the following:

1. Perform locomotor movements, such as run, jog, skip, slide, hop, jump, gallop, and walk. (psychomotor)

2. Practice making twisted, straight, and curved or round shapes with their body and holding the shape still for 8 counts. (psychomotor)

3. Create and perform a dance using twisted, straight, curved, or round shapes and locomotor movements. (cognitive and psychomotor)

Organization

Children dance individually with the whole class.

Equipment Needed

- A whiteboard or chart paper listing locomotor movements and shapes
- Plastic poly spots

Introduction and Warm-Up

Today's lesson is focused on creating a dance that uses locomotor movements and still (also called frozen) shapes. The warm-up is a review of locomotor movements and shapes. It is called move and freeze. When the music is on, you will move using a locomotor movement. When the music is paused, you will freeze in a shape. First, I will call out a locomotor movement, and you will move using that movement. When the music is paused, I will call out a type of shape and you will freeze your body in that shape. [Following is a list of locomotor movements and shapes to call out. The music can be played for 10 to 15 seconds and the shapes held still for 5 to 10 seconds.]

Walk slowly taking giant steps (twisted shape).

Skip and swing your arms (tall, stretched shape).

Jog at a medium speed (low, round shape).

Gallop alternating right and left feet (wide shape).

Slide sideways to the right (curved shape).

Hop on right foot 4 times then the left foot 4 times and repeat the pattern (twisted shape with stretched arms).

Run forward using small steps (big shape on one foot).

Slide sideways to the left (stretched shape from the waist down and a twisted shape from the waist up).

Walk backward taking giant steps (low, twisted shape).

Ask children to suggest a locomotor movement and a shape. This can be repeated two or three times.

Development

Next, you will choose three plastic poly spots, and you will use them to mark spots in the space for your connect-the-spots dance. (See figure 8.11.) The first spot is like first base, and on this spot you will freeze in a twisted shape for 8 counts. Go to your first spot, place the poly spot on the floor, and freeze in a twisted shape and let's all count to 8. [Set a medium tempo for the 8 counts and ask the children to count out loud at the same tempo.] Next, point to another spot in the space; this is like second base. On this spot you will freeze on your second poly spot in a round, low shape for 8 counts. Now, go to that spot and freeze in a round, low shape and let's all count to 8. Finally, choose a third spot that is far away from the other two spots and on this poly spot freeze in a stretched shape that is tall or wide. Move to that spot, freeze in a stretched shape, and let's all count to 8. Let's review the three spots. Move to your first spot and freeze in a twisted shape and count out loud for 8 counts, now move to your second spot and freeze in a low, round shape and count out loud for 8 counts, and now to your third spot and freeze in a stretched shape and count out loud for 8 counts. Now, practice by yourself moving to each spot, freezing in your shape, and counting to 8. [Observe to see if the children are freezing in the shapes and counting to 8.]

Now it's time to create a dance called connect the spots. You will choose a locomotor movement that will take you from one spot to another. For example, you can begin on spot 1, skip to spot 2 and make your shape, and skip to spot 3 and freeze in your third shape. Or, you can use two different locomotor movements—one movement to go from spot 1 to 2 and a different movement to go from spot 2 to 3. Let's do the dance together. Everyone go to spot 1, make your twisted shape, and let's count to 8. Now, show me how you are going to move to spot 2. Freeze in your low, round shape and let's count to 8. Now, show me how you are going to move to spot 3. Freeze in your stretched shape and let's count to 8. Everyone practice the dance again. Begin on spot 1 in your twisted shape and count out loud to 8. Now, do your locomotor movement to spot 2. Freeze in the low rounded shape and count to 8. Now, use another locomotor movement to travel to the third spot and show me how still you can be in the stretched shape while you count to 8. Now, go back to the beginning and do the whole dance by yourself. Remember your shapes and locomotor movements. [Observe whether the children can hold the shapes and use locomotor movements to travel to the spots; also listen for the counting.]

Culminating Dance

[As a way to provide imagery and meaning to the shapes and movement, ask the children to think about an animal who will be dancing their connect-the-spots dance.] Think of an animal you would like to be while performing your connect-the-spots dance. The dance will tell the story about the animal. On spot 1, the animal is sleeping in a twisted shape, then it wakes up and goes out to play while moving to spot 2. Let's try this first part of the story. Show me your sleeping animal on spot 1. Is it in a twisted shape? Now wake up and move using a locomotor movement to spot 2. [Observe the children's actions; you can choose to repeat this first part of the story if needed.] On spot 2 your animal is frozen in a low, round shape to show they are looking for food on the ground. Can you stay still and just move your fingers? Next, the animal goes out to play while it moves to spot 3. Show me how you move to spot 3 and freeze in a stretched shape. In this shape the animal is showing how happy they are. This is the end of the dance and the story. Let's try it again from the beginning. Ready? On spot 1 your animal is still and sleeping. Quietly count to 8. Wake up and move to spot 2. Freeze and nibble on some delicious food. Quietly count to 8. Okay, time to go out to play and move to spot 3. Freeze in your stretched happy shape. Quietly count to 8. Try the whole dance by yourself. Remember your shapes and counting to 8. [The children all perform their individual dances at the same time while you observe.]

Closure

There are a couple ways to bring closure to the learning experience. One way is to add music to

Figure 8.11 Children use poly spots to mark spots in the general space for their connect-the-spots dance.

(continued)

the dance. You can use children's popular songs or use folk or square dance music that has a lively tempo. A second way is to ask half of the class to be the audience and watch while the other half of the class performs their dances. Before the children perform, they can tell the audience the type of animal they have selected for their dance. Then switch groups to allow each child to be an audience member and a performer.

Look For

- Children who are having difficulty holding the shapes still for 8 counts. You can stand next to the child while they make the still shapes and count with them, or ask them to move with a peer buddy who can help with the counting.

- A child who may need help remembering where his or her three spots are located. You can mark their poly spots with a number to identify the dance order.

How Can I Change This?

- The next step is to add a pathway to the locomotor movements. What are different pathways you can move along? Chantelle says straight or curvy, and Gina suggested a circle pathway or zigzag. Any others? Karen came up with pathways with lots of angles or a pathway that looks like someone scribbled on the page. These are all great ideas. Let's try them with the locomotor movements. [Following are tasks you can use to combine locomotor movements and pathways.]

    Run forward on a curvy pathway, and on my signal, stop and freeze in a low, round shape.

    Skip on a straight pathway and when you come close to the wall, turn and move on another straight pathway. Stop and freeze in a wide, stretched shape.

    Gallop on a spiral pathway that begins in a big circle and becomes smaller and smaller. When the pathway becomes very small, reverse the spiral, moving from a small circle back to the big circle. Stop and freeze in a twisted shape using one hand and one foot to support your body.

    Slide using a zigzag pathway using two slides before you change the angle.

    Now, choose a locomotor movement, and each time you hear the drum sound move

on a different pathway. Ready, go! [Allow the children to move for 5 to 10 seconds and then complete on a beat of a handheld drum. This task is repeated several times to allow children to practice moving on different pathways.]

Assessment Suggestion

- Teacher assessment—psychomotor and cognitive: Use a rating scale and recording sheet, and note whether the child can remain still in the correct shape for a count of 8. While students are practicing or performing, observe the accuracy of the shape and their ability to hold the shape still. You can select a spot to focus on for the observation. This strategy will work with a class with many students all moving at the same time. (outcomes 2 and 3)

    Record ++ if the child has made the correct shape on the corresponding spot and can hold it for 8 counts.

    Record +S if the child has made the correct shape on the corresponding spot but cannot hold still for the 8 counts.

    Record +C if the child is not using the correct shape on the corresponding spot but can hold still for the 8 counts.

    Record O if the child is not using the correct shape on the corresponding spot and cannot hold still for the 8 counts.

- Peer assessment—cognitive and psychomotor: Ask one partner to be an observer and one partner to be the performer. After the performer completes the dance, the observer tells the partner what locomotor movements he or she observed. Then partners switch roles. (outcomes 1 and 3)

Interdisciplinary Connections

- Language arts (writing or storytelling): The children can develop their own story to illustrate the shapes and locomotor movements.

- Math: Children can count how many steps they are using to travel from one spot to another or use standard or nonstandard measurement to measure the space from one spot to another.

- Visual art: Children can draw a map of the spots in the space and include a drawing of how their bodies appear in the shapes.

Frog Dance

Outcomes

As a result of participating in this learning experience, children will be able to do the following:

1. Demonstrate locomotor and nonlocomotor movements that are big and small. (psychomotor)

2. Remember and perform the sequence of actions used in dancing the story of the frog dance. (cognitive and psychomotor)

3. Choose their favorite part of the frog story to dance. (affective)

Organization

Children dance individually among others in the class.

Equipment Needed

- Pictures of frogs
- The following list of words on a single sign or multiple signs in the following order (see figure 8.12; also found on the bound-in CD-ROM in full-size posters):

Sleep

Wake up and look around

Stretch

Wave

Jump

Eat bugs

Jump

Sleep

- Music of sounds of tropical forest or frog vocal sounds

Introduction and Warm-Up

Today, we are going to do a dance about the day in the life of a frog. I have placed some pictures of frogs on the wall. Can someone describe one of the frogs? Yes, Carly says that one is small and has red spots. [Ask several other children to share their descriptions.] Next, we need to warm up our frog bodies before we dance. Let's start by walking in the space. Find a way to take very small steps as you walk forward, now backward. Change your steps to giant steps. How big can you step? Show

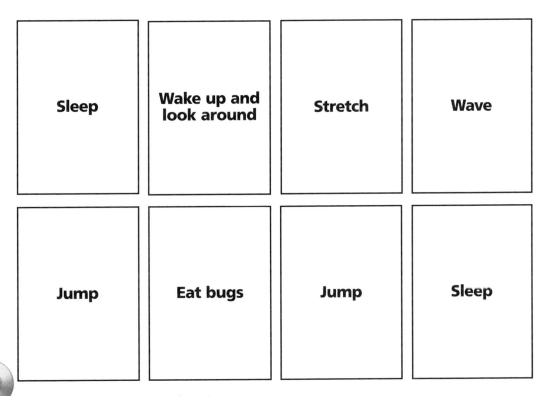

Figure 8.12   Signs for the frog dance.

(continued)

me how you can do the smallest stretch and bend movement with your body reaching up and down. Now what does that movement look like when you make it as big as you can? Who can tell me a movement they did this morning on their way to school? Yes, Anthony says he was swinging his backpack while waiting for the school bus. Great! Everyone, show me a small swinging movement with your arms. Now make it a little bigger, now bigger, and now as big as you can. Okay, I think we are warmed up. Let's find out what happens in the frog dance.

Development

While I tell the story, you can create your frog movements to go along with the story. I have posted the actions the frog will do in the story on the wall. Let's read them: sleep, wake up, stretch, wave, jump, eat bugs, jump, sleep. [Point to each word.] First, each person find a personal space and lie on the floor. Now, I will begin the story. Once upon a time, there was a very small pond filled with very small frogs who were all sleeping on very small lily pads. [Children make a small shape curled up on the floor.] One morning, the little frogs woke up and looked around with their small heads. The frogs could only make little movements looking up and down and side to side. [Children sit on the floor and look up and down, right and left.] Then the frogs began to stretch, but they could only do small stretches using their arms, legs, and back. [Children stretch arms, legs, and back, reaching up and down.] The small frogs stood up on the little lily pads and made a tiny wave to each other. [Children wave to each other using small waving movements.] Next, the little frogs decided to go out and find something to eat. So they did small jumps all over the pond. Some were jumping forward, some backward, and some sideward. [Children perform many small jumps in the space in different directions.] Then the frogs stopped and began to quickly grab tiny bugs to eat. They found bugs high over their head, behind them, out to the side, and low to the ground. [Children pretend to quickly grab bugs out of the air and place them in their mouth to eat.] Now the little frogs were very full from eating all those bugs, so they did small jumps back to their little lily pads and slowly went back to sleep. [Children jump back to the spot where they began the dance and curl up in a small shape on the floor as if they are sleeping.]

That night, something strange happened to the little frogs. They grew bigger and bigger and bigger. [Children stretch out, changing from a small shape on the floor to a large stretched shape.] That morning, when the frogs woke up, they were very surprised to see how big they had become during the night. They sat up in a big stretched shape and looked around the pond that was also very big. They could look up and down and side to side using big head movements. [Children sit in a wide stretched shape with arms stretched out and move their heads up and down and side to side using big movements.] Then the frogs began to stretch, and because they were so big, they did big stretches using the arms, legs, and back. [Children perform big stretch movements with their arms, legs, and back.] The big frogs stood up on the huge lily pads and did a huge wave to each other. [Children wave to each other using big, exaggerated waving movements.] Next, the big frogs decided to go out and find something to eat. So, they did huge jumps all over the pond. Some were jumping forward, some backward, and some sideward. [Children perform many big jumps in the space.] Then the frogs stopped and began to quickly grab huge bugs to eat. They found bugs high over their heads, behind them, out to the side, low to the ground. [Children pretend to grab bugs out of the air using two hands and place them in their mouths to eat.] Now the big frogs were so full from eating all those bugs that they did big jumps back to their huge lily pads and went back to sleep. [Children jump back to the spot where they began the dance and lie down in a large stretched shape on the floor as if they are sleeping.]

That night, something strange happened to the big frogs. They began to shrink and became smaller and smaller and smaller. And for the rest of their lives, the frogs spent one day as a small frog and the next day as a big frog and then again as a small frog, and so on and so on and so on. The end.

Culminating Dance

This time you can choose which part of the frog dance you would like to do. The small frog dance is first and then the big frog dance is second. Those of you who want to do the little frog dance will find a place to start. This time I will not tell the story; you need to remember all the parts by yourself. Those of you who are waiting to dance the big frog story can be the audience for the little frog dance, and then the little frog dancers will be the audience for the big frog dancers. When I put the music on, the little frogs can begin.

Closure

Ask, "Can someone who danced the part of the little frog tell me why you chose that part? Now can someone who danced the part of the big frog tell me why you chose to dance that part?"

Look for

- Children who need a reminder to take off and land on two feet to perform a jump correctly and safely.
- How well children move between each other while jumping in the pond and not bump into each other.
- How well the children use light energy in the small movements and how they can isolate moving the small body parts such as hands, head, and feet.

How Can I Change This?

- Add other events into the day in the life of the frog, such as swimming or lying on a rock and feeling the warm sun.
- Change the story to the life of another animal, bird, or sea creature.
- Ask children to dance with a partner like twin frogs moving in unison.

Assessment Suggestions

- Teacher assessment—psychomotor: Observe to see whether students can perform the same movement sequence using small and then big movements. Do you observe students demonstrating a clear difference in the big and small sizes of the movement? (outcome 1)
- Teacher assessment—cognitive and psychomotor: Observe during the culminating dance to see how many children can remember and perform all the parts of the dance. (outcome 2)
- Student self-assessment—affective: Students identify and perform their preference to dance as the small frog or the big frog during the culminating dance. At the end of the performance, students share their reasons for why they preferred to dance as the small or the big frog. (outcome 3)

Interdisciplinary Connections

- Language arts (reading): Read a story about frogs at the beginning of the learning experience, such as *Frogs Sing Songs* (Winer and Oliver 2003) or *Hop Jump* (Walsh 1993) or *Jump, Frog, Jump* (Kalan and Barton 1981).
- Language arts (writing and reading): Children can write and read their own frog stories and then create a dance to reflect the actions in the story.
- Math: Children can count the number of jumps or number of bugs they eat.
- Theater arts: Children create costumes with scarves, paper streamers, or construction paper.

nine

Learning Experiences for Third, Fourth, and Fifth Grades

Students in third through fifth grades have experienced the basic locomotor and nonlocomotor movements and can use these movements to create dances as individuals, in partners, or in small groups. They can recall sequences of movements, move in unison to counted phrases of movements, and organize movements when composing a dance. You can conduct discussions regarding the historical, social, and cultural contexts of the dance content and ask students to assess themselves and their peers. Although you may find some students in this age group are reluctant to dance, the learning experiences in this chapter offer nonthreatening ways to engage in dance using familiar movements. To facilitate your selection of learning experiences, we have summarized each learning experience in table 9.1.

You will find that each learning experience is outlined in 12 sections that identify outcomes and assessments, equipment and organization, and a detailed description of how to implement the introduction, warm-up, development, culminating dance, and closure. Additional ideas for varying the learning experience and connecting to other subject areas are also included. The description of each learning experience follows this format:

◈ Title

◈ Outcomes

◈ Organization

◈ Equipment needed

◈ Introduction and warm-up

◈ Development

◈ Culminating dance

◈ Closure

◈ Look for

◈ How can I change this?

◈ Assessment suggestions

◈ Interdisciplinary connections

The instructions for each dance learning experience are similar to the dialogue you would use when talking with your students. Any text in brackets indicates suggested instructions that you might use. All of the learning experiences in this chapter appear on the CD-ROM.

Table 9.1 Index of Learning Experiences for Third, Fourth, and Fifth Grades

Name of dance learning experience	Description of dance learning experience
Dancing Homework Machine	A learning experience that begins with students individually exploring the concept of repetition and concludes with a collaborative effort using repetitive movements to create parts of a moving homework machine.
Creative Square Dance	This creative dance experience is a wonderful addition to a traditional unit on square dance. Students have the opportunity to use their knowledge of square dance to create new movements and call their own creative square dance.
Action Words	Students explore directions, levels, shapes, ranges, and tempos through creating ways to perform the action words *run, pause, spin,* and *collapse.* The words are then linked together to form a dance. Students also create their own action word dances using words they select.
Baseball Dance	This popular learning experience is a great way to celebrate the opening of baseball season or the World Series. Students create movement variations for pitching, running, batting, and catching emphasizing tempo, levels, and direction. These movements are then combined into a dance performed in unison using a double-circle formation.
Birthday Celebration	Birthday celebrations are part of the traditions of many cultures. This learning experience focuses on expressing the events at a birthday celebration such as traveling to the party, blowing out the candles, unwrapping gifts, playing a game, and traveling back home. The culminating dance is performed in unison in a circle formation and includes all the birthday events.
Partner Dance	Learning to collaborate with another person is the focus of this learning experience. Students learn four partner relationships—mirror, shadow, echo, and call and response—and then use the relationships to choreograph a dance using the ABA choreographic structure.
Three Sport Dances	The sport dance is a great learning experience to introduce to students who may be reluctant to dance. The sport dance uses sport actions familiar to the students and explores ways to perform the actions using time, range, and levels. Three ways to create sport dances are included. Each way can be taught as a single session, or the three ways can be combined to form a complete creative dance unit.
Dance Maps	Students create shapes and pathways that result in drawn maps of their dance. Initially, students create an individual map and then collaborate with a small group to combine their dances into one dance. This learning experience offers a step-by-step process for creating the dances and requires the students to work independently with the teacher in the role of facilitator.
Create Your Own Hip-Hop Dance	Students demonstrate and teach their own hip-hop movements to the class. Next, they collaborate in a small group to create a new hip-hop dance using the movements they learned.
Funky Shape Museum	This dance experience uses locomotor movements and still shapes to create individual and group dances. Students dance the role of the funky shapes and the visitors to the museum.
Stick Figures Come Alive	Stick-figure drawings are the inspiration for students to create partner and small-group dances.

Dancing Homework Machine

Outcomes

As a result of participating in this learning experience, children will be able to do the following:

1. Create repetitive movements using the whole body and isolated body parts. (cognitive)

2. Perform repetitive movements that vary in level, direction, tempo, range, and amount of force. (psychomotor)

3. Create repetitive movements that represent the parts of the homework machine. (cognitive)

4. Collaborate with a small group to create a machine part using repetitive movements. (affective)

Organization

Students move individually, in partners, and then in small groups.

Equipment Needed

- MP3 or CD player
- Music with a steady beat
- Drum or wood block
- Whiteboard or chart paper
- Signs attached to cones naming parts of the machine: in slot, smoother, computer, checker, out slot, homework

Introduction and Warm-Up

Today, we are going to create movements that are repeated exactly the same way over and over. These are called *repetitive* movements. We will use these movements to create a dance about a machine that does your homework. Now, let's warm up.

In your personal space, move your arms up and down exactly the same way each time as I play the drum. [Students move their arms on each beat of the drum.] Now, take a step forward on each drumbeat. Make each step exactly the same. Now, move backward. As I play the drum at different tempos, see if you can take one step on each beat. [Alternate the drumbeat between fast and slow tempos.] Change the direction of your steps as you move fast and slow.

Now, I will play a steady beat on the drum. I want you to use your head to create a repetitive move-ment at the same tempo as the drum. Now try a repetitive movement with your shoulders, now one arm, alternating arms, now the legs.

Choose a body part that can repeat the same movement as I play the drum faster and then slower. Make the movement faster as you hear the drum played faster and then slower as the drum is played slower.

This time, choose two different body parts and alternate them as you do a repetitive movement to the drumbeat. For example, if you choose head and arms, move your head up and down for 8 beats, then move your arms apart and together for 8 beats, then repeat the head movement, and then the arm movement. [Students choose body parts and practice to the drumbeat.]

Create a repetitive movement that uses your whole body and changes levels. Travel forward while changing levels.

Development

I will assign partners, and then you will create a repetitive sequence of movements that you can perform in unison. Your sequence should have three different movements. Each movement uses 8 counts before you change to the next movement. Agree on a tempo and practice staying together. [Students explore, select, and practice their sequence of movements.] Now, you and your partner will perform your sequence for another set of partners, who are the observers. Then you will switch places. The observers will be looking to see how well you can perform in unison. After the performance, the observers will tell the performers if they moved in unison while doing three different movements for 8 counts each. [You can call on two sets of partners to model the performance and observation task.]

Today, we are going to build a human homework machine using repetitive movements. I have listed the five parts for our homework machine on the whiteboard: the in slot, which pulls the homework into the machine; the smoother, which smoothes out the homework after it comes out crumpled from your backpack; the computer, which does the homework; the checker, which makes sure the homework is correct; and the out slot, which pushes the homework out of the machine. We will also need

(continued)

some human homework to travel through all the parts of the machine. First, everyone will create a repetitive movement for each part of the machine. I will play the drum to provide a tempo to accompany your movements.

Let's begin with the in slot. Create a movement that repeats a reaching and pulling movement to pull the homework into the machine. Begin small and make the movement bigger and bigger. You may need to take a few steps forward and backward as you reach and pull. [Play a medium-tempo steady beat as students practice a pulling and reaching repetitive movement.] Can someone share an in-slot movement? Let's observe how the movement repeats over and over again. [Several students share their movements.]

The next machine part is the smoother. Show me a movement that demonstrates how you would smooth out the crumpled homework. Choose a level for the movement—high, medium, or low. Make sure you can keep repeating the movement. What body parts can you use to smooth the homework? [Play a medium-tempo steady beat as students practice a smoothing repetitive movement.] Let's share your ideas like we did for the in slot.

The next machine part is the computer. What kind of movements can you create that would show the inside of a working computer? Make this movement very big, using your whole body; exaggerate the size of the movement. Keep repeating the movement over and over again. Again, let's share ideas.

Next is the checker, which is going to make sure the homework is done well. Create two different movements for the checker. Can you alternate the movements every 8 beats of the drum? I will play a steady beat while you create your movement and

practice. [Students share their ideas, either with the whole class or with another student.]

The last machine part is the out slot. Create a movement that pushes the homework out of the machine. Try this move using light force. Now, try the same movement using strong force. How does the change of force change the way the movement feels? Can you use different body parts to push? Let's share again.

Now, we need to work on making the homework that travels through the machine. What are some ways you think the homework will move? [Students offer locomotor movements.] Let's all try Sarina's suggestion to skip. Can you change levels as you skip? Now, let's try Jamal's idea to walk in a curvy pathway. Can you start low and become higher as you walk and then go lower again? [You can ask for additional responses and use the elements of space, time, and force to create variations.]

Culminating Dance

Now, you are going to work with others in a small group and put together the movements you created for each machine part. Each group will be a different part of the homework machine. I have placed cones around the space in a semicircle with a sign marking the area for each machine part. (See figure 9.1.) The first time we do the dance, I will choose the machine part or homework for you; the second time, you can choose the part you would like to dance. [Assign students to a machine part and ask them to work together to create a repetitive movement that represents their part of the homework machine. Next, assign a few students to be the human homework.] While the groups are creating and practicing their machine movements,

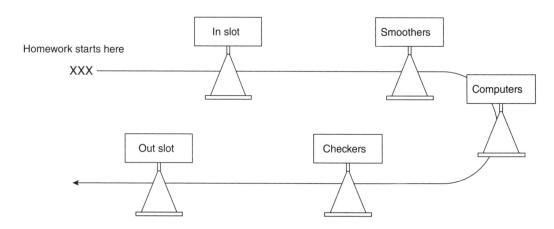

Figure 9.1 Space plan for the dancing homework machine.

the students who are the human homework should practice using locomotor movements in different ways to travel through the machine parts.

Now, each group will share what they have created and practiced. [Have each machine-part group demonstrate while the remaining students observe.] Now, let's start up the machine and all dance together. The machine parts begin in a still shape. [Play the music and direct the students when to begin moving.] First, one piece of homework begins to travel to the in slot. Now, the in slot begins and keeps working as each piece of homework passes through. Next, the second piece of homework begins as the first piece travels to the smoother. Next, the smoother begins. Each part of the machine begins to move as the first piece of homework travels by; the parts keep moving while the other pieces of homework move by. Now, the computer starts to move, then the checker, and then the out slot—all perform their repetitive movement. Keep going! I want the homework to show us different ways you would move as you pass each machine part. As the homework approaches the smoother, show me what shape you would be in before you are smoothed out. Start curved and then stretch out as you pass through the smoother. When all the homework has gone through the machine once, stop. Let's try that again.

Now, I am going to add a story to the homework machine. Listen to the sequence first, and then we'll do it. The machine starts up slowly beginning with the in slot, then the smoother, the computer, the checker, and the out slot. As the machine is moving slowly, homework begins to travel through the machine parts. After all the homework passes through the first time, the machine picks up speed, and the homework travels through again, this time a little faster. There is a lot of homework that needs to get done. So, the machine begins to move faster and faster until it explodes and breaks apart! The machine parts travel through the space in individual pieces, stopping in different places to perform the movement they did when the machine was all together. The homework calls the machine parts back together, and the machine parts slowly reassemble in their original places. The homework travels through the machine once more, and the machine slows down and comes to a complete stop. The parts freeze in a shape.

Let's try the story with our machine. I will tell you the story again as you dance. This time you can choose which machine part you would like to be. Some groups may have a lot of people who need to work together. We will get organized, create the machine part, practice, and then dance the story.

Closure

This activity makes you think about how a machine works, doesn't it? All the parts have to work together. What are other times when you need to work together with others? Let's talk about repetition in movement and how we use it in our daily lives. When do we need to use repetitive movement to accomplish a task? What machines have been invented to replace human movement?

Look For

- How well students can perform repetitive movement in an isolated body part and alternating body parts.
- How well students can coordinate a change in the tempo of their movements.
- Groups that need help to collaborate and share ideas and practice together.
- The variety of locomotor movements performed by the homework dancers as they travel through the machine.

How Can I Change This?

- The dance can be repeated several times with students choosing to dance a different part each time.
- Small groups of students can design smaller homework machines instead of designating the whole class as one large machine.
- Students create their own stories about what happens to the machine in the dance.
- Students create their own list of machine parts and then create repetitive movements that express each part.
- Students can add props, costumes, and vocal sounds or percussion instruments to accompany the dance.
- Students create a dance about another type of machine.

Assessment Suggestions

- Student self-assessment—cognitive: The students write in their physical education or dance journals about how to perform the movements

(continued)

in their favorite part of the machine. They name the machine part and describe how they used one or more elements of dance. (outcome 1)

- Teacher assessment—psychomotor: Complete a rating scale of performance criteria for assessing the partner sequence and check off the corresponding level of performance for each student (see figure 9.2). (outcome 2)

- Student self-assessment—cognitive and affective: Individually, students complete a recording sheet that reflects how their group's machine part performed. The sheet should include the following information. (outcomes 3 and 4)

  - Names of group members
  - Machine part
  - A movement that changes levels
  - A movement that changes direction
  - Description of the group's level of cooperation when creating and performing the machine part
  - Suggested changes for this dance

Interdisciplinary Connections

- Language arts (poetry): Read Shel Silverstein's (1981) poem "Homework Machine" to introduce the dance.

- Language arts and science: Display books or pictures of various types of machines. Talk about how repetition is used in the machine parts.

- Science: Connect to science concepts focused on ways in which force is exerted, such as push, pull, squeeze, swing, twist, and lift.

Students' names	1	2

Criteria

  1 = Student can perform a sequence composed of three different repetitive movements with each performed for 8 counts at the correct tempo.

  2 = Student can perform all three movements but not at the correct tempo.

Figure 9.2   Assessment tool for dancing homework machine.

Creative Square Dance

Outcomes

As a result of participating in this learning experience, children will be able to do the following:

1. Apply their knowledge of traditional square dance movements and formations to create their own new square dance movements. (cognitive)

2. Teach others the movements they created. (psychomotor)

3. Create, identify, and perform a square dance movement with a partner. (cognitive and psychomotor)

4. Perform a creative square dance called by you or a student. (psychomotor)

5. Cooperate as a group to create and perform a creative square dance. (affective, cognitive, and psychomotor)

6. Demonstrate respect for individual ideas and take responsibility as a contributing member of a group. (affective)

Organization

Students are in a square dance formation in partners. When a class does not have complete sets of eight, you can use fewer students on a side of the square or use a triangle formation.

Equipment Needed

- MP3 or CD player
- Music that is either chosen by the students and appropriate for use in a school environment or traditional square dance music
- Whiteboard or chart paper
- Microphone for calling the dance cues

Introduction and Warm-Up

Today, we are going to create, teach, and perform a new square dance using movements you create. [This learning experience can be an extension of a unit on traditional square dancing.] First, we need to warm up. Find a personal space. What are some ways you can travel while moving on 8 counts? Lisa suggests running. I want you to run through general space taking one run on each of the 8 counts and then stop. Ready, run, 1, 2, 3, 4, 5, 6, 7, 8. Try it again. What other ways can you travel? Nick suggests skipping, Yuh-lin says sliding, Evan says walking, and Keisha suggests jumping and hopping. Choose one of the ways to travel that was mentioned, and move using 8 counts and stop. Choose another way to travel. [You can specify the locomotor movements and the number of counts.]

Development

Now, I will organize you into groups of four. Stand in a square or circle formation and practice the following movement phrase that has 32 counts. Slide to your right for 8 counts and then left for 8. Next, take 4 steps forward into the square and 4 steps backward out of the square, and repeat the 4 steps forward and 4 steps back. The goal is to move in unison by finding a way to begin at the same time and perform the movements at exactly the same time. After you practice a few times, add arm movements while performing the slides and the steps forward and backward. [Before students practice, call on one group to demonstrate the sequence of steps.] How did you decide when to start all together?

Next, I will combine two groups of four to make a group of eight and ask you to choose a leader to signal the group to start and move in unison to the 32 counts of movement. [Students practice working on the same sequence of movement they performed as a group of four.]

Now, I will join all the groups of eight to form one large group performing the movement sequence. [Organize the class and select a student to be the leader who signals for the group to start and count out the sequence to keep everyone moving in unison. Each time the class dances this sequence, a new leader can be selected.] We have been moving in unison using the same movements; now, I will organize you into sets of six or eight and you will create, teach, and practice your own square dance. [It is helpful if students have had some experience with traditional square dancing to provide a reference for creating a new dance.]

Next, each set of partners will create a movement and a name for the movement in one of the following four categories written on the whiteboard or chart paper.

(continued)

Honor your home partner and corner partner. [This is a movement that greets and acknowledges the home partner and corner partner, such as a high five, funky bow, or clap pattern.]

Circle right and left. [Students can choose a way to travel, such as running steps, jumping, walking steps, grapevine steps, or a combination of traveling steps they create. They can also add arm movements.]

Turn in place. [Students can create ways to turn by changing levels, supporting themselves on various body parts, and adding movements as they turn, such as wiggling or moving their arms up and down.]

Exchange partners. [This exchange is similar to the do-si-do in traditional square dance. Students can jump, walk, skip, move at different levels, or connect using different body parts as they change places and then return to their original spot.]

[Assign each set of partners a category of movements to create.]

After you have created your category movement, each set of partners will teach their movement to the other students in their group so everyone knows how to perform all the movements in each category. [Students establish an order to teach and practice the movements.] Also, give your movement a creative name. [Ask one group to demonstrate for the class.]

Please show us your movements to honor your partner and corner. [Students demonstrate.] Now, let's see the circle-right-and-left movement. [Students demonstrate.] Now, the turn-in-place movement. [Students demonstrate.] And the partner-exchange movement. [Students demonstrate.] Next, let's see another group's movements. [Each group of students demonstrates the movements they created.]

Culminating Dance

In the next part of the session, I will call a dance sequence that I have designed using the four categories. [Point to the whiteboard or chart paper where the sequence is written.] When I call the category, your group will perform your movement that you created that corresponds to the category. Ready? Stand in your square formation and number each set of partners. Remember from our square dance lessons how each set of partners has a number like this diagram on the whiteboard. (See figure 9.3.) Ready, here's the first call:

- Partners honor each other.
- Corner partners honor each other.
- Everyone circles 8 counts to the right.
- Everyone circles 8 counts to the left.
- Face your partner and turn in place.
- Face your corner partner and turn in place.
- Partners 1 and 3, move to the middle and do partner exchange.
- Partners 2 and 4, move to the middle and do partner exchange.
- Partners 1 and 3, move to the middle and do partner exchange.
- Partners 2 and 4, move to the middle and do partner exchange.
- Everyone go to the middle and do the turn in place.
- Everyone go back home and say, "Good-bye."

That is the end of the dance. Now, let's try it to music as I call the dance again.

Next, each group will practice their dance using the sequence on the whiteboard; however, this time substitute the names of your movements instead of using the category term. For example, say "happy high five" instead of "honor your partner," or "the tornado twirl" for "turn in place." Select one person in your group to call the dance. They will also dance at the same time. [After students practice, they can

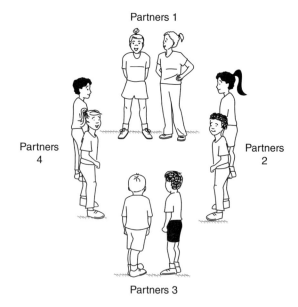

Figure 9.3 Numerical arrangement for square dance partners.

share their dances with the class. The caller can use a microphone to call the dance, and another student can take his or her place in the dance.]

Closure

Did you observe any movements in another group that you thought were creative? Can you describe or show the movement and tell us why you thought so? How did your group show respect for one another?

Look For

- How well students can perform the 32-count sequence in unison. You may need to offer cues to help them start the sequence.

- How partners collaborate to create a movement in the assigned category.

- The strategies that students use to teach their movements to others. Do they use words, do they demonstrate, or do they combine words and demonstrations?

- The process students use to choose leaders. Did they vote? Do they share the leadership? Do they change leaders? Did students volunteer eagerly?

How Can I Change This?

- Suggest other square dance sequences. Look at the sequence of steps from other square dances for ideas.

- Students can design their own sequences.

- Students can write the name of the movements they created and place them in front of their feet so everyone in the square can see the name of the movement.

- Each student in the square can call any of the created movements for the groups to perform. This way, each student has an opportunity to call one of the moves.

Assessment Suggestions

- Teacher assessment—cognitive and psychomotor: Have an assessment station. While students are practicing their dances, each student, or students in partners, can record on video their response to a question at a preset assessment station. They will state their name and the response. Examples of questions are as follows: Describe the name of the dance movement you and your partner created, describe how to perform it, and then demonstrate your movement. (outcomes 1 and 3)

- Teacher assessment—cognitive: Each student draws a diagram of their dance group and labels the partners by number and writes the name of the movements they created. (outcomes 1 and 5)

- Teacher assessment—affective and psychomotor: The teacher writes anecdotal notes about how well the group collaborated to teach and practice and perform the movements in their dance. (outcomes 2, 5, and 6)

- Student self-assessment—psychomotor: Students complete a rating scale that evaluates their ability to perform a creative square dance. Rubric—awesome criteria: I performed all the steps correctly when called. Rubric—good criteria: I made one or two mistakes and did not do the correct move when called. Rubric—need more time criteria: I could not perform most of the correct steps when called. (outcome 4)

Interdisciplinary Connections

- Language arts (literature): Use children's literature focused on square dance as an introduction to square dancing. Use books such as *Barn Dance* (Martin and Archambault 1986), *Barnyard Dance* (Boynton 1993), or *Pigs in the Corner* (Axelrod and McGinley-Nally 2001).

- Music: Introduce music through showing and talking about the instruments that are used for traditional square dance music.

- Social studies: Discuss the history and cultural contributions of square dance.

- Social studies: Tell students about the square dance legislation collection (1975 to present) at the Library of Congress American Folklife Center (www.loc.gov/folklife/guides/square-dance.html). This site documents the history of legislation to designate square dance as the national or state folk dance. Include a discussion on other national symbols that are representative of the United States.

Outcomes

As a result of participating in this learning experience, children will be able to do the following:

1. Perform, with control, movement variations using the elements of dance for the action words *run, pause, spin,* and *collapse.* (psychomotor)

2. Identify and record the action words selected for their dance. Include the order used in the dance and the number of counts for each action word movement. (cognitive)

3. Collaborate as a small group to create and perform a dance using a sequence of selected action words. (psychomotor, cognitive, and affective)

Organization

Students dance individually and then are organized into small groups.

Equipment Needed

- Whiteboard or large sheet of paper to list action words
- Smaller pieces of paper and pencils for students
- A list of action words for each student (see figure 9.4)

Introduction and Warm-Up

Today, we are going to explore four action words using various directions, levels, shapes, tempos, and body parts. The words are *run, pause, spin,* and *collapse.* We will use these words to create a dance.

The warm-up today is called quick response. I will call out a word, and I want you to show me a shape that you think represents the word. Find a personal space and begin by standing in a straight shape. Ready? Reach, twist, stretch, bend, reach, twist, stretch, bend. Now, let's try jump, swing, squeeze, inflate, jump, swing, squeeze, inflate. Can you suggest other words we could do in our personal space for our warm-up? [Write the words on the whiteboard or large sheet of paper and then call them out.]

Development

The first word we are going to explore is *run.* [Write the word on the board.] Begin running in a forward direction at a medium tempo. Now change the direction to sideways—right then left. [To prevent

Run	Shake	Wiggle	Skate	Wait	Freeze
Jump	Bend	Stretch	Spin	Turn	Pop
Skip	Vibrate	Shiver	Twirl	Burst	Open
Hop	Swing	Reach	Sneak	Close	Slink
Leap	Squirm	Fidget	Shuffle	Prowl	Fling
Walk	Twist	Wring	Roll	Grow	Rise
Step	Bounce	Spring	Pounce	Swell	Shrink
Slide	Fall	Collapse	Squeeze	Explode	Flick
March	Drop	Melt	Dab	Tap	Press
Stamp	Fold	Crumple	Punch	Float	Glide
Crawl	Compress	Contract	Slash	Splatter	Stab
Slither	Inflate	Deflate	Flip	Bump	Push
Gallop	Recede	Advance	Pull	Slam	Kick
Dart	Lift	Dash	Stop	Pause	Pump

Figure 9.4 List of action words.

falling, do not let children run backward.] Change direction after 8 runs in one direction. You can choose to run sideways right, then forward, and then sideways left, or choose another order. Now, change direction after 4 runs. [Play a drumbeat or use music with a clear steady beat.] Now, run using 8 small steps and then 8 large steps. Repeat this running pattern a few times and add different directions.

The next word is *pause.* [Write it on the board next to the word *run.*] What is a pause? Gina says it is a short stop, and your body is still. Can you think of any other words that mean the same as *pause*? Now, I want you to make a different paused shape on each drumbeat. Can you make shapes that are wide? Narrow? Twisted? Curved? Balanced on one foot? Low to the floor? Stretched up high? This time you will add a pause shape to the run. Begin running when you hear the drum, then pause on the one loud drumbeat. [Play the drumbeats faster for the run and then one loud beat to signal the pause.] Hold your body still. Notice your shape. What is the shape of your arms? Are you leaning in a particular direction? Where are you looking? How are your feet placed on the floor? After the next run, pause in a different shape. [Play the drum.] Is your shape straight? Twisted? Round? Tall? Wide? Stretched? Balanced on one foot? Run again, changing the direction and size of the steps and pause in a different shape. Keep your body very still. [Play the drum.] Try the run and pause again. [Again, play the drum.]

The next word to explore is *spin.* [Write the word on the board next to the word *pause.*] Spin while changing to different levels. Can you spin low to the floor? What are the ways you can spin low? What other levels can you use to spin? How high off the floor can you spin? Is there a way to start your spin low to the floor and end on a high level? Can you do the opposite? Now, we will combine run, pause, and spin into a sequence, like a sentence of movements. I will play the drum for the run, the one loud beat for the pause, and fast, light beats for the spin. Each part will be 8 counts. [Play the drum and call out the words while the students perform the sequence.] Let's repeat this sequence again, making the movements different each time.

The last word is *collapse.* [Write the word on the board next to *spin.*] What happens to your body in a collapse movement? Yes, Kareem, that's it. I see your body carefully falling to the floor; your muscles look loose. Now, everyone raise your arm up high and let it collapse. Try the collapse with both arms at the same time. Now, let your head collapse forward. Now, collapse the top of your body forward from the waist. Stretch your whole body reaching up to the ceiling, and then slowly collapse to the floor. Which direction did you use? Try the collapse forward, backward, and sideways. I'm going to watch as you collapse; remember to keep it slow and controlled.

When you perform the four words in this order, you are creating an action word dance. The order is run, pause, spin, and collapse. Let's do this dance all together using the same movements. Which direction will we run and for how many counts? Sue suggests we run forward at a fast speed for 12 counts. What shape and counts will we use for the pause? Aaron suggests a 5-count stretched shape. At what level and counts will we do the spin? Kara suggests we spin at a high level that takes us off the floor for 3 counts. How will we collapse and how long will it take? Travis suggests the whole body collapses slowly in a forward direction for 10 counts. [Write the counts under the words and review the sequence before the students dance.] Everyone find a place to begin the dance. Ready? [Play the drum or use music to accompany the dance.] Run forward for 12, pause in a stretched shape for 5, spin high off the floor for 3 counts, and slowly collapse forward to the floor counting to 10. Let's try the dance again. [The students practice the dance.]

Let's try the same dance, but now we will do it in a different order, using the same counts for each word. [Students suggest this sequence: spin, collapse, pause, and run.]

I will assign partners and you will create your own dance using the four words—run, pause, spin, and collapse. You can change the order of the words and the tempo, direction, level, size, shape, and counts of each movement. Make your decisions, write the word order and number of counts on a piece of paper, and then practice your dance. I will ask one set of partners to share their dance while another pair observes. [Students work together to write and practice their dance.] Now, one set of partners will demonstrate their dance and when the dance is over, the students watching will tell the dancers the order of the words they observed. Then switch places.

Culminating Dance

In the next part of this learning experience, you will collaborate with a group of three or four people to make your own choice of action words for your dance. I have provided you with a list. (See figure 9.4 on page 164.) Choose four words, decide how you

(continued)

will perform the words, and choose how many counts each word will take. Each person selects a word for the dance. Write each word on a separate piece of paper and rearrange the words until you find an order you like. Try several orders before you make a final choice. Then, practice your dance.

Decide how your group will be organized in the space. Will you use a circle, a line, or a scattered formation? Will the dance be performed in unison, or will different people start and end the dance at different times?

Each group will perform their dance for another group. Then, you will switch. The observers will write down the sequence of action words they observed.

Closure

Ask the students "What did you like about this learning experience? Can you suggest any changes for the next time? Describe a new way you learned to move."

Look For

- The variety of shapes students create for the pause.

- Spins with control at different levels.

- How carefully students control their bodies on the collapse (safety is important when children use action words such as *fall, melt, deflate, drop,* or *sink*).

- How smoothly students can transition from one movement to another.

- Students who need help choosing action words from the list.

- Strategies that groups use to cooperate as they create their action word dance.

- How leadership appears while the group is creating and practicing their dance. Does one person assume leadership? Did everyone have an opportunity to contribute to the dance?

How Can I Change This?

- Select a category for the action word dances such as words associated with traveling, sports, animals, food, clothing, or words used in comics.

- Read a story or poem to the students and select action words from the text.

- Choose more or fewer words for the dance.

- Add descriptive adjectives to the word list.

- Students can create a story that uses the order of the words in their dance. For example, one day, three girls were running to the playground. They paused when they saw a beehive. The bees came out and the girls began to spin around, waving their arms to get away from the bees. They all got stung in the arm and collapsed to the ground.

- Encourage students to explore many possibilities of how the action words can be performed. Provide a list of the elements of dance to help them make choices of how to vary the action words.

- Students can add percussion instruments or sounds to accompany the movements.

Assessment Suggestions

- Student self-assessment—cognitive: Each student in the group records the selected action words and notes the order of the words for their dance. Next to each word is the number of counts. (outcome 2)

- Peer assessment—psychomotor, cognitive, and affective: Students and you compose criteria and a rubric for assessing the dance. Then assessment is conducted with one peer group as the observers and another peer group as the performers (see figure 9.5). (outcome 3)

Group name _____

Check the box next to the word that describes how the group performed.

Super	The dance had four words. Everyone showed a lot of energy.
Okay	The dance had four words, but some of the dancers did not show a lot of energy.
Needs practice	The dance was missing an action word, not all dancers showed energy.

Figure 9.5   Example of an assessment composed by a teacher and students.

- Teacher assessment—psychomotor: Using a checklist, note how well the students perform each of the four words. The + symbol can denote using balance, coordination, smooth transitions using control, and the ? symbol can denote a performance where the child loses balance, falls, or uses an inappropriate amount of energy to maintain control. (outcome 1)

Interdisciplinary Connections

- Language arts (parts of speech): Integrate language arts concepts about verbs, adverbs, adjectives, and nouns. Include books such as *To Root, To Toot, Parachute: What Is a Verb?* (Cleary and Prosmitsky 2001).

- Language arts (writing): Use the concept of a sentence in comparison to a dance sequence.

- Language arts (spelling): Ask the students about spelling words they could use for their dances.

- Language arts (writing): Students can use writing and composition skills to write stories that reflect the action word dances they created.

- Language arts (reading): Students can create dances based on the action words used in novels and poems they are reading in the classroom or at home.

Baseball Dance

Outcomes

As a result of participating in this learning experience, children will be able to do the following:

1. Perform movement sequences accurately based on baseball skills: running, pitching, batting, and catching. (psychomotor)

2. Move in unison with others to the same rhythm. (psychomotor)

Organization

Students will learn the dance movements individually and with a partner, and then the whole class forms a double circle for the culminating dance.

Equipment Needed

- MP3 or CD player
- Music (locate a version of "Take Me Out to the Ball Game")
- Pictures of baseball players using the movements in the dance: pitching, catching, running, and batting

Introduction and Warm-Up

Today, we are going to celebrate the opening of baseball season across America by learning a new dance that uses baseball movements. I have selected pitching, batting, running, and catching for the dance. Look on the board at the pictures of players using these skills. What do you see? Can someone choose a picture and make their body into the shape in the picture? [Several students are selected to demonstrate the shapes. Ask the students to describe the shape.]

Let's begin the warm-up pretending we are jogging around the bases. Stand on a spot that will be home plate, and now point to a place for first base; now point to second base and third base. When I say go, everyone will take 7 jogs to each of your bases and 1 jump on the base on the count of 8. Ready, go. Jog 1, 2, 3, 4, 5, 6, 7, and jump on 8. Let's repeat. Remember to take one step on each count. Ready, and jog 1, 2, 3, 4, 5, 6, 7, jump 8! Let's try that again.

The second part of our warm-up is stretching movements you do before a game. Can anyone suggest a stretch? [One student demonstrates and the other students perform the stretch.] Can anyone else suggest a stretch?

Development

The first baseball movement is the pitch. First, show me how you would pitch a ball to the batter. Try it several times and think about how your arms move, how your feet move, and how the movement starts and ends. [Students practice pitching overhand.] Now, do the pitch as slowly as possible. Make the movement big, with a feeling of stretching. Practice several times, and hold your shape at the end of the pitch. [Students practice.] Add the following counts to the pitch: 4 slow counts for the windup and 4 slow counts for the follow-through. Ready! Windup, 1, 2, 3, 4, 5, 6, 7, 8. Remember to keep the movement slow and continuous and lean back on the windup and forward on the follow-through. Let's try again, and hold your shape still on count 8. Ready? Windup, 1, 2, 3, 4, 5, 6, 7, and hold 8. I can see that you are coordinating your movement with the counts and are moving slowly. We will use this slow pitch in our dance.

Now, let's change our movement to batting. First, bat the way you usually do. Remember how your feet are placed, your knees are bent, the body twists, your hands hold the bat with elbows lifted, and your eyes look at the pitcher. Try a few swings. [Students practice.] You are going to take 3 swings. The first 2 swings take 2 counts each, and on the third swing you will follow up with a complete one-foot spin for 4 counts. Now, add a stop at the end of your spin and hold your body still. Ready? Swing, swing, and swing and spin, hold. One more time. Ready? 1, 2, 3, 4, 5, 6, 7, and 8. Let's practice this part again.

The third movement you will need to learn for the dance is running. This part you already know. I want you to repeat the 7 runs and 1 jump from the warm-up. Can someone show us how they performed the runs and jump? Yes, Isabel, it is 7 runs and a jump on the eighth count. Do the runs and a jump four times. The first run begins to the right and the jump pretends to land on first base, then 7 more runs and a second jump on second base, then turn left and do 7 runs and jump on third base, and finally the fourth set of runs and jump on home plate. I want you to practice the runs and jumps in a circle of six to eight students. See if everyone can run and jump on the counts at the same time. Designate a leader to count out loud for the group. See if your group can do the entire sequence of 32 counts with everyone running and jumping at the same time. Remember 16 counts to the right, then 16 counts to the left. [Students practice as you observe and help where needed.]

The fourth movement is catching. We are going to do four catches in a sequence. Show me a catch reaching up high, now a low catch, a catch lunging and reaching to the right at a medium level, and then lunging and reaching to the left at a medium level. Together, let's practice the sequence. Ready? Catch high, catch low, catch right, and catch left. Use 2 counts for each catch. Try it again using the counts 1, 2, 3, 4, 5, 6, 7, and 8. Now, I will assign you a partner. You and your partner will face each other and perform the 8-count catching sequence in unison. Practice several times with your partner.

Now, let's review all the movements in the four sequences. Everyone find a personal space. Ready? Pitching, 1, 2, 3, 4, 5, 6, 7, and hold 8. Now, the batting sequence. Swing, 1, 2, swing, 3, 4, swing and spin, 5, 6, 7, hold 8. Next, 32 counts of running and jumping. Run 7 counts to each base and jump on 8 four times through. Ready, go. And now, the 8-count catch repeated two times. Catch high, low, right, and left; catch high, low, right, and left.

Culminating Dance

We are going to combine all the movements we practiced today into a dance. The dance will not be exactly like a baseball game; however, parts of the game will be in the dance. The formation for the dance is a double circle. (See figure 9.6.) I will assign you a place on the inside circle or the outside circle. The dancers standing in the inside

circle are the pitchers, and the dancers standing in the outside circle are the batters. You are facing a partner. Let's combine the pitching and batting sequences. First, the pitcher will pitch for 8 counts and hold still while the batters perform the batting swings and a turn sequence. Then, the pitchers go again and hold, and then the batters perform. Alternating sequences with a partner in dance is called call and response. The pitcher's sequence is the call, and the batter's sequence is the response. Pitchers get ready, and batters get in your batting stance. Pitchers, begin the 8-count pitch and hold your follow-through at the end. Ready, pitchers? Pitch, 1, 2, 3, 4, 5, 6, 7, and hold on 8. Batters, now do the batting sequence you practiced. Swing, swing, swing, and spin. Now, the pitchers go again and repeat their pitch. Keep the movement slow, stretched, and continuous as you look the batter in the eye. Batters go again.

The next part of the dance uses the 32 counts of running with a jump on the eighth count. Turn to your right, and get ready to run on my signal. Remember, the inner circle will need to take smaller runs and jumps because you have less space to move in, and the outer circle can take a little bigger run and jump because you have more space. Everyone ready! Run, 1, 2, 3, 4, 5, 6, 7, and jump. And, 1, 2, 3, 4, 5, 6, 7, and jump. Turn left 1, 2, 3, 4, 5, 6, 7, and jump. And 1, 2, 3, 4, 5, 6, 7, and jump! Turn and face your partner at the end of the running and jumping. If you are not standing in front of your partner, the inner circle should stay still and the outer circle can take a few more running steps until you meet your partner. Let's try it again, and see if you can coordinate your runs and jumps with

Figure 9.6 The dancers are organized into a double circle for the baseball dance.

(continued)

my counts. [You can play the music and count with the students.]

The third part of the dance uses the catching sequence: catch high, catch low, catch right, and catch left. This sequence is repeated two times by everyone as you face your partner. You and your partner try to move in unison. Practice as I count. Ready? Catch high, 1, 2, catch low, 3, 4, right, 5, 6, and left, 7, 8. Again, high, low, right, and left.

Next, the pitcher and batter change places. On the change, they give each other a high five or another type of greeting. If you were the batter, you are now the pitcher; and, if you were the pitcher, you are now the batter. [Students switch places and take their new positions.] Let's try the dance again in these new positions. [Students repeat the dance again.] At the end of the second time you complete the dance, you can freeze in a high five with your partner so the dance ends in a still shape or everyone in their circle can jog to the right and high five the dancers in the circle with their left hand as they pass by each other. Let's try the dance from the beginning. Return to your original places.

Closure

Conduct a discussion about how baseball is part of the American culture and how it affects people's lives. Explore the concept that dance is a way of recording and representing one's culture. What other events that occur annually as part of our lives could be represented in dance form?

Look For

- A slow and exaggerated pitching movement. Use the image of a slow-motion instant replay.

- How the batters coordinate the three swings and spin. Can they maintain their balance on the spin?

- How well the students can run in a circle in unison and maintain appropriate spacing. When students run in a circle, the circle tends to become smaller, and they may bump into one another.

- Clear changes in level in the catching sequence.

How Can I Change This?

- Any of the movement phrases can be varied. For example, in the pitching phrase you can have the pitchers do slow pitches the first time and fast pitches the second time.

- Before the students begin the dance, add 16 counts of stretching movements as a game warm-up.

- Ask the students to greet each other using different ways they have seen in athletic events, such as different handshakes or bumping elbows.

- Assign other students to do the counting for different sections of the dance.

- Create a dance using movements from another sport.

Assessment Suggestions

- Student self-assessment and teacher assessment—psychomotor: The dance is recorded on a video, and the students observe themselves performing each baseball movement sequence of the dance. They reflect on their performance and write about what part they did well and what part they would like to improve. They perform the dance again and write or talk about how they improved their performance. Also observe the video and the live dancing and note how well the whole class moves in unison to the same rhythm for each baseball movement sequence. (outcome 1)

- Peer assessment—psychomotor: One half of the class performs the dance while the other half observes to see how well the whole performing group can perform in unison. The observers raise two hands up if everyone was in unison and one hand up if unison was not observed. (outcome 2)

Interdisciplinary Connections

- Language arts (literature): Introduce children's literature by reading books on baseball such as *Ballpark* (Cooper 1998) or other children's novels or biographies.

- Music: Integrate music through using the song "Take Me Out to the Ball Game," with lyrics by Jack Norworth and music by Albert Von Tilzer, composed in 1908. Use the book *Take Me Out to the Ballgame* (Gillman 1999) as a companion to the music.

- Math: Connect math by adding the number of beats for each movement to complete a total of beats for the entire dance.

Birthday Celebration

Outcomes

As a result of participating in this learning experience, children will be able to do the following:

1. Recall and perform a sequence of dance movements that reflect the events at a birthday party. (cognitive and psychomotor)

2. Move in a circle formation in unison, maintaining an even space among dancers. (psychomotor)

3. Move using the specific rhythms designated in each section of the dance. (psychomotor)

4. Describe the part of the dance they liked to perform and which part they felt they performed best. (affective)

Organization

The dance uses a single large-circle formation. For the gift section of the dance, students are assigned partners.

Equipment Needed

- MP3 or CD player

- Music that has a steady beat

- On a whiteboard or a chart paper, a list of events that are related to a birthday celebration, such as traveling to the birthday party, blowing out the candles, unwrapping the gifts, playing a game, and traveling back home

- A piñata if available

Introduction and Warm-Up

Today, we are going to learn a dance that expresses the events and feelings we experience at a birthday party. Does anyone have a birthday today? This week? This month? Let's celebrate everyone's birthday today. [Ask students about how they celebrate birthdays. Also, before presenting this learning experience, check with students to see if they are able to participate in a dance that celebrates birthdays. Not all cultures or religions celebrate birthdays.]

During the dance, all of you will be running in a circle for 32 counts—16 counts to the right and 16 counts to the left. For the warm-up, practice moving to the 32 counts; however, be sure to run in your own pathway. How shall we travel first? Mike says

we should jog. Okay, ready to jog to the right? [Beat the drum for 32 counts.] Jog—1, 2, 3, 4, 5, 6, 7, 8, 9, 10, 11, 12, 13, 14, 15, 16. Turn left and jog—1, 2, 3, 4, 5, 6, 7, 8, 9, 10, 11, 12, 13, 14, 15, 16. What is another way we can travel? Raina says we can skip. Skip for 32 counts. [Ask for several more ways to travel in the warm-up.]

Development

Listed on the board are the birthday party events that we will express in the dance. We will begin traveling to the party. I'd like everyone to organize themselves in a large single circle with a space in between each person. [Students assemble in a large circle.] We are going to travel to the party by riding a bicycle or riding a skateboard. How do you think your hands and arms will move? Kevin says that our hands will hold the bike grips, and we'll twist to show how we steer. Good, good. I also want you to jog lifting your knees up high as if you are pedaling a bike, or jog leaning to the right and left like you are on a skateboard. Turn so your left shoulder is facing in to the middle of the circle. Notice how much space is between you and the person in front of you. Now, take 4 jogging steps forward, keeping the same space between each person. Ready? 1, 2, 3, 4. Stop. Do you have the same amount of space between you and the person in front of you? Now, let's try 8 runs. Ready? 1, 2, 3, 4, 5, 6, 7, 8, stop. Now, look at the space. Is it still the same? Let's try 16 counts. Ready? 1, 2, 3, 4, 5, 6, 7, 8, 9, 10, 11, 12, 13, 14, 15, 16, stop. Now, look at the space. What did you do to keep the same amount of space as you jogged? At the end of our 16 jogs, we are going to turn our bikes and skateboards around and go in the opposite direction just like in the warm-up. Then, your right shoulder will face in to the center of the circle. In your space, show me how you will turn your bike or skateboard around. Will you use a jump turn? A one-foot turn? A two-foot turn? Let's practice adding your turn at the end of the 16 counts. Ready? All together, 1, 2, 3, 4, 5, 6, 7, 8, 9, 10, 11, 12, 13, 14, 15, 16, and turn on 1, 2, 3, 4, 5, 6, 7, 8, 9, 10, 11, 12, 13, 14, 15, 16, and stop. Great, you are all taking one step on each count and keeping a space between each person. Let's try it again. [You can add the music or continue to use the drum.]

(continued)

The second part of the dance is blowing out the candles. Pretend there is a giant cake in the middle of the circle. Show me how your body moves when you blow out candles on a birthday cake. How does your body move when you inhale? I see you are leaning backward. I want everyone to exaggerate the inhaling movement and lean backward for 4 counts. Stretch and reach up and backward with your arms. Inhale and stretch backward, 1, 2, 3, and 4. Next, move this stretched shape toward the middle of the circle, taking 4 steps, 1, 2, 3, 4. To blow out the candles, lunge forward and make a strong exhaling movement for 4 counts. (See figure 9.7.) Then, take 4 large steps backward to where you began inhaling. Blowing out the candles uses 16 counts. Let's combine the inhaling movement with walking 4 steps forward, then exhaling, and then walking 4 steps backward. Ready? Inhale, lean backward, 1, 2, 3, 4. Walk forward, 1, 2, 3, 4. Lunge and exhale strong, 1, 2, 3, 4. Walk backward, 1, 2, 3, 4. Let's try the sequence again and move in unison.

The next part of the party is when the gifts are unwrapped. You will dance two parts—a gift and a child who unwraps the gifts. First, we will practice the gift part. I want each person to think about a toy for the gift and make your body into a shape that represents the toy. Is your shape low to the floor, at a medium level, or at a high level? Each student will tell the class what toy his or her shape represents. Let's start with Trent and go around the circle. [Each student shows his or her shape and identifies the toy.] Remember your shape. Next, we will create

movements that express the excitement you feel when you unwrap a gift. First, I will assign partners and you will take turns dancing the part of the gift and the person who unwraps the gift. [Assign partners by selecting students who are standing next to each other. One partner is identified as happy, and the other partner is identified as birthday.] The birthday people will be the gifts first, and the happy people will unwrap the gifts first. Birthday people, make your gift shapes. Now, the happy people skip, gallop, or jog in a circle around the gift, using fast arm movements that represent pulling off the ribbon and paper. You have 8 counts. [Students practice the unwrapping movements.] Now, switch parts with your partner so they can practice the unwrapping. Let's practice this section of the dance again.

Now, before we play the party game, let's see if we can combine the first three parts. You travel to the party on your bikes or skateboards, blow out the candles twice, and unwrap the gifts twice. Start in a big circle with your left shoulder facing in to the center of the circle. Remember to keep the same space between each person and perform the movements together to the music. [Turn the music on.] Ready? Begin. [Students practice the first three parts of the dance while you cue the counts.]

The next part of the dance is the party game. Today, we are going to hit a piñata. [Show the class a piñata, a decorated container filled with candies and gifts that is hung and broken open by hitting it with a stick.] Has anyone played this game at a party? In this part of the dance, the happy students

Figure 9.7 Blowing out the candles during the birthday celebration dance.

172

take 4 walking steps toward the center of the circle and pretend they are holding a stick performing this sequence: swing, swing, and spin around for 4 counts. [You or a student demonstrates the swing-and-spin sequence.] This movement sequence represents swinging a stick at the piñata. Then you will open your arms and reach up to catch all the candy for 4 counts and walk backward 4 steps to your place in the circle. Ready? Happy people walk forward, 1, 2, 3, 4, and swing, swing, and spin around, 1, 2, 3, 4, open your arms and catch candy, 1, 2, 3, 4, and walk backward, 1, 2, 3, 4. Now, the birthday people do the same. Now, each group will practice this part of the dance again.

Now, it is time to go home after the party. In this section of the dance, the happy people will go home first. They begin riding their bicycles or their skateboards to the right, weaving in and out of the circle among the birthday people without bumping into them. How would you describe the pathway they are traveling on? Keep jogging until you get back to your place. Next, the birthday people do the same. Let's try this once. [Both groups of students practice this weaving pathway.]

Culminating Dance

Now, let's combine all the sections of the dance we learned into one dance. Can someone tell us what happens first? What is one important thing to remember in the traveling-to-the-party section? What section is second? Can someone show us the sequence of movements for blowing out the candles? What happens in the third part? Can one set of partners demonstrate the gift and the unwrapping? Now, the piñata game. Can someone describe how to do it and then show the movements? Finally, the party is over and the guests travel home. How is this part the same as traveling to the party, and how is it different?

Now, we are ready to put it all together. I will play the music and cue the counts for each section. [Call out the counts as the students dance.] Now, you perform the dance by yourselves. I will ask five students to count out loud so everyone can dance in unison. [Select a different student to count each section while she or he also dances.]

Closure

Ask students to describe the part of the dance they enjoyed most. Ask students what they learned about dancing in this learning experience.

Look For

- How well students can maintain an even space between each other as they travel in the circle.
- How well students perform the movements in each section of the dance using the appropriate tempo and space.
- Whether students can coordinate the 32-count run with a change of direction after 16 counts.
- How well students can move between each other without bumping.

How Can I Change This?

- Suggest other means of traveling to the party such as driving a car, taking a subway, using roller skates, using a skateboard, or flying in a plane.
- The whole class can represent the same gift instead of making individual choices.
- Use a different game played at a party.
- Students dance in groups of eight to demonstrate different birthday parties happening in the neighborhood.

Assessment Suggestions

- Student self-assessment—cognitive: On one sheet of paper, students can draw and label a series of pictures on one sheet of paper that describe the correct order of events in the dance. (outcome 1)
- Teacher assessment—psychomotor: Use a checklist to note students who demonstrate difficulty with performing movements on the beat and maintaining appropriate space in the dance. (outcome 2)
- Peer assessment—psychomotor: Students are organized into observers and performers. Each observer is assigned a performer to assess. While the performers are dancing, the observers note if the dancer is on the music beat during each birthday event. They receive a + if they are on the beat and a √ if they are not on the beat. (outcome 3)
- Student self-assessment—affective and psychomotor: Students verbally share with another peer which part of the dance they liked performing and which part of the dance they feel they stayed on the beat. (outcomes 3 and 4)

(continued)

Interdisciplinary Connections

- Social studies: Combine this dance with a social studies unit focused on cultural traditions. A birthday is one cultural tradition that is celebrated in many ways. Incorporate these cultural traditions into the birthday dance.

- Math: Integrate math concepts by adding together the ages of all the students, then use the total number as the number of counts for the dance. Students can divide the total counts and assign a number of counts to each section of the dance. The total counts for the five sections will equal the total age of the students.

- Music or world language: Students can combine the dance with music as they sing "Happy Birthday" during the dance. They can also sing the song in other languages.

Partner Dance

Outcomes

As a result of participating in this learning experience, students will be able to do the following:

1. Create, perform, and observe movements that use four partner relationships: mirror, shadow, echo, and call and response. (cognitive and psychomotor)

2. Identify the four partner relationships. (cognitive)

3. Create and perform a dance with a partner using the ABA choreographic structure. (cognitive and psychomotor)

4. Identify preferences for moving using four partner relationships. (affective)

Organization

Students will collaborate with various partners during the learning experience.

Equipment Needed

- MP3 or CD player
- Lively music in fast and slow tempos
- Whiteboard or chart paper listing the four partner relationships and the definition
- Paper and pencils for students to record their choreography

Introduction and Warm-Up

Who can tell us what they know about the word *duet?* How is a duet used in music? Any other ideas about duets? In this dance unit, we are going to create duets with a partner. You will have the opportunity to create and perform movements with many partners.

First, we are going to warm up. Sit on the floor in a personal space. Pretend your arms and hands are partners. Can you move your arms so they both do exactly the same movement at the same time? Try using slow motion. Now, increase the tempo faster and faster. Can you move both legs exactly the same way in a leg dance duet? Can you move your legs far apart and close together? Can they change shape and levels? Now, try moving both your arms and legs in unison. [You can play music that will be used during the lesson.]

In the next part of the warm-up, we will all stand in a circle. One student will volunteer to be the leader in the center of the circle, and everyone will follow. He or she will move using one of the elements of dance that I call out, and then another person will lead. Ready? Who will be first? Create a slow movement. Next person, do quick and light movements. [Continue to change leaders after 15 seconds and call a way to move, such as one body part, twisting movements, changing frozen shapes, jumping apart and together, low movements, small movements using the hands, bending and stretching, turning, or strong and slow movements.]

Development

This unit will focus on four ways to dance with another person: mirror, shadow, echo, and call and response. These relationships are called partner relationships. You and a partner will create and perform movements for each relationship and choose two of the relationships to compose a dance.

The first one is mirror. In mirroring, you face your partner and move at the same time using the same movement. (See figure 9.8.) One person is the leader, and one is the follower. If the leader is using the right hand, the person following will use the left hand, like looking in a mirror. The leader moves slowly so it is easy to follow. [Demonstrate mirroring with a student.] I will assign partners, and you decide who will lead first. Begin when I play the slow music, and stop and switch leaders when the music stops. [Play the music for 1 minute, and when the music stops students switch places.] Now, I will assign you a different partner, and we will try the mirroring again.

The second relationship is shadow. In the shadowing relationship, the leader moves with his or her back facing the follower; one partner stands behind the other. The partners do the same movement at the same time. This time the leader chooses different ways to travel in the space using locomotor movements, stopping occasionally to freeze in a shape. [You and a student demonstrate.] I will assign new partners, and, again, you decide who will lead first. When I play the music, you will begin, and when the music stops, switch places. [Play medium-tempo music.] Remember to stop and make a shape. [Students practice.] Now, I will assign you a different partner, and we will try the shadowing again.

(continued)

Figure 9.8 Mirroring is performing a movement with your partner as if you are looking in a mirror.

The third relationship is echo. Can someone tell us what you know about the word *echo?* What do you think it would look like in movement? [Ask several students to share their responses with the class.] In the echo, one person performs one or two movements and then freezes while the partner observes. After the freeze, the observing partner repeats the same movement. Then the partners switch roles. Partners keep switching the echo leader role with the echo follower role. [The students and you discuss what makes the echoing relationship successful and then demonstrate.] When you perform the echoing movements, make small and big movements and slow and fast movements. I will assign you a new partner; you decide who will be the first leader. When I play the music, you will begin, and keep switching on your own time. [Play medium-tempo music while the students practice echoing.] Now, I will assign you a different partner, and we will try echoing again.

The fourth relationship is call and response. This relationship is like having a conversation with someone. First, one person briefly expresses a feeling or thought through performing one or two movements and then freezes in a still shape. Next, the other partner responds using a different movement and freezes. It is like having a conversation using movement instead of words. You may say something

using small, light, and quick movements or strong, slow, and big movements. What are other types of movements you could use? I would like two students to demonstrate this relationship for the class. [Students demonstrate the call and response using a variety of movements.] The movements can contrast with each other or be similar. Be creative and try different amounts of force and a variety of ranges of movement, body parts, tempos, and levels. I will assign new partners, and you decide who will start the conversation. When I play the music, you will begin, and when the music stops, freeze. [Play medium-tempo music while the students practice the call and response.] Now, I will assign you a different partner, and we will try the call and response again.

Culminating Dance

You will work together with your partner to create a dance that includes two of the four partner relationships using the ABA choreographic structure. The ABA structure is like a pattern. For example, if you chose call and response and echo for the dance, the sequence in ABA would be call and response, echo, call and response. You and your partner will create the movements and decide on the tempo for each part and the range (size) of the movements. Let me know if you need help. Be prepared to write down the type of relationship you are using and how it follows the ABA structure. After everyone has created and practiced their dance, you will perform your dance for another set of partners who will be the observers. Then, you will become the observers as they perform.

Closure

What part of the dance did you practice the most before the performance? Why did that part need extra practice? I will call the four types of relationships; raise your hand when I mention the one you liked the best. Now, someone shares which one they liked and why they liked it.

Look For

- Smooth, slow movements in the mirror relationship. Moving slowly is a challenge for some students.

- How children cooperate and relate to each other positively when you change partners.

- How well students can accurately reproduce the movements their partner is performing in the mirror, shadow, and echo relationships.

How Can I Change This?

- Introduce different partner relationships such as connected, supported, or meeting and parting.

- Organize students in groups of three or four instead of in partners. One student is the leader and the others follow. Students take turns as leaders.

- Assign different choreographic structures such as ABC or ABAB or ABCD.

Assessment Suggestions

- Teacher assessment—cognitive: Students identify the two relationships they used in their dance and write down the definitions. (outcome 3)

- Student self-assessment—affective: Students verbalize, draw, or write the partner relationship they liked the best and the one that was the hardest to perform. (outcome 4)

- Peer assessment—cognitive: Peer observers watch the performance of another set of partners and write the partner relationships the performers used as they appeared in the ABA choreographic structure. (outcome 2)

- Teacher assessment—psychomotor and cognitive: During the partner performance, use a checklist to record how well each student performs the selected partner relationships. (outcomes 1 and 3)

Interdisciplinary Connections

- Science: Integrate the dance with a science lesson focused on the sun and shadows.

- Social studies: Use this dance as a way to illustrate a social studies concept that looks at roles and responsibilities of leaders and followers in a community or partnership.

- Music: Connect the choreographic structure ABA to the ABA music composition form.

- Science: Use the dance as a way to illustrate the science concept of echoing.

Three Sport Dances: Sport Add-On, Sport Web, and Sport Pictures in Action

Outcomes

As a result of participating in this learning experience, students will be able to do the following:

1. Create and perform individual, partner, and group dances using sport actions. (affective, cognitive, and psychomotor)

2. Create and perform variations to sport actions using the elements of dance. (cognitive and psychomotor)

3. Select and use pictures of sport actions in creating and performing a partner dance. (cognitive and psychomotor)

4. Perform the sport add-on dance in unison. (psychomotor)

5. Respond to their performance of one of the three sport dances. (affective)

Organization

Students dance individually for the sport web dance and as part of a small group for the sport add-on dance and the sport pictures in action dance.

Equipment Needed

- MP3 or CD player
- Music with a clear beat
- Whiteboard or chart paper
- Sport web dance recording sheets
- Pencils
- Pictures of sport actions (sport pictures can be obtained from magazines, the newspaper, the Internet, photographs, or a display of books)

Introduction and Warm-Up

This dance unit uses sport actions and sport pictures as the topic for creating and performing dances. Sports are part of our everyday world. We see sports in person, on the Internet, and on television. We hear sports on the radio. We read about sports in magazines, in books, on the Internet, or in the newspaper. We view sport movies, videos, photographs, or works of art. We wear clothing with sport logos. You may choose a career in sport as a writer, an announcer, an official, or a coach, or you can participate as an athlete.

Can each person share your favorite sport you like to play or watch? [Each student in the class comments on a sport. You can write the sports on the whiteboard or chart paper.] Before we start our dances, we need to warm up all parts of the body. Let's begin with jogging in place, and when I call out one of the sports you mentioned, I want you to freeze in an action shape from that sport. Ready, jog in place and freeze in a tennis shape. [Repeat the sequence of jogging and still shapes several times, calling out different sports on the freeze.]

Development

Students participate in three activities in which they learn three ways to create and perform a sport dance.

Sport Add-On Dance

The first sport dance is the sport add-on dance. I will organize you into groups of five or six, and I want you to stand in a circle. [Give each student in your group a number that follows consecutively around the circle.] Next, each student selects a sport and one action from the sport. Practice performing the action in 4 counts. [Students practice individually while in the group circle.]

I will demonstrate how your group will add the actions together. I'll use this group to demonstrate. The first student demonstrates her action to the group, and in unison the group members repeat the movement. [One student demonstrates, and then everyone in the group repeats the action.] You may need to practice a couple times to repeat it accurately. Next, the second person in the group demonstrates his action, and in unison the group members repeat the movement. Then, the first movement is repeated followed by the second movement, which is added to the first. [Students demonstrate.] Then, the third person demonstrates her action, and in unison the group repeats the action. Now, the group combines the actions beginning with the first, then the second, and then the third. This pattern of demonstrating, repeating, and adding the movement on to the sequence is repeated until everyone in the group has contributed an action to the sequence. The goal is to remember the sequence, perform in unison as a group, and continue to do each movement in 4 counts. [Direct the demonstration, adding two more actions.] The options for using the 4 beats are as follows: One action is performed four times, once on each beat; one action is performed twice, taking 2 beats for the action; or one action is performed once, taking all 4 beats for the action. [Observe the groups and offer help where needed.]

Now, each group will demonstrate their dance to the class. The other class members will observe the performance. After the performance, I will ask the observers to tell us what they saw. Here are the questions I will ask: Did the group perform in unison? What sport actions did you observe? How did the performers use their 4 beats? [Groups can be paired as performers and observers instead of one group performing for the entire class.]

Next, your group is going to revise your sport dance. Each person will make a change in the size or the level of his or her action. You will show the change to the group, the group members will try the change, and then the whole group will practice the dance again using the changes.

Next, I will combine all the groups into one large circle. You will maintain the same order you had in your small-group circle. As you become organized, notice that there will be people from the other groups mixed in between your group members. [Organize all the groups into one combined circle.] Point to the members of your group so you can see where they are. Now, all the group dances will be performed at the same time. Freeze in your last shape until all the groups have finished. Ready, begin. [Students perform their dances.] How did it feel to perform your dance while all the groups danced at the same time? Did you notice any of the other group's movements? [You can omit the whole-class dance with all the groups combined into one circle. The sport add-on dance can be completed in a single dance session as a lesson in a unit on creating sport dances.]

Sport Web Dance

The second way to create a dance using sport actions is the sport web dance (Cone and Cone 2002). In this experience, you will create and perform an individual sport dance using your favorite sport. First, we will create a dance together to demonstrate how you will create your individual dance. Let's select a sport, and I will write it in the

center of the web. (See figure 9.9.) [The students and you select a sport, and you write the sport in the center oval of the web drawn on the whiteboard or a large sheet of paper.] On the lines of the web, I will write the actions performed by someone playing the sport. We selected basketball. Tell me some of the actions used in basketball. [Students respond with passing, shooting, rebounding, dribbling, and guarding.] I will write one action on each line of the web.

Now, make a still shape for each basketball action when I call it out. This is similar to a photograph of a player caught in action. [Call out the actions, and all the students perform the same action at the same time in their own way.] Hold the shape for 8 counts. Ready? Shooting, 1, 2, 3, 4, 5, 6, 7, 8. [Call out the actions of dribbling, guarding, passing, and rebounding and direct the class to hold each shape for 8 counts.] Now, can someone show us one of your shapes? [One student makes a shape.] Now look at Mariah's shape. Is the shape high, low, big, small, reaching forward, or leaning backward? What action do you think the shape represents?

Next, we are going to choose three of the basketball actions and create an action shape dance. [The students choose the actions jump shot, rebound, and dribble.] Everyone make one still shape for each action you selected. Freeze in each shape for 8 beats. [Students make the shapes while you count to 8 for each shape.] Next, you are going to connect the three shapes by moving in slow motion from one

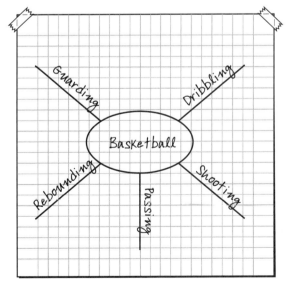

Figure 9.9 Sport dance web using basketball actions.

(continued)

shape to another. Begin by making the first shape. Hold it for 8 beats, and then slowly move into the second shape. Hold the second shape for 8 beats, and end the dance by moving into the third shape and holding it for 8 beats. [Students practice their dance several times to music.]

Now, you will create your own sport dance using the same process we used for the basketball dance. I will give each of you a sport web sheet. Choose a sport and write the sport in the center of the web and the actions on the web lines. Then, create a shape for each of the actions. Next, choose three actions for your dance. You can select the number of beats to hold each sport shape. [Students complete the web, practice the actions, choose three actions, and connect the actions with slow motion.] You can travel slowly to another space between the action shapes. [Students practice while you observe and help where needed.]

To finish this web dance, I want everyone with the same sport to perform at the same time. I know you will all have a different dance using the same sport. Can all the football players perform? Now, swimmers. Now, ice hockey players. What other sports have you selected for your dances? [The sport web dance can be a lesson within a unit on creating sport dances or taught as an individual dance lesson.]

Sport Pictures in Action Dance

The third way to create a sport dance is sport pictures in action. I have a box of sport action pictures that I have collected. They are from newspapers and magazines and show one or more players caught in the action. I have organized the pictures into a large circle on the floor facing out of the circle. Each student stand behind one of the pictures so you are on the outside of the circle. Look at the picture and make your body into the same shape of the athlete in the picture. Hold the shape for 8 counts. On my signal to switch, you will move to the picture on your left. Ready? Switch. Now, look at this picture and make the same shape for 8 counts. [Repeat the switch until the students have reproduced 15 to 20 pictures. You can also offer a way to change from one picture to the next, such as move slowly, jump, turn, take small steps, or move quickly. Another arrangement for the pictures instead of the floor circle is to tape the pictures to cones placed randomly in the space. Students begin at one cone and then switch to another.] Now, I will organize you into partners or small groups and you will select one

picture for your dance. The dance is composed of three parts. In the beginning of the dance, movements are performed that represent actions that may have occurred before the picture was taken. Use 8 counts for this section. The second part is a frozen shape that represents the player's shape in the picture. Use 8 counts for this section. In the third section of the dance, create your own movements that may have occurred after the picture was taken. Use 8 counts for this section.

When you choose a photo, look at a picture and talk about what you see. What are the players doing in the picture? What shapes are the players using? Are the players in a high, medium, or low level? In what direction are they facing? What type of energy do you think the players are showing? Can you make your body into the shape of the person in the picture? Practice holding that shape for 8 counts.

The whole dance takes 24 counts: 8 counts of what happened before the picture, 8 counts showing what is in the picture, and 8 counts of what happened after the picture. [Students choose pictures and collaborate to create the dance. Observe and help where needed.] Now that everyone is finished, one group or set of partners will perform for another group or set of partners who will be the observers and then switch places. Before you begin, hold up the picture. Observers, take a look at the pictures you will see in the dance. [Students perform their dances.]

Culminating Dance

For your final sport dance, you will be in a group of four or five. The group will choose one of the three ways you learned to create a sport dance: sport add-on, sport web, or sport pictures in action. If you have selected the sport add-on dance, each person chooses a sport action. If you have selected the sport web dance, the group decides on a sport and the actions and performs all together. If you have selected sport pictures in action, your group selects one picture and performs the movements together. Give your group a name and then create and practice your dance. When each group is finished, you will perform your dance for another group.

Closure

Ask the students, "Which way of creating a sport dance did you find most interesting? Why? How did you change your sport action to make it different from the way it is performed in a real game?"

Look For

- How children create variations for a sport movement. How did they apply the elements of dance to make a movement variation?
- Children who need help with transforming a sport action or picture into a movement or shape. They may need to see how another student has transformed words and pictures into movement.

How Can I Change This?

- Use categories of sports such as winter sports, Olympic sports, water sports, team sports, or extreme sports.
- The sport web dance can become a partner dance.
- Students can bring in photos of themselves playing sports or use drawings for the sport pictures in action dance.

- Students create a dance that uses a group sport tableau (see Rovegno and Bandhauer 2000) using sport action shapes designed by the students.

Assessment Suggestions

- Teacher assessment—psychomotor: Observe each group's sport add-on dance and record the group's ability to move in unison using a checklist (see figure 9.10). (outcome 4)
- Teacher assessment—psychomotor: Observe individual students' performance of the sport web dance and record the student's ability to hold the shapes still and move slowly from one shape to another (figure 9.11). (outcome 1)
- Peer assessment—cognitive: Peer assessment for the sport pictures in action dances. The following questions are presented to the observing

Group	Excellent: All students remembered the sequence and performed in unison using 4 beats for each sport action.	Very good: Some students (one or two) had trouble moving in unison with the other members of the group.	Needs improvement: Most students in the group were not in unison.
A			
B			
C			
D			

Figure 9.10 Group assessment tool for the sport add-on dance.

Name	Excellent: Student held still in all three shapes and clearly demonstrated slow movements between shapes.	Very good: Student had trouble holding the shapes still, or did not move slowly to connect one shape to another.	Needs improvement: Student was unable to hold any of the shapes still and could not move slowly from one shape to another.
Samir	X		
Cara		X *Wiggled in shapes.*	
Star			X *Held balance for 1 count and did not use slow movement.*
Loren	X		

Figure 9.11 Assessment tool for the sport web dance.

(continued)

group. Their answers can be either spoken or written: What sport did the dancers use for their dance? What types of pathways did the dancers use in their dance? Did the dancers change level or direction during their dance? Can you suggest any variations for the dance? (outcomes 2 and 3)

- Teacher assessment—affective: Use a checklist to note which of the three dances the group chose for their culminating dance (see figure 9.12). Use the letter A for the sport add-on dance, the letter B for the sport web dance, and a C for the sport pictures in action dance. The checklist also notes the level of cooperation that you observed as the group selected, created, and practiced their culminating dance. A rubric can be used, such as excellent (E), which means that the group worked well together or independently to practice and perform their dance, or needed help (NH), which means the group

needed the teacher's assistance to organize and practice their dance. (outcome 1)

- Student self-assessment—affective: Each student in the group writes a response to the following questions: What dance did your group choose for their culminating sport dance? Why did they make that choice? How did you feel about your performance in the dance as a part of the group? (outcome 5)

Interdisciplinary Connections

- Language arts (writing): Discuss how using a web for developing the sport dance is similar to using a web for developing ideas when writing.
- Language arts (literature): Use the text and illustrations in children's literature books and poems based on sports, such as *Hoops* (Burleigh and Johnson 1997), for initiating ideas for a sport dance.

Students' names	Group name	Type of sport dance	Cooperation used in creating, practicing, and performing
Snam	Red Dogs	A	E
Bart	Magic Steppers	B	NH
Christos	Super Dancers	C	E

A = sport add-on dance, B = sport web dance, C = sport pictures in action dance, E = excellent, NH = needed help.

Figure 9.12 Sample teacher checklist for culminating dance.

Dance Maps

Outcomes

As a result of participating in this learning experience, students will be able to do the following:

1. Create, perform, and record an individual dance using pathways and still shapes as the theme of the dance. (cognitive and psychomotor)

2. Collaborate with a small group to create and perform a group dance. (affective and psychomotor)

3. Observe a group's dance and identify shapes, locomotor movements, and pathways. (cognitive)

4. Choose a music selection to accompany their dance and explain why they chose the selection. (cognitive)

Organization

Students will work individually and then as part of a small group.

Equipment Needed

- MP3 or CD player
- Three different selections of music (choose from a variety of styles such as classical, jazz, contemporary, new age, cultural, blues, hip-hop, or rock)
- Four place markers for each student such as rubber spot markers, beanbags, construction-paper shapes, foam cylinders, or hoops
- Whiteboard or chart paper listing the instructions for the map dance
- Paper and crayons for recording dance maps

Introduction and Warm-Up

This dance experience will focus on making a map of a dance. The map will show the pathways that are straight, curvy, spiral, circular, or zigzag; the different shapes; and locomotor movements that you use in your dance. You will also select music to go with your dance.

First, we are going to do a warm-up focusing on shapes and pathways. Find a personal space, and pretend you have a giant crayon in your hand and you are standing inside a huge cylinder of paper.

Begin to draw curved pathways. Reach high, low, out to the side, and over your head. Place the crayon on another body part, perhaps your elbow, nose, knee, or heel, and draw straight pathways vertically, horizontally, and diagonally. Can you place the crayon in the middle of your back and draw zigzag pathways? What other body parts can you use to draw? Each time you hear me call out the word "change," draw with a different body part using a different pathway. Ready, change, change, change, and change. [Pause for a few seconds before calling out the next change of body part.]

Now, step out of your cylinder and pretend you have a giant bucket of paint in front of you. Jump in and out of the paint bucket, and walk in a spiral pathway in the general space. See if you are leaving a painted pathway behind you. Return to the bucket and jump in and out, and then travel in the space using another locomotor movement and a different pathway. Each time you hear me call out the word "change," travel using another locomotor movement on a different pathway. Ready, change, change, change, and change. [Again, pause for a few seconds before calling out the next change of movement and pathway.]

The last part of the warm-up is pretending you are a rubber band. Stretch your body as wide as you can, and hold the shape still while you count to 5. You can make your shape while standing, sitting, kneeling, or lying down. Now, try stretching as high as you can. This time stretch and hold a shape for a count of 5, and then slowly retract the rubber band and stretch into another shape. Move in and out of your shapes slowly. [You can use a drum to keep an even beat for the counting.]

Development

The step-by-step instructions for completing the map dance are listed on the whiteboard. (See figure 9.13 on page 184.) We will create each step and then you will have time to put the dance together. First, you will receive four space markers. These markers will show the places you will make still shapes in your dance. Find a different place on the floor to put down each marker. Now, identify each of your markers as 1, 2, 3, and 4. Stand on marker 1; now go to 2; now 3, then 4. [You can have students stand on the markers in numerical order a

(continued)

Step 1: Make a different shape on each of the markers.

Step 2: Create a pathway between each marker.

Step 3: Choose a locomotor movement for traveling on each pathway.

Step 4: Combine the shapes and locomotor movements to create your dance.

Step 5: Practice performing your dance.

Figure 9.13 Instructions for the map dance.

few times to help them establish a sequence for the dance.] This will be the order of the spaces you move to in your dance.

In step 1, you will make a different shape on each of the markers. Shapes can be wide, tall, low to the floor, twisted, curved, straight, or a combination of shapes. Hold still in each shape. You can choose the number of counts. [Provide time for students to create and practice their shapes on each of the markers.] I want you to show the shapes you have created. This half of the class will observe, and this half of the class will demonstrate their shapes. Demonstrators, you will begin on your first marker, hold each shape still for the number of counts you have chosen, and then go to each of the next three markers. Sit down when you have finished. [The students demonstrate, and then the demonstrators and observers switch roles.]

Now, let's go to step 2. Create a pathway between each marker. You can use straight, curved, zigzag, or a combination of pathways. Look at this example on the whiteboard [Show the students a sample drawing. See figure 9.14.] Try a couple ideas and then use a piece of paper to draw your pathways. You can use different-colored crayons for the different pathways. [The students create and practice making the pathways, then they draw the pathways connecting the four markers as shown in the example.]

Next, we have step 3. Choose a way to travel on each pathway. Incorporate a locomotor movement, a level change, and a direction for each part of the pathway. For example, you may walk backward slowly taking big steps on your first pathway, then quickly slide sideways to the third marker, and walk on your hands and feet while turning to the fourth marker. Remember to practice your shape when you arrive at each marker. [You or a student can demonstrate the example. The students work on their traveling movements.] When you finish, next to the pathway on your map write down how you are traveling.

Last, let's work on step 4. Combine the shapes and locomotor movements to complete your dance. Make your beginning shape on your first marker, then travel on your pathway to your second marker and make your second shape. Next, travel on your second pathway to your third marker and make a shape. And, finally, travel on your third pathway to your fourth marker to make your ending shape. Do you want to make any changes to your dance? Work on making the transitions smooth between the shapes and the traveling movements. Now finish with step 5: Practice your whole dance several times. [Provide time for the students to practice and make changes to the dance.] Now, I want everyone to perform their dance all at the same time. Be careful of others who may be moving across one of

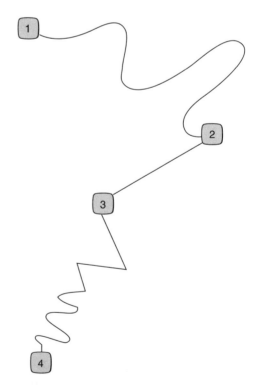

Figure 9.14 Teacher's example of pathways connecting four place markers.

your pathways. Ready? Start in your first shape. At the end hold your fourth shape until everyone has finished. [You can complete an informal observation to see if the students have all completed the components of the dance.]

Culminating Dance

In the final dance, three or four students will combine their individual dances into one dance. I will organize you into small groups, and each person will demonstrate her or his dance to the others in the group. First, explain your map to the group and show them where you have placed your markers. Then perform your dance. [Each student in the group performs while the others in the group observe.] Now, I would like everyone in each group to perform her or his dance at the same time. As you dance, make eye contact with each other, and notice when others in your group are in their still shapes and where they are traveling in the space.

Before you perform the dance again, your group will agree on a beginning place in the space to make a connected group shape and decide for how many counts you will hold the shape. Then everyone will agree on one way to travel from the group shape to her or his first marker. This is now the beginning of your group dance. In the middle part of the dance, everyone performs his or her individual dance. To end the dance, the group returns to the same place they started using the same way to travel and freezes in the same group shape. [Students collaborate to create a group shape and a way to travel to and from their individual dance.]

The final decision your group needs to make is to select a piece of music to accompany your dance. You will listen to each piece of music, practice your dance to each piece, and then choose the one you want to use. I will play 30 seconds of three different pieces of music. [Play each music selection twice while the students listen.] Now, I will play each piece of music again, and I would like your group to perform their dance while the music is playing. [Students perform their dance three times, once to each piece of music.] Now, after listening and dancing to each selection, your group can make a decision on the music selection.

To conclude this learning experience, each group will perform their dance for the class. Tell us which piece of music you selected, and take your beginning place in the group shape. When the music begins, start your dance. I will stop the music when everyone returns to the group shape to signal the end of your dance. Which group would like to perform first? After each group performs, the observers will complete the group observation form. (See figure 9.15 on page 186.) Before you perform, tell us why you chose the music piece for the dance. [Each group performs for the class, and the observers assign a recorder for their group and jointly complete the observation form or each observer completes a form.] Now, on one large piece of paper, each person in the group will draw their dance. Assign a different-colored crayon to represent each person. At the end, all the pathways of each of your dances will overlap one another to form one drawing. Then, clip your individual drawings to the group drawing and give them to me. [You can display the drawings as part of a bulletin board display about dance maps.]

Closure

What part of this learning experience did you enjoy the most? What ideas would you add to this learning experience to make it different? What was the most challenging part of the learning experience?

Look For

- How students use different pathways and locomotor movements. Help students to expand their choices so all movements and shapes are not the same.

- Students who need help drawing the pathways and writing the words.

- Students who may have trouble getting started with the shapes and locomotor movements. Ask guiding questions such as these: What type of shape do you want to start in? What level do you want your shape to be in? What are some ways you like to move? These guiding questions can provide students with ideas yet still allow them to make their own decisions.

How Can I Change This?

- Reduce or increase the number of shapes and pathways.

- Students can work in pairs to create the dance.

- Individuals or groups can create stories to accompany their dance.

- Students can enlarge their paper maps by drawing them on the facility's sidewalk or blacktop with chalk. They can label the movements and

(continued)

Dance Maps *(continued)*

___

Names of dancers: _____

Names of observers: _____

Write three words that describe the beginning and ending shape of the group.

    1. _____

    2. _____

    3. _____

What was the common locomotor movement the group used in the beginning and the ending of the dance?

_____

_____

List three different pathways you observed the students using in their dance.

    1. _____

    2. _____

    3. _____

Figure 9.15 Group observation form.

draw the markers and then move on the chalk pathways.

Assessment Suggestions

- Teacher assessment and student-self assessment—cognitive: Students complete a drawing of the pathways used in their dance and identify the locomotor movements. They may also include a description of each shape and the number of counts. (outcome 1)

- Teacher assessment—psychomotor: During the performances, use a checklist to note whether the students have performed the four shapes and three pathways in their individual and group dances. (outcomes 1 and 2)

- Peer assessment—cognitive: Students, organized into groups, complete an observation form after observing a performance of another group (see figure 9.15). (outcome 3)

- Student self-assessment—cognitive: Before the group performs their dance, they identify which of the three music selections they chose and explain their reasons for the choice. (outcome 4)

Interdisciplinary Connections

- Social studies: Connect with social studies by discussing the purposes of maps. Bring a variety of maps to the dance lessons.

- Math: Use math to estimate and measure the distance between the markers used in the dance.

- Language arts (writing): Create a story that describes an imaginary journey taken along the pathways of the dance.

- Music: Integrate music by talking about and listening to different styles of music that will accompany the dance.

Create Your Own Hip-Hop Dance

Outcomes

As a result of participating in this learning experience, children will be able to do the following:

1. Learn and perform four hip-hop movements demonstrated by their peers and learn a link step and identify their preferences. (psychomotor and affective)

2. Create and perform a hip-hop dance using all five movements (the link step + the four peer-taught movements) and include a change in tempo and level. (cognitive and psychomotor)

3. Collaborate with their group to practice and perform their hip-hop dance. (affective and psychomotor)

Organization

Students warm up individually and then collaborate in groups of four or five to compose, practice, and perform a hip-hop dance.

Equipment Needed

- MP3 or CD player
- Student self-assessment forms
- Paper and markers for writing the hip-hop steps
- Composition sequence cards
- Poster
- Whiteboard or chart paper and markers
- Appropriate music brought to class by the students

Introduction and Warm-Up

Today we are going to create a hip-hop dance using movements that you suggest. Remember, you were asked to watch TV or online videos, or look in magazines, or ask friends for hip-hop moves that you could bring to class. Today is the day—we are going to use your ideas. Where have you seen hip-hop dancing? What did you think about the movements you saw? Before we begin to list and learn your moves, we need to warm up our bodies. Find a personal space. When I say go, begin to jog in place slowly for 10 seconds. When I call stop, freeze in a straight, round, or twisted shape. Ready? Jog slowly, stop, and freeze. Next, jog at a medium speed for 10 seconds. Ready, go. Stop and freeze in a different shape. This time you will jog in place at a fast tempo. Ready, go. Stop and freeze in a low shape. The last jog is at a superfast speed. Ready, go. Stop and freeze in a stretched shape. Stay in the stretched shape and bend it slowly forward, then to the right side and to the left side. Finally, I want you to practice a link step that will be used in the hip-hop dance. [Demonstrate a side-to-side step and ask the students to mirror]. Stand and face me. As I step to my left with my left foot, you will step to your right with your right foot. Then my right foot will move beside the left and your left foot will move beside your right. This is called a side step. Let's practice moving to the right and left. Here we go. Step together, step together, step together, step together. Great! Now you have step 1, called the link step, ready for your dance.

Development

Now, we will create the movements for the dance. Can someone demonstrate a hip-hop movement? I see Roberto is showing us his step. What is the name of your step? I call it the double cross. [Record the name of the step on the whiteboard or chart paper.] Everyone observe Roberto and follow him as his demonstrates his step. [Students observe and practice the step. In this way, student leadership is used in teaching a step.] This step will be step 2. [Continue to ask for students to demonstrate a step, name it, and teach it to their peers while you write it on the whiteboard or chart paper and give it a number. This continues until there are four student-suggested and student-demonstrated steps.] Now you all know five hip-hop movements that you will use in composing your dance. I will organize you into a group and you will practice the five movements. [Groups of four or five are organized and students collaborate to remember the dance movements and practice together]. Refer to the list of five movements on the whiteboard or chart paper and practice each one. Also, remember the number next to each movement. (See figure 9.16 on page 188.)

I will now give each group a recording form that identifies the order of the hip-hop steps for your dance. [Determine a different order for each group. If there are five groups, there are five orders of the

(continued)

1. Link step
2. Double cross
3. Sprinkler
4. Spin jump
5. Body pop

Figure 9.16   Steps and numbers.

hip-hop steps.] (See figure 9.17.) On the form, next to the number, write the name of the corresponding hip-hop step. This is your dance order. You can decide how many times to repeat each step before you add the next one. Practice the order with your group. [Students practice the movements in the assigned order of the hip-hop steps while you observe and offer help where needed.] Next, you need to make two changes to your dance. First, one of the movements is performed very slowly and another movement is performed at a low level. [Students decide on which of the five movements will be performed slowly and which one is performed low. They practice their dance with the added changes.] I have one more part to add to your dance. Find a still beginning shape and a still ending shape. Everyone can be in the same shape or you can all be different. This is like the group is posed for a picture in the beginning and at the end. Practice the whole dance with the new beginning and ending. [Students practice making different group shapes and add one to the beginning and to the end of their dance.]

Culminating Dance

Each group will now perform their dance for another group. I will organize you into paired groups. One group is the observers and the other group is the performers. Then you will switch. The observers will look for one slow movement and one low movement and give the performing group two thumbs up if they see the slow and low movements or one thumb up if they see only the slow or only the low and no thumbs if the slow and low movements are not seen.

Closure

Students complete a self-assessment of their performance (see figure 9.18) and identify their movement preferences.

Look For

- Students who are reluctant to try any of the movements and feel they cannot perform.
- Student-suggested movements that are not safe or are inappropriate for elementary-level students.

Group 1

Step order	Hip-hop step
5	Body pop
3	Sprinkler
2	Double cross
4	Spin jump
1	Link step

Group 2

Step order	Hip-hop step
3	Sprinkler
1	Link step
4	Spin jump
2	Double cross
5	Body pop

Figure 9.17   Recording form for composition order.

- Students who have a background in hip-hop and can be used as student leaders to help others learn.

How Can I Change This?

- Students can add more steps or decrease the number of steps in the dance.

- Show a video, DVD, or online video of appropriate hip-hop movements as the movements students can choose for their dance.

- Ask students to bring in music that is appropriate for use in a school environment.

- Students can create their own order for the dance movements.

- Students can add solo performances that are variations on the selected movements. For example, to vary the link step, students can add waving their arms overhead or making the body twist on each step.

- Students can add a prop to their dance such as a playground ball, hoop, scarf, or other equipment that is easily manipulated.

Assessment Suggestions

- Student self-assessment—affective and psycho-motor: At the end of the learning experience, students complete a self-assessment describing how well they perform each step. They will also identify their favorite and least favorite movement and provide a reason for their choice (see figure 9.18). (outcome 1)

- Peer assessment—cognitive: Students will complete a peer assessment after observing a group's performance and identify whether the performing group's dance used a slow tempo and a low level. (outcome 2)

- Teacher assessment—psychomotor and affective: Observe students as they are in the process of organizing and practicing their dance. Use a checklist for recording the observation (see figure 9.19 on page 190). (outcome 3)

Interdisciplinary Connections

- Visual art: Students can create a poster using graffiti-type letters or pictures to accompany their dance.

STUDENT SELF-ASSESSMENT OF HIP-HOP STEPS

Name: _____

Rate how well you can perform the following steps. List the steps in the left column. Complete the two questions at the end of the form.

Step name	I am excellent. This step was easy for me.	I am still working on learning to do this step accurately. I can do some of it well.	I was not able to perform this step today. More practice is needed.
Link step			

What was your favorite step and why did you like that one?

Suggest a change to one of the steps to make it better.

Figure 9.18 Student self-assessment.

(continued)

TEACHER OBSERVATION OF HIP-HOP DANCE

Group name: _____

Criteria	Observed	Not observed	Comments
Group included all 5 movements in their dance.			
Group members agreed on which step has a tempo change and which step has a level change.			
Group created a beginning and ending shape.			
Group was focused and practiced movements.			
Group members encouraged each other.			

Figure 9.19 Teacher observation assessment.

- Theater art: Students can create costumes using scarves or their own clothing such as hats, hooded sweatshirts, gloves, or belts.

- Music and language arts: Students can create a rhyming rap to accompany their dance or use it to introduce the dancers or the dance.

- Math and music: Students can add the counts for each step and then complete a count total for the entire dance.

- Social studies: Students can research information on the origin of hip-hop, break dance, crumping, B-boys, or B-girls.

Funky Shape Museum

Outcomes

As a result of participating in this learning experience, students will be able to do the following:

1. Create and perform a variety of still shapes that use levels, range, direction, and different body parts for support. (cognitive and psychomotor)

2. Observe and reproduce a variety of shapes created by their peers. (psychomotor)

3. Move between the still sculptures using locomotor movements that travel in slow and fast tempos. (psychomotor)

Organization

Students will create and practice the shapes individually and then collaborate with a partner or small group to create group shapes.

Equipment Needed

- MP3 or CD player
- Music that has a slow tempo
- Music that has a fast tempo

Introduction and Warm-Up

Today we are going on a visit to an imaginary funky shape museum. You will all have an opportunity to be a funky shape in the museum and a museum visitor. Has anyone been to a museum and seen still sculptures? Yes, Matt says that he's been to the Philadelphia Museum of Art and saw a metal sculpture that used old car parts. Matt, can you make your body or a part of your body in a shape you saw in the sculpture? [Student demonstrates what he observed. Ask one or two other students to share their observations of a sculpture.] Now, we are going to do a warm-up called stuck like glue. When I say go, you will skip forward on any pathway. When I say, "Stuck like glue," you will connect to another person. Two or three people can be connected. I will call out the body part that gets stuck together. Ready? Stuck like glue with your elbow. Ready, now skip again on a straight pathway. Stuck like glue with a knee. This time skip backward. Stuck like glue with five toes and one finger. Now, skip on a curvy pathway, swinging your arms as big as you can. Stuck like glue with a shoulder and be in a stretched shape. Skip and add a turn. Stuck like glue with one person in a round shape and another person in a wide shape. Last time, skip and clap your hands. Stuck like glue in a twisted shape and connected by three body parts.

Development

Now, you will create a variety of funky shapes. Each person find a personal space. I will call out a funky shape and you will have two seconds to quickly make your interpretation of the shape with your body. Stay in your personal space. Ready? Wide shape like a stretched piece of bubble gum. Hold it still. Great. Make a shape like a piece of clothing thrown down on the floor; go. Now, a shape like a pencil with a broken point. [Continue to offer ideas for shapes such as in the following list.]

- A deflated basketball
- A letter in your name
- A giant balloon ready to burst
- A flat pancake
- A piece of gum stuck to a shoe
- A backpack that is heavy on one side
- A giant's sneaker that is untied

Now, I will organize you into groups of four or five. One person will be the funky shape teller and the others will make the shape. Each person takes two turns to tell the group what funky shape to make. [Students are organized and each person offers an idea for a funky shape for the group to complete.]

Culminating Dance

For our final dance, half of the class will be the statues in the funky shape museum and the other half will be the visitors. [Assign the students as statues and visitors.] First, the statues find a personal space and make a shape that you did when I called out a shape or you did in your group. Hold your shape still. Next, the visitors will use a locomotor movement as they move around and between the shapes. They will stop by a shape and make the same exact shape and hold still for 8 counts and move to another shape. Chris, show the class what you will do as a visitor. [Student models the visitor's role to clarify the task.] Ready, visitors all skip as you tour the museum. [Observe students as

(continued)

they travel through the statues and make shapes.] Great, now switch roles. The visitors become the statues and the statues are now the visitors. This time the visitors will jog at a medium speed. Ready, go. Everyone stop. Switch roles again. This time the visitors must move using slow motion as they walk through the museum. It is like time is distorted in the museum. This time the sculptures change slowly to another shape after a visitor has copied them for 8 counts. The sculptures change after each visitor. I will play slow music to help your movements stay slow. [Students perform this new part of the dance and then you announce to switch roles.]

In the final dance, the visitors will move through the museum as fast as they can, and when they stop by a sculpture, they freeze. This makes the sculpture come alive, and now the sculpture becomes a visitor and the visitor is a sculpture. In this way the visitors and sculpture will keep changing places. I will play the fast music for this final part of the dance. Ready? Here we go.

Closure

Who can show us a shape and they created and tell us what the shape represents? [Ask several students to share their shapes with the class.]

Look For

- When students are in the group and offering ideas for shapes, and they cannot think of what to say and may need a prompt.

- Students who need a reminder to move slowly. Tell them to feel how slowly their muscles can move.

- Students who move fast and are unable to stop quickly without falling or bumping into the sculpture.

How Can I Change This?

- Use a category of shapes for the museum, such as the baseball player museum, the cartoon character museum, the monster museum, or the machine museum.

- Sculptures can add a nonlocomotor movement to part of their body while in their shape.

- Visitors can pretend to take a picture of the sculpture and then make the shape.

- Visitors can move the hand of the sculpture into a different position.

- Add a story to the dance. For example, the visitors fall asleep on the museum floor and the sculptures come alive and dance around the visitors, matching their sleeping shapes. Then when the visitors wake up, the sculptures are back in their original places.

Assessment Suggestions

- Teacher assessment—cognitive and psychomotor: Use a checklist to assess whether students can create a body shape and hold it still for 8 counts. (outcome 1)

- Peer assessment—psychomotor: While the visitor is making the sculpture shape, the sculpture looks to see how accurate the visitor's shape is and says "Okay" if the shape is correct or "Do again" if the shape is not correct. (outcome 2)

- Student self-assessment—psychomotor: Students reflect on how well they were able to move slowly and fast using body control. At the end of the learning experience, ask the students to place two thumbs up if they were able to move slowly and quickly without falling down or bumping into another visitor or sculpture. One thumb up if they fell down or bumped into another person or sculpture. (outcome 3)

Interdisciplinary Connections

- Visual art: Talk with the art teacher about books he or she could suggest on sculpture and share the books in class.

- Visual art and language arts: Students can draw or write a description of a shape they created.

- Language arts: Students can create a story about what happens to their sculpture when the museum closes at night.

Stick Figures Come Alive

Outcomes

As a result of participating in this learning experience, children will be able to do the following:

1. Reproduce the shape of a drawn stick figure and demonstrate the shape with their bodies. (psychomotor)
2. Perform the dance using the sequence outline of selected stick figures and transitions between figures. (psychomotor)
3. Collaborate with a partner or small group to select stick figures, organize a dance order, create a formation, and practice and perform a dance. (affective, cognitive, and psychomotor)

Organization

Students dance individually and then with a partner or small group.

Equipment Needed

- Stick figures drawn on poster paper, each figure on a separate poster (see figure 9.20 on page 194)
- Individual stick figure sheets with 14 figures on one side and a space for students to draw a figure (see figure 9.21 on page 195)
- A dance outline on the other side of the figure sheet (see figure 9.22 on page 196)

Introduction and Warm-Up

Today you are going to be transformed into a stick figure and create a dance that jumps off the page. For the warm-up, we are going to do the aerobic alphabet. This warm-up uses locomotor movements and letters of the alphabet. Begin to jog in the space. When I call out stop, listen for the letter I call out and then make that letter with your body. Ready, go. Stop. Make an uppercase letter that has all straight lines. [Students hold the shape still for 5 seconds and then the go signal is repeated. Following is a list of tasks for the letter shapes.]

- A lowercase letter that is curved.
- A letter lying on the floor.
- A letter in the school's name. Now, find a way to twist the letter.
- A letter that has a straight line and a curved line.

- The first letter of your name. Find a way to make the letter travel in the space.
- Make two different letters with your body at the same time.
- Find a partner and together form one letter.
- Four or five people get together and make a word; each person is a letter. Try it lying on the floor.

Development

In this part of the lesson I will show you a stick figure drawn on a poster and ask you to make the same shape with your body. Ready, here is the first figure. [Show the drawings listed in figure 9.20 on page 194 (also found on the bound-in CD-ROM in full-size posters) and add the following tasks to each stick figure. Then place the figure poster on the wall.]

- Figure 1. Now, I want you to slowly turn your body while staying in this shape.
- Figure 2. Can you switch the arm shapes? Try it a couple times and increase your speed.
- Figure 3. Show me how you can slowly bend and stretch your supporting leg. Try the same shape on the other foot.
- Figure 4. See if you can add a twist to this shape. Now turn over so the front of your body is facing the floor and add a twist.
- Figure 5. Find a way to make this shape rock forward and backward and then side to side.
- Figure 6. Keep still and move only your head. Now stop, and move only one leg. Now move only one arm.
- Figure 7. Hold the figure for a count of 5 then run and jump and freeze in the figure again. Repeat this a couple times, each time facing a different wall.
- Figure 8. How would this figure travel in the space? Find another way, and now one more way.

Now, I am going to assign you a partner or a group of three people and give you a sheet (see figure 9.21 on page 195) that has a variety of figures and an empty space for you to draw your own, if you

(continued)

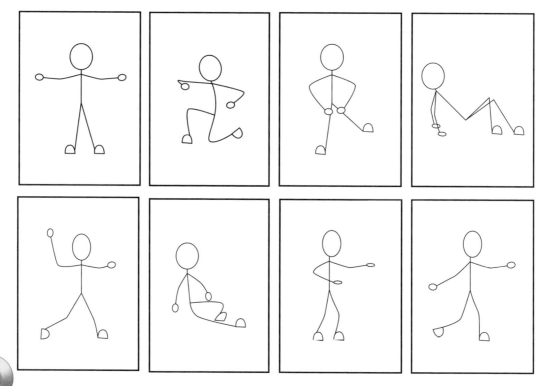

Figure 9.20 Teacher's stick figures for posters.

would like to add another figure. [Assign partners or groups and distribute figure sheets.] Here are the rest of the instructions. First, you and your partner or group will have three minutes to try making as many of the figures as you can. Begin on the top left and continue across the page, like when you read, to complete as many shapes as you can. Hold each shape without moving for a count of 5. [Students practice making the shapes while you circulate and help where needed.] That was great. Now, here is the next part of the instructions. Choose four different stick figures. Under each figure write the order you would like to perform them. You can choose a horizontal or vertical line as your order or choose at random. Then practice making each shape. [Students choose shapes and an order and practice.] You are all doing great. I can see how similar the figures are to your body shapes. Now, I will give you the last part of the instructions for you to complete your dance. The first shape is the beginning of your dance, then in superslow motion transform into the second shape. It is like the first shape melts and re-forms into the second shape. Everyone try this part of the dance. Fantastic! That was really slow and controlled. Now as fast as you can, make the third shape. Ready, go. Practice beginning in shape 1, slowly transforming into shape 2. Then quickly make shape 3. [Students

practice while you circulate and comment on body control and accuracy of the body in reproducing the figure shapes.] Next, make the third shape travel in the space and then melt it into the floor and grow into the fourth shape. The fourth shape is the end of your dance. You can decide how long to hold each shape and the locomotor movements you want to use to travel in the space. I have listed the dance outline (see figure 9.22 on page 196) on the back of your figure sheet. [While the students practice, check with students to make sure they have completed the dance outline.]

Culminating Dance

Now, it's time for the performance of stick figures come alive. I will pair your set of partners or group with two other partners or groups. One group will perform first. They show the four stick figures they selected for their dance to the observers and then perform the dance. Then the second and third partners or groups perform.

Closure

Gather the students and ask if anyone drew their own stick figure and used it in their dance. If so, the students are asked to show the shape. If not, point to the figures on the sheet and students can

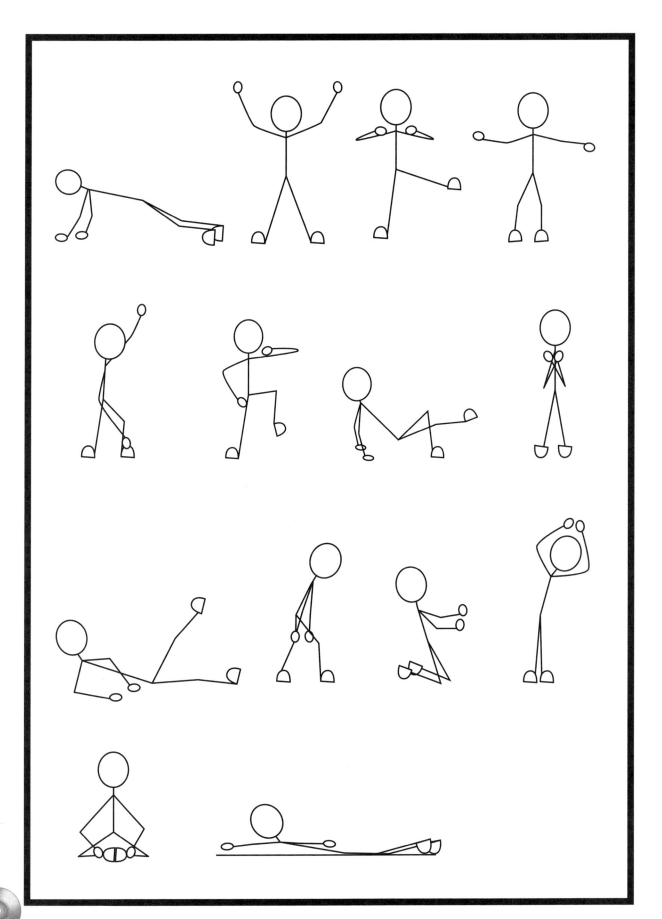

Figure 9.21 Student's stick figure sheet.

(continued)

1. Hold stick figure 1 for beginning shape.

2. Use slow motion to change into stick figure 2.

3. Use fast motion to change into stick figure 3.

4. Travel in the space using stick figure 3.

5. Stop and melt down out of stick figure 3.

6. Grow slowly into stick figure 4.

7. Hold stick figure 4 for the end shape.

Figure 9.22 Dance outline for Stick Figures Come Alive.

raise their hands if they used the designated figure in their dance.

Look For

- Students who need help translating the stick-figure drawing into a body shape. They could begin with symmetrical figures and then use asymmetrical figures.

- How well students can use the slow-motion and quick transitions. Before placing this into the dance, the students can practice while in the warm-up.

How Can I Change This?

- Students draw their own stick figures.

- Substitute stick figures for pictures of people in a variety of poses.

- Ask students to take pictures of themselves in various positions using the pictures in place of the stick figures.

Assessment Suggestions

- Teacher assessment—psychomotor: Observe students' accuracy in reproducing shapes from the posters. If students have difficulty, repeat the poster and offer a demonstration by a student who is accurate. (outcome 1)

- Teacher assessment—affective: Observe students collaborating in partners or small groups to complete the dance outline. Check with each group and clarify instructions when needed. (outcome 3)

- Student self-assessment—cognitive: Students place a check next to the parts of the dance outline (see figure 9.22) indicating that they have completed the process from selection to performance. (outcome 3)

- Peer assessment—psychomotor: Peers observe the performance of their peers and use a deck of cards to show their assessment. The observers share cards from 1 to 10 in a suit, such as hearts, clubs, spades, or diamonds. They watch the performance and observe whether the shapes were held still and the transitions from one shape to another were clear. At the end of the performance they hold up a card from 1 to 10 to indicate how well they believe the performers completed the dance. (outcome 2)

Interdisciplinary Connections

- Visual art: Ask the art teacher to help students draw a variety of stick figures in different positions.

- Language arts (writing): Students write a descriptive word to correspond to a stick figure's shape.

- Math: Students create stick figures that represent letters and numbers.

References

Alperstein, C., and Weyl, R. (1992). *Arts for everykid: A handbook for change.* Trenton, NJ: New Jersey State Council of the Arts, Department of State and Alliance for Arts Education.

Anderson, A. (2002). Engaging student learning in physical education. *Journal of Physical Education, Recreation and Dance* 73 (7): 35-39.

Anderson, L.W., and Krathwohl, D.R. (Eds.). (2001). *A taxonomy for learning, teaching, and assessing: A revision of Bloom's taxonomy of educational objectives.* New York: Longman.

Apache, R. (2004). A developmentally appropriate lesson supports an inclusive physical education class. *Teaching Elementary Physical Education* 15 (5). Champaign, IL: Human Kinetics.

ASCD. (2011). The whole child. www.wholechildeducation.org/about.

Axelrod, A., and McGinley-Nally, S. (2001). *Pigs in the corner: Fun with math and dance.* New York: Simon & Schuster.

Ball, D., and Forzani, F. (2011). Teaching skillful teaching. *Educational Leadership* 68 (4): 40-45.

Bartholomew, B. (2008). Sustaining the fire. *Educational Leadership* 65 (6): 55-60.

Benzwie, T. (2011). *Numbers on the move: 1 2 3 dance and count with me.* Philadelphia: Temple University Press.

Benzwie, T. (2002). *Alphabet movers.* Bethesda: National Dance Education Organization.

Benzwie, T. (2000). *More moving experiences: Connecting arts, feelings and imagination.* Bethesda: National Dance Education Organization.

Benzwie, T. (1987). *A moving experience: Dance for lovers of children and the child within.* Tucson: Zephyr Press.

Boynton, S. (1993). *Barnyard dance.* New York: Workman.

Brady, K., Forton, M., Porter, D., and Wood, C. (2003). *Rules in school.* Greenfield, MA: Northeast Foundation for Children.

Brehm, M., and McNett, L. (2008). *Creative dance for learning: The kinesthetic link.* Boston: McGraw-Hill.

Brookfield, S. (1995). *Becoming a critically reflective teacher.* San Francisco: Jossey-Bass.

Burleigh, R., and Johnson, S. (1997). *Hoops.* San Diego: Harcourt Brace.

Carle, E. (1996). *Little cloud.* New York: Philomel Books.

Chandra, D. (1993). *Balloons and other poems.* London: Sunburst Books.

Clark, J. (2007). On the problem of motor skill development. *Journal of Physical Education, Recreation and Dance* 78 (5): 39-44.

Cleary, B., and Prosmitsky, J. (2001). *To root, to toot, to parachute: What is a verb?* Minneapolis: Carolrhoda Books.

Cone, T. (2002). *Off the page: Children's creative dance as a response to children's literature.* Unpublished doctoral dissertation, Temple University.

Cone, T. (2000). Off the page: Responding to children's literature through dance. *Teaching Elementary Physical Education* 11 (5): 11-34.

Cone, T., and Cone, S. (2011). Strategies for teaching dancers of all abilities. *Journal of Physical Education, Recreation and Dance* 82 (2): 24-31.

Cone, T, and Cone, S. (2005). *Assessing dance in elementary physical education.* Reston, VA: National Association for Sport and Physical Education.

Cone, S., and Cone, T. (2003). Dancing, learning, creating, knowing. *Teaching Elementary Physical Education* 14 (5): 7-11.

Cone, S., and Cone, T. (2002). Using sport themes in creative dance. *Strategies* 16 (1): 9-12.

Cone, T., Werner, P., and Cone, S. (2009). *Interdisciplinary elementary physical education: Connection, sharing, partnering.* Champaign, IL: Human Kinetics.

Cookson, P. (2009). What would Socrates say? *Educational Leadership* 67 (1): 8-14.

Cooper, E. (1998). *Ballpark.* New York: Greenwillow Books.

de Mille, A. (1991, April 7). Measuring the steps of a giant. *New York Times.*

Donnelly, F. (2002). Make learning an electric experience! *Teaching elementary physical education* 13 (2): 25-27.

Dunphy, K., and Scott, J. (2003). *Freedom to move: Movement and dance for people with intellectual disabilities.* Sydney, Australia: MacLennan and Petty.

Eisner, E. (1998). *The kind of schools we need: Personal essays.* Portsmouth, NH: Heinemann.

Elin, J., and Boswell, B. (2004). *Re-envisioning dance: Perceiving the aesthetics of disability.* Dubuque, IA: Kendall/Hunt.

Endicott, J. (1988). *Listen to the rain.* New York: Holt.

Fleming, D. (1993). *In the small, small pond.* New York: Holt.

Fowler, C. (1994). *Music: Its role and importance in our lives.* New York: Glencoe.

Fraleigh, S. (1987). *Dance and the lived body: A descriptive aesthetics.* Pittsburgh: University of Pittsburgh Press.

Gardner, H. (1983). *Frames of mind: The theory of multiple intelligences.* New York: Basic Books.

Gilbert, A.G. (1992). *Creative dance for all ages.* Reston, VA: American Alliance for Health, Physical Education, Recreation and Dance/National Dance Association.

Gilbert, A.G. (1977). *Teaching the three R's through movement experiences.* New York: Macmillan.

Gillman, A.G. (1999). *Take me out to the ballgame.* New York: Simon & Schuster.

Goodrich, H. (1997). Understanding rubrics. *Educational Leadership* 54 (4): 14-17.

Graham, G. (2008). *Teaching children physical education: Becoming a master teacher.* 3rd ed. Champaign, IL: Human Kinetics.

Hall, Z., and Halpern, S. (2000). *Fall leaves fall.* New York: Scholastic Press.

Halsey, M. (2000). *Circus 1-2-3.* New York: Harper Collins.

Hanna, J. (1987). *To dance is human: A theory of nonverbal communication.* Chicago: University of Chicago Press.

Hawkins, A.M. (1988). *Creating through dance.* Hightstown, NJ: Princeton Books.

Huebner, T. (2010). Differentiated learning. *Educational Leadership* 67 (5): 79-81.

Jacobs, H. (1989). *Interdisciplinary curriculum: Design and implementation.* Alexandria, VA: Association for Supervision and Curriculum Development.

Johnson, I. (2002). Liven up those line dances. *Teaching Elementary Physical Education* 13 (1): 30-32.

Joyce, M. (1984). *Dance technique for children.* Palo Alto, CA: Mayfield.

Kalan, R., and Barton, B. (1981). *Jump, frog, jump.* New York: Scholastic.

Kane, K. (1998). *Move and learn: A kaleidoscope of creative movement activities for literacy development.* Grand Rapids, MI: Instructional Fair TS Denison.

Kaufmann, K. (2006). *Inclusive creative movement and dance.* Champaign, IL: Human Kinetics.

Kaufmann, K. (2002). Adaptation techniques for modeling diversity in the dance class. *Journal of Physical Education, Recreation and Dance* 73 (7): 16-19.

Laban, R. (1976). *Modern educational dance.* 3rd ed. London: Macdonald & Evans.

Landsman, J., Moore, T, and Simmons, R. (2008). Reluctant teachers, reluctant learners, *Educational Leadership* 65 (6): 62-66.

Lazaroff, E. (2001). Performance and motivation in dance education. *Arts Education Policy Review* 103 (2): 23-29.

Leahy, S., Lyon, C., Thompson, M., and Wiliam, D. (2005). Classroom assessment minute by minute, day by day. *Educational Leadership* 63 (3): 19-24.

Martin, B., and Archambault, J. (1986). *Barn dance.* New York: Holt.

McCarthy-Brown, N. (2009). The need for culturally relevant dance education. *Journal of Dance Education* 9 (4): 120-125.

McCollum, S. (2002). Reflection: A key for effective teaching. *Teaching Elementary Physical Education* 13 (6): 6-7.

McTighe, J. (1997). What happens between assessments? *Educational Leadership* 54 (4): 6-12.

Meyer, F. (Ed). (2010). *Implementing the national dance education standards.* Champaign, IL: Human Kinetics.

Mosston, M., and Ashworth, S. (2002). *Teaching physical education.* 5th ed. Boston: Benjamin Cummings.

Murray, R. (1963). *Dance in elementary education.* 2nd ed. New York: Harper & Row.

National Association for Sport and Physical Education. (2009). *Opportunity to learn: Guidelines for elementary school physical education.* Reston, VA: Author.

National Association for Sport and Physical Education. (2004). *Moving into the future: National standards for physical education.* 2nd ed. Reston, VA: Author.

National Dance Association. (1995). *Opportunity-to-learn standards for dance instruction.* Reston, VA: Author.

Nelson, H. (2009). High-quality arts programs can contribute to the intellectual, physical, and emotional well-being of children. *Principal* 14-17.

Newnam, H. (2002). Overcoming your fears of teaching educational dance. *Teaching Elementary Physical Education* 13 (3): 10-12.

Niguidula, D. (2005). Documenting learning with digital portfolios. *Educational Leadership* 63 (3): 44-47.

Overby, L., Post, B., and Newman, D. (2005). *Interdisciplinary learning through dance: 101 moventures.* Champaign, IL: Human Kinetics.

Root-Bernstein, R., and Root-Bernstein, M. (2000). Learning to think with emotion. *Chronicle of Higher Education* 46: A 64.

Rovegno, I. (2003). Children's literature and dance. *Teaching elementary physical education* 14 (4): 24-29.

Rovegno, I., and Bandhauer, D. (2000). Teaching elements of choreography. *Teaching Elementary Physical Education* 11 (5): 6-10.

Silverstein, S. (1981). *A light in the attic.* New York: Harper & Row.

Silverstein, S. (1974). *Where the sidewalk ends.* New York: Harper & Row.

Sprague, M., Scheff, H., and McGreevy-Nichols, S. (2006). *Dance about anything.* Champaign, IL: Human Kinetics.

Square Dance Legislation Collection. (2004). Library of Congress American Folklife Center. www.loc.gov/folklife/guides/squaredance.html.

Stinson, S. (1998). Seeking a feminist pedagogy for children's dance. In *Dance, power, and difference: Critical and feminist perspectives on dance education*. Edited by S. Shapiro, 23-47. Champaign, IL: Human Kinetics.

Stinson, S. (1988). *Dance for young children: Finding the magic in movement*. Reston, VA: National Dance Association/American Alliance for Health, Physical Education, Recreation and Dance.

Tanis, C., and Hebel, S. (2010). Developing an emergency action plan for the physical education class. *CAPHERD Journal* 73 (1): 28-39.

Tomlinson, C. (1999). *The differentiated classroom: Responding to the needs of all learners*. Alexandria, VA: Association for Supervision and Curriculum Development.

Tortora, S. (2006). *The dancing dialogue: Using the communicative power of movement with young children*. Baltimore: Brookes.

Townsend, J.S., and Mohr, D. (2002). Review and implications of peer teaching research. *Teaching Elementary Physical Education* 13 (6): 28-31.

United States Department of Health and Human Services. (2008). *2008 Physical activity guidelines*. www.health.gov/paguidelines/guidelines/default.aspx.

United States Department of Justice. (2010). *Final regulatory impact analysis of the final revised regulations implementing titles II and III of the ADA, including revised ADA standards for accessible design*. http://www.ada.gov/regs2010/RIA_2010regs/ria_appendix02.htm.

Wall, J., and Murray, N. (1990). *Children and movement: Physical education in the elementary school*. Dubuque, IA: Brown.

Walsh, E. (1993). *Hop jump*. San Diego: Harcourt Brace.

Weeks, S., and Carter, D. (1996). *Noodles*. New York: Harper Collins.

Wiggins, G. (1998). *Educative assessment: Designing assessments to inform and improve performance*. San Francisco: Jossey-Bass.

Wiggins, G., and McTighe, J. (2005). *Understanding by design*. Alexandria, VA: Association for Supervision and Curriculum Development.

Wildsmith, B. (1970). *Circus*. New York: Franklin Watts.

Winer, Y., and Oliver, T. (2003). *Frogs sing songs*. Watertown, MA: Charlesbridge.

Worrell, V., Evans-Fletcher, C., and Kovar, S. (2002). Assessing the cognitive and affective progress of children. *Journal of Physical Education, Recreation and Dance* 73 (7): 29-34.

Zakkai, J. (1997). *Dance as a way of knowing*. Portland, ME: Stenhouse.

Suggested Readings

Bennett, J., and Riemer, P. (2006). *Rhythmic activities and dance.* 2nd ed. Champaign, IL: Human Kinetics.

More than 190 activities applicable for an elementary dance program in addition to guidelines for developing social dance units and lessons.

Benzwie, T. (2011). *Numbers on the move: 1 2 3 dance and count with me.* Philadelphia: Temple University Press.

A children's picture book that uses locomotor and non-locomotor movements to help children learn to count and identify numbers. Illustrations depict children moving and making shapes.

Benzwie, T. (2002). *Alphabet movers.* Bethesda: National Dance Education Organization.

A children's picture book that uses locomotor and non-locomotor movements to help children identify the letters of the alphabet and connect action words with the letters. Illustrations depict children moving and making shapes.

Benzwie, T. (2000). *More moving experiences: Connecting arts, feelings, and imagination.* Bethesda: National Dance Education Organization.

This book offers activities that integrate the arts and promote creativity. Ideas are applicable for students in the K-5 educational setting.

Benzwie, T. (1987). *A moving experience: Dance for lovers of children and the child within.* Tucson: Zephyr Press.

A collection of ideas for designing dance activities. Ideas include props, space, sculpting, art, music with movement, communication, language, rhythm, name games, fantasy, range, and movement games and warm-ups. It lists suggestions for music selections to accompany activities.

Brehm, M., and McNett, L. (2008). *Creative dance for learning: The kinesthetic link.* Boston: McGraw-Hill.

A collection of lessons for teaching creative dance and integrating dance with other subject areas. Includes feasible worksheets and teaching resources applicable for elementary-age students to adults.

Cone, T., and Cone, S. (2005). *Assessing dance in elementary physical education.* Reston, VA: National Association for Sport and Physical Education.

Assessing social, cultural, and creative dance in the cognitive, psychomotor, and affective domains. Included are descriptions and examples of assessment instruments.

Cone, T. (2000). Off the page: Responding to children's literature through dance. *Teaching Elementary Physical Education* 11 (5): 11-34.

Outlines the benefits of integrating children's literature and dance, strategies for selecting and presenting appropriate literature, and strategies for translating the text and illustrations into dance movement.

Cone, T., Werner, P., and Cone, S. (2009). *Interdisciplinary elementary physical education: Connection, sharing, partnering.* Champaign, IL: Human Kinetics.

Includes a model and strategies for integrating physical activity with social studies, language arts, math, science, and the arts. Twenty-four complete lessons are described with over 100 ideas for successful connecting, sharing, and partnering with other subject areas.

Donnelly, F. (2002). Make learning an electric experience! *Teaching elementary physical education* 13 (2): 25-27.

An article on the application for exploring the elements of dance and developing a dance using the science topic of electricity.

Dunkin, A. 2006. *Dancing in your school: A guide for preschool and elementary school teachers.* Hightstown, NJ: Princeton Books.

Over 70 dance activities outlined in an easy-to-follow progression. Suggestions for lesson development and program organization are included.

Dunphy, K., and Scott, J. (2003). *Freedom to move: Movement and dance for people with intellectual disabilities.* Sydney, Australia: MacLennan and Petty.

Lessons for teaching creative dance to children and adults with intellectual disabilities. Ideas for program planning, developing a performance, and assessment are included.

Elin, J., and Boswell, B. (2004). *Re-envisioning dance: Perceiving the aesthetics of disability.* Dubuque, IA: Kendall/Hunt.

Includes a discussion of a new way of seeing dance and dancers with distinctions as creators and performers. Information for teaching individuals with a range of disabilities is offered along with references for further study.

Fraser, D.L. (1991). *Playdancing.* Pennington, NJ: Princeton.

A discussion of the creative process and the part it plays in education. Fraser provides activities that integrate movement with development of self-awareness, language, and interpersonal skills.

Gilbert, A.G. (2006). *Brain-compatible dance education.* Reston, VA: National Dance Association.

Includes background information on brain anatomy and development and connects this information to dance movements. The "brain dance" components are outlined along with numerous dance activities for young children.

Ideas for developing lesson plans and resources are provided.

Gilbert, A.G. (1977). *Teaching the three R's through movement experiences.* New York: Macmillan.

Activities for integrating movement with other subject areas such as language arts, math, science, social studies, and visual arts. Each chapter focuses on a different subject.

Gilbert, A.G. (1992). *Creative dance for all ages.* Reston, VA: National Dance Association/American Alliance for Health, Physical Education, Recreation and Dance.

A comprehensive resource of activities for teaching dance to students of all ages. The chapters focus on the elements of dance: space, time, force, the body, and movement. Includes information on assessment, integrating dance with other curricular areas, props, accompaniment for dance classes, and a music and video list.

Graham, G., Holt/Hale, S., and Parker, M. (2004). *Children moving: A reflective approach to teaching physical education.* 6th ed. New York: McGraw-Hill.

Information on movement concepts with examples for application to teaching dance. Also included is a chapter on teaching creative dance, which presents content for a creative dance experience and a process for teachers and children on creating create dances.

Grant, J. (1995). *Shake, rattle, and learn.* Markham, ON: Pembroke.

Support movement-based learning as an essential component of a child's education. Each chapter focuses on a different theme that ranges from individual to whole-class activities. Themes integrate movement with language arts, science, drama, music, visual arts, social studies, and math. Activities are fun and appropriate for developing into dance lessons.

Humphrey, J. (1987). *Child development and learning through dance.* New York: AMS Press.

Presents an approach to teaching dance based on the stages of child development. Also suggests ways to integrate dance into teaching reading and math and to improve general learning ability through dance.

Joyce, M. (1973). *First steps in teaching dance.* Palo Alto, CA: National Press Books.

Contains information on the content and process of teaching dance. Author includes easy-to-follow lessons that are applicable for elementary-school-aged children. Well illustrated with photographs.

Joyce, M. (1984). *Dance technique for children.* Palo Alto, CA: Mayfield.

Presents content that focuses on teaching children the essential technical skills for becoming more proficient in creative movement in order to fully express their ideas. Provides descriptive experiences to help children understand how their bodies move efficiently and expressively. Chapters cover basic locomotor movements, opposition, rhythm, alignment, and use of energy.

Kane, K. (1998). *Move and learn: A kaleidoscope of creative movement activities for literacy development.* Grand Rapids, MI: Instructional Fair TS Denison.

Integrates children's literature with creative movement by offering activities applicable for the dance program. The author highlights 67 popular children's picture books and provides ideas for expressing the text and illustrations through movement in addition to visual arts, language arts, math, science, and social studies.

Kassing, G., and Jay, D. (2003). *Dance teaching methods and curriculum design.* Champaign, IL: Human Kinetics.

Includes an overview of the essential information for planning a dance program in the K-12 setting. Gain access to program models, dance education theory, and skills that emphasize effective teaching and program design.

Kaufmann, K. (2006). *Inclusive creative movement and dance.* Champaign, IL: Human Kinetics.

Describes how to teach dance to children with disabilities using the elements of space, time, force, and relationships. Included are lessons, student characteristics, and ideas for modifying instruction.

Kogan, K. (1982). *Step by step: A complete movement education from preschool to sixth grade.* Byron, CA: Front Row Experience.

Provides experiences that can be used by teachers beginning to teach dance. Each experience is sequenced and offers specific language and instructions for teaching.

Kooyackers, P. (1996). *101 dance games for children.* Alameda, CA: Hunter House.

Includes a variety of ideas for developing creative dance lessons for children. Offers suggestions for choosing and organizing dance lessons based on available space, age of participants, amount of time, size of the group, and props required.

Laban, R. (1976). *Modern educational dance.* 3rd ed. London: Macdonald & Evans.

Provides the theoretical background for movement education and educational dance. Describes 16 basic movement themes, 8 effort actions, and the use of the body and its movements in space. Laban is the pioneer in defining the movement principles used for dance.

Lane, C. (1995). *Christy Lane's complete book of line dancing.* Reston, VA: American Alliance for Health, Physical Education, Recreation and Dance.

A comprehensive resource of line dances for a social dance unit. Includes easy-to-follow instructions and diagrams.

Lloyd, M. (1998). *Adventures in creative movement activities: A guide for teaching.* 2nd ed. Dubuque, IA: Eddie Bowers.

An approach to developing a creative movement lesson. The book is filled with illustrations, sample lessons, and specific ideas for developing a meaningful experience for children.

McGreevy-Nichols, S., and Scheff, H. (1995). *Building dances: A guide to putting movements together*. Champaign, IL: Human Kinetics.

Introduces educators to a clear approach to creating dance lessons for elementary students. Includes strategies for observing dances and assessing dance learning along with over 200 easy-to-use cards that provide ideas for designing dance units and lessons.

McGreevy-Nichols, S., Scheff, H., and Sprague, M. (2001). *Building more dances: Blueprints for putting movements together*. Champaign, IL: Human Kinetics.

Expands on *Building Dances* with over 100 new ideas for creating dances and strategies for interdisciplinary connections.

Murray, R. (1953). *Dance in the elementary school: A program for boys and girls*. New York: Harper & Row.

One of the foundational texts used by many dance educators. A comprehensive description of the basic locomotor and nonlocomotor movements and the use of rhythm and music in dance. The process of creating new dances and learning dances is accompanied by many ideas and resources.

National Dance Association/American Alliance for Health, Physical Education, Recreation and Dance. (1990). *Guide to creative dance for the young child*. Reston, VA: Author.

Information on the content and process of teaching dance for the early childhood level.

Oliver, W. (ed.) (2009). *Dance and culture: An introductory reader*. Reston, VA: National Dance Association.

Suitable for upper-elementary students for a dance class text. Information includes cultures from Africa, the Middle East, Asia and Pacific Islands, Eastern and Western Europe, Latin America, Canada, North America (Native American Indian), and ancient Egypt, Mesopotamia, and the Indus Valley. Review questions and supplemental activities are provided.

Overby, L., Post, B., and Newman, D. (2005). *Interdisciplinary learning through dance: 101 moventures*. Champaign, IL: Human Kinetics.

Lesson plans integrating dance with social studies, language arts, science, math, physical education and creative arts. Includes a DVD and music CD.

Overby, L. (ed.). (1991). *Early childhood creative arts: Proceedings of the international early childhood creative arts conference 1990*. Reston, VA: American Alliance for Health, Physical Education, Recreation and Dance.

Several sections of the proceedings address dance for young children. Includes a resource for integrating dance with other art forms.

Parker, P., Fenton, M., Holme, J., Ireland-Echols, A., and Phillips, G. (1988). *Creative dance*. Ottawa, ON: Canadian Association for Health, Physical Education, Recreation and Dance.

A detailed description of how to approach teaching creative dance. Explains the selection of content, planning for a unit and lesson, and teaching strategies. Includes sample lessons.

Ross, F. (2010). *Soul dancing: The essential African American cultural dance book*. Reston, VA: National Dance Association.

A collection of African American folk and social dances for all ages. Includes lesson plans and historical information for traditional and popular dances.

Rovegno, I. (2003). Children's literature and dance. *Teaching elementary physical education* 14 (4): 24-29.

Criteria for selecting children's literature, steps in lesson planning, and a detailed description of a dance lesson based on Denise Fleming's (1993) children's book *In the small, small pond*.

Scheff, H., Sprague, M., and McGreevy-Nichols, S. (2010). *Exploring dance forms and styles: A guide to concert, world, social, and historical dance*. Champaign, IL: Human Kinetics.

Comprehensive resource on teaching dance forms for novice and experienced educators. Each described dance includes background information, teaching strategies, resources, and worksheets. A DVD is included that illustrates a majority of the dances.

Sprague, M., Scheff, H., and McGreevy-Nichols, S. (2006). *Dance about anything*. Champaign, IL: Human Kinetics.

A process for creating dances focused on a theme that is integrated with other subjects. Includes examples and reproducibles on a CD-ROM.

Stinson, S. (1988). *Dance for young children: Finding the magic in movement*. Reston, VA: National Dance Association/American Alliance for Health, Physical Education, Recreation and Dance.

Content and processes for teaching dance to young children. Contains examples of experiences that teachers beginning to teach dance can use easily. Includes excellent appendix citing children's literature that can be a resource for developing experiences.

Tortora, S. (2006). *The dancing dialogue: Using the communicative power of movement with young children*. Baltimore: Brookes.

Strategies for interacting and making connections with children who are nonverbal. Designed for teachers, therapists, and parents with children from birth to seven years.

Wall, J., and Murray, N. (1990). *Children and movement: Physical education in the elementary school*. Dubuque, IA: Brown.

A general text on physical education based on Rudolf Laban's descriptive analysis of human movement. A section focuses on dance and includes the elements of dance, how to teach dance, and how to design learning experiences for singing games, folk dance, and creative dance. Examples are specific and helpful to teachers beginning to teach dance.

Willis, C. (2004). *Dance education tips from the trenches.* Champaign, IL: Human Kinetics.

An approach to organizing, managing, and planning dance lessons and performances. Tips and suggestions for guiding students through the creative process, from exploring to choreographing a dance.

Zakkai, J. (1997). *Dance as a way of knowing.* Portland, ME: Stenhouse.

Addresses how dance is foundational to learning and offers an approach to including dance in the class-room and physical education curriculums. Information on how the elements of dance are developed into lessons that include learning, creating, and observing dance. Ideas for interdisciplinary connections are also included.

Zukowski, G., and Dickson, A. (1990). *On the move: A handbook for exploring creative movement with young children.* Carbondale: Southern Illinois University Press.

A guide for presenting creative movement in the class-room, physical education, and dance education curriculums. Included are movement games and activities appropriate for initiating dance lessons that integrate music, language arts, drama, literature, math, and science.

About the Authors

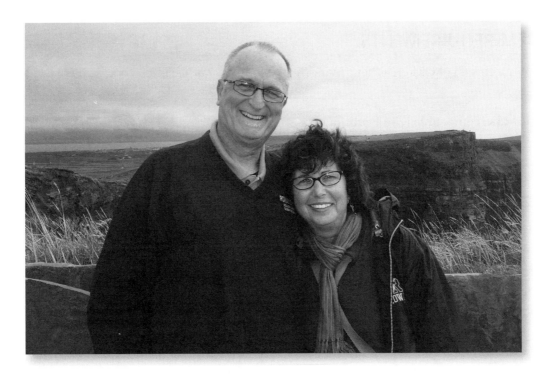

Theresa Purcell Cone, PhD, is an associate professor in the department of health and exercise science at Rowan University in New Jersey. Previously, she was a physical education and dance teacher at Brunswick Acres Elementary School in Kendall Park, New Jersey, where she also directed a children's dance company.

Dr. Cone is a past president of the National Dance Association and was named its first K-12 Dance Educator of the Year. Dr. Cone was coauthor of *Interdisciplinary Teaching Through Physical Education* (Human Kinetics 1998) and *Interdisciplinary Elementary Physical Education* (Human Kinetics 2009). She currently serves as an assistant editor of the *Journal of Dance Education*.

In 2004, Dr. Cone was awarded a Presidential Citation by the American Alliance for Health, Physical Education, Recreation and Dance and has also received their Honor Award. She also was awarded the Margie R. Hanson Distinguished Service Award by the National Association for Sport and Physical Education. Dr. Cone received her doctorate in dance from Temple University.

Stephen L. Cone, PhD, is a professor in the department of health and exercise science at Rowan University in New Jersey. Previously, he was a dean and professor at Keene State College in New Hampshire.

Dr. Cone is past president of the American Alliance for Health, Physical Education, Recreation and Dance (AAHPERD) and received their Honor Award in 2000. He has written dozens of articles for physical education publications and was coauthor of *Interdisciplinary Teaching Through Physical Education* (Human Kinetics 1998) and *Interdisciplinary Elementary Physical Education* (Human Kinetics 2009).

Dr. Cone was made a charter fellow in the North American Society for Health, Physical Education, Recreation, Sport and Dance Professionals in 2000. He also was named an American Council on Education fellow in 1993-94 and received a Presidential Citation from the National Dance Association. Dr. Cone earned his doctorate in motor learning and sport psychology from Texas A&M University.

CD-ROM User Instructions

SYSTEM REQUIREMENTS

You can use this CD-ROM on either a Windows-based PC or a Macintosh computer.

Windows

- ◆ IBM PC compatible with Pentium processor
- ◆ Windows 2000/XP/Vista/7
- ◆ Adobe Reader 8.0/9.0/10.0
- ◆ Microsoft Office 2003 or higher
- ◆ 4x CD-ROM drive

Macintosh

- ◆ Power Mac recommended
- ◆ System 10.4/10.5/10.6/10.7+
- ◆ Adobe Reader 8.0/9.0/10.0
- ◆ Microsoft Office 2004 for MAC or higher
- ◆ 4x CD-ROM drive

USER INSTRUCTIONS

Windows

1. Insert the *Teaching Children Dance, Third Edition* CD-ROM. (Note: The CD-ROM must be present in the drive at all times.)
2. Open the "My Computer" window.
3. Select the CD-ROM drive.
4. Open the file you wish to view. See the "00Start.pdf" file for a list of the contents.

Macintosh

1. Insert the *Teaching Children Dance, Third Edition* CD-ROM. (Note: The CD-ROM must be present in the drive at all times.)
2. Double-click the CD icon located on the desktop.
3. Open the file you wish to view. See the "00Start" file for a list of the contents.

For customer support, contact Technical Support:

Phone: 217-351-5076 Monday through Friday (excluding holidays) between 7:00 a.m. and 7:00 p.m. (CST).

Fax: 217-351-2674

E-mail: support@hkusa.com